A NEW SOCIAL QUESTION?

CHANGING WELFARE STATES

Processes of socio-economic change – individualising society and globalising economics and politics – cause large problems for modern welfare states. Welfare states, organised on the level of nation-states and built on one or the other form of national solidarity, are increasingly confronted with – for instance – fiscal problems, costs control difficulties, and the unintended use of welfare programs. Such problems – generally speaking – raise the issue of sustainability because they tend to undermine the legitimacy of the programs of the welfare state and in the end induce the necessity of change, be it the complete abolishment of programs, retrenchment of programs, or attempts to preserve programs by modernising them.

This series of studies on welfare states focuses on the changing institutions and programs of modern welfare states. These changes are the product of external pressures on welfare states, for example because of the economic and political consequences of globalisation or individualisation, or result from the internal, political or institutional dynamics of welfare arrangements.

By studying the development of welfare state arrangements in different countries, in different institutional contexts, or by comparing developments between countries or different types of welfare states, this series hopes to enlarge the body of knowledge on the functioning and development of welfare states and their programs.

EDITORS OF THE SERIES

Gøsta Esping-Andersen, University of Pompeu Fabra, Barcelona, Spain
Anton Hemerijck, the Netherlands Scientific Council for Government
    Policy (Wetenschappelijke Raad voor het Regeringsbeleid – WRR)
Kees van Kersbergen, Free University Amsterdam, the Netherlands
Jelle Visser, University of Amsterdam, the Netherlands
Romke van der Veen, Erasmus University, Rotterdam, the Netherlands

A New Social Question?

On Minimum Income Protection in the Postindustrial Era

Ive Marx

AMSTERDAM UNIVERSITY PRESS

The publication of this book is made possible with a grant of the GAK-Foundation (Stichting Instituut GAK, Hilversum).

Cover illustration: Mario Sironi, *Periferia* (1922), oil on canvas, private collection

Cover design: Jaak Crasborn BNO, Valkenburg a/d Geul
Layout: V3-Services, Baarn

ISBN-13 978 90 5356 925 2
ISBN-10 90 5356 925 1
NUR   754

© Amsterdam University Press, Amsterdam 2007

All rights reserved. Without limiting the rights under copyright reserved above, no part of this book may be reproduced, stored in or introduced into a retrieval system, or transmitted, in any form or by any means (electronic, mechanical, photocopying, recording or otherwise) without the written permission of both the copyright owner and the author of the book.

Library
University of Texas
at San Antonio

Table of Contents

Introduction 9
The Rise of Economic Redundancy 10
Welfare State Failure(s) 12
Limits to Incrementalism 14
Beyond Incrementalism 17
Organisation of This Book 19
Acknowledgements 20

PART 1   THE DECLINE OF SELF-RELIANCE AND THE LABOUR DEMAND SHIFT AGAINST THE LESS-SKILLED: CONJECTURES, FACTS AND EXPLANATIONS

1   **The Decline of Self-Reliance in Advanced Welfare States** 23
   1 Introduction 23
   2 A Note on the Relevance of Self-Reliance in Social Policy 25
   3 The Decline of Self-Reliance: General Evidence 30
   4 Evidence for Belgium, with a Particular Focus on the Less-Skilled 38
   5 Difficulties of Interpretation 51
   6 Some Direct Evidence that the Capacity for Economic Self-Reliance Has Declined 56
   7 Conclusion 58

2   **The Demand Shift against the Less-Skilled** 61
   1 Introduction 61
   2 Jobless Growth and the Demand for Less-Skilled Labour 62
   3 Is There Evidence of a Universal and Structural Deterioration of the Labour Market Position of the Less-Skilled? 65
   4 The Role of Trade and Technological Change Empirically Assessed 78
   5 Accounting for Divergent Country Trajectories: The Role of Education, Institutions and Social Norms 86
   6 Conclusion 93

PART 2   NEW SOCIAL RISKS, POVERTY AND THE ADEQUACY OF SOCIAL PROTECTION

3 **Low Pay and Poverty: Anatomy of a 'New' Social Risk**   97
   1 Introduction   97
   2 What Is Low Pay?   98
   3 Low Pay and Poverty   99
   4 Why the Overlap between Low Pay and Poverty Is Limited   106
   5 Further Considerations   109
   6 The Impact of Traditional Policy Instruments and the Role for New Policy Instruments   115
   7 Conclusion   119

4 **On the Limits to Incrementalism in Income Protection Policy: The Case of Structural Unemployment in Belgium**   123
   1 Introduction   123
   2 Unemployment Insurance in Belgium   124
   3 Policy Responses to Mass Unemployment   125
   4 Outcomes in a Comparative Perspective   134
   5 How the UI System Started Failing the Most Vulnerable   139
   6 Why the UI System Started Failing the Most Vulnerable   142
   7 On the Economic Limits to Incrementalism   147
   8 On the Political Limits to Incrementalism   156
   9 Conclusion   162

PART 3   NEW POLICY RESPONSES ASSESSED

5 **How Responsive Are Poverty Rates to Job Growth?**   167
   1 Introduction   167
   2 The Renewed Primacy of Work in Social Policy   168
   3 Employment and Poverty: Some Basic Facts   170
   4 Workless Households   173
   5 Households with Work   183
   6 The Case of the Netherlands   186
   7 Conclusion   194

6 **Alternatives to Passive Income Support: The Verdict of Empirical Evaluation Studies**   201
   1 Introduction   201
   2 Employers' Subsidies   201

3 Subsidising the Low-Paid 218
4 Conclusion 233

Overall Conclusion **235**

List of Tables and Figures **243**

References **249**

Index **283**

Introduction

A pervasive sense of pessimism and even a degree of defeatism have dominated the welfare state literature ever since the first oil shock put an abrupt end to the now-mythical 'Golden Age' of welfare capitalism. That a general sense of dread came to prevail in the years immediately after the oil price shocks of the mid- to late 1970s is scarcely surprising; the consequences of the economic crisis that ensued were after all both brutal and profound. The general economic slowdown brought about a collapse in the demand for labour precisely at a time when many youngsters (the sizable post-war baby boom cohort) and women were entering the labour market. In addition, the energy price shock severely affected employment in manufacturing, which up until then had been sustained by historically unprecedented levels of economic growth. The social consequences of sudden and massive job shedding in industry were particularly disruptive because manufacturing had traditionally provided stable, relatively well-paid employment to many a breadwinner, even to those with little formal education. The economic crisis directly affected the central supporting pillar of the welfare capitalist system, the (male) breadwinner and it created a particularly unwelcoming climate for the scores of newcomers on the labour market.

During the bleak late 1970s and early 1980s, unemployment exploded and benefit dependency soared. As is evident from the literature at the time, there was much speculation that the welfare state would eventually collapse under the weight of its apparently inexorably mounting budgetary and economic cost. The sense of malaise was aggravated by the perception that, despite the massive and apparently unsustainable increases in social spending, the welfare state seemed to be failing in alleviating the poverty and deprivation created by the economic crisis and the rise of mass unemployment. The talk was increasingly of new poverty, social exclusion and the underclass. While it is true that income surveys, where available, suggested that income poverty was not generally rising in the OECD area, it is not difficult to understand why a perception of welfare state failure prevailed; it was a time when seemingly never-ending reports of factory closings, mass layoffs and growing welfare lines dominated the news and public consciousness.

I think it is fair to say that, generally speaking, even in the darkest years of the late 1970s and 1980s the hope still lived that the economic crisis would be transitory and that Western economies would eventually recover – aided or not by economic stimuli and/or reform, and that unemployment would come down again. This is not to say that many people believed that the golden years of welfare capitalism would return. The crisis had blown away the illusion that the historically atypical growth rates of the 1950s and 1960s could be restored. Also, it had become clear to all that some things had changed quite fundamentally or were in the process of doing so. On the socio-demographic front there was the decline of the traditional nuclear two adult household and the rise of female labour market participation. And it was evident that the transition from an industrial to a post-industrial economy was bringing with it the demise of the traditional life-long, full-time job.

Yet the economic recovery of the mid-to late 1980s did not bring the expected improvement. Unemployment fell, but it did not fall as much as some had expected or hoped for. Benefit dependency rates came down only hesitantly, and, again, much less than hoped for. As a consequence, neither did social expenditure. Poverty rates remained stagnant or increased, especially for those of working age. Clearly, economic growth no longer produced social progress in the way it had during the 'Golden Age' of welfare capitalism.

It was around this time that talk arose of advanced welfare states facing, in the words of French sociologist Pierre Rosanvallon (1995), *A New Social Question*.

The Rise of Economic Redundancy

Clearly, high levels of involuntary labour market exclusion and benefit dependency among those of working age have become permanent features of post-oil shock welfare states. It is a well-documented fact that the less-skilled are disproportionally affected.

The situation we witness today seems consistent with writings predicting a growing divide between 'winners' and 'losers' in post-industrial societies. Deindustrialisation, economic globalisation and technological progress play a central role in such arguments. One recurrent claim is that the less-skilled are in danger of becoming 'economically superfluous' in the increasingly skill- and talent-driven Western economies, and that countries are increasingly faced with a choice between more structural labour market exclusion or more low-paid employment, unless government is willing to provide adequately paid employment (which, in the context of increasing economic openness and competition, is deemed increasingly difficult).

To illustrate this point, let me quote at some length from 'A new welfare architecture for Europe', a report written for the Belgian presidency of the EU by four leading social policy writers, Esping-Andersen, Gallie, Hemerijck and Myles (2002):

> The tide is now unfavourable because market inequalities are intensifying. This is a long-term and structural trend that stems from demographic factors (the rise of more vulnerable households) and changes in labour markets (higher risks of unemployment, precarious employment and increasing earnings disparities). Over the past two decades, primary income inequality has grown by 10 to 30 per cent in most advanced countries... It is evident that welfare states face an uphill battle to sustain egalitarian ambitions...
>
> This 'big picture' puts the menace of a polarised future society into focus. Widening welfare gaps are unlikely to be reversed without policy intervention simply because the driving forces are of a long-term, structural nature. This is why we encounter so many pessimistic scenarios. In one, the gulf between the post-industrial 'winners' and 'losers' is widening. The 'winners' are those with skills and excellent mobility chances, united in high-income dual career households. The 'losers' are, above all, those with low qualifications and little schooling who are likely to circulate between low paid, precarious jobs and unemployment, as well as those in weak households such as lone mothers or work poor couples.
>
> We no longer live in a world in which low-skilled workers can support the entire family. The basic requisite for a good life is *increasingly* strong cognitive skills and professional qualifications... Employment remains as always the sine qua non for good life chances, but the requirements for access to quality jobs are rising and are likely to continue to do so.

As the excerpt above indicates, it is not only structural shifts in labour demand which are considered to be at the detriment of the low-skilled. Socio-demographic changes too are thought to be widening the economic gap between the lower- and the higher-skilled. The rise of double earnership, for example, has driven up general living standards, and hence relative poverty thresholds, but it has also brought with it increased exposure to relative poverty among the remaining single-earner households, especially among those with low earnings capacity, i.e., the less-skilled. Also take into account that the proportion of single people and single-parent households has risen.

It is precisely the interaction between economic and socio-demographic trends which is thought to be driving up economic inequality between the low-skilled and the high-skilled. Simply put, the idea is that economic inequality among those of working age used to be determined primarily by the differences in earnings between low- and high-skilled male breadwinners, almost all of whom had lifelong full-time jobs. Now, we appear to have entered an era in which the upper end of the income spectrum is occupied by highly educated dual-earner couples who accumulate income from two relatively well-paid full-time jobs, while, on the other end, and far removed from the highly educated, there are the less-educated single earners who have to make ends meet on one income, and given their limited earnings capacity, usually below-average income. The most severe disadvantage is faced by low-skilled lone parents; they obviously lack two incomes and generally have a low earning potential, which, moreover, they find difficult to realise because of work-care incompatibilities.

On top of all this, there is the alleged inequality-enhancing impact of the welfare state itself. The argument here is that some of the core institutions of the traditional welfare state itself are effectively responsible for the alleged economic divergence between the less and the more highly skilled. The proliferation of double earnership among the lesser skilled is said to have been obstructed in many countries by the maintenance of the breadwinner bias in the institutional organisation of the labour market. Minimum wages, for example, are said to be particularly harmful to the employment chances and hence (relative) living standards of less-skilled women.

Welfare State Failure(s)

The apparent demand shift away from the less-skilled in conjunction with other aspects of economic and social change creates both shared and specific problems for European welfare states.

The general and also fundamental problem, I would contend, is that the declining demand for less-educated labour is making it increasingly hard for a growing number of work-eligible people to acquire adequate incomes in the labour market, even if they do everything they reasonably can to achieve their full earnings potential. The days that people with limited years of schooling but an appetite for work could make a decent living in the (then still heavily unionised) manufacturing sector are finally gone it would seem. Service sector jobs for the less-skilled tend to be less stable and often lack the degree of social protection and benefits that industrial jobs used to offer. In countries with extensive labour market regulation, the less-skilled are confronted with structural job scarcity.

This is a fundamental problem because minimum income protection regimes in the advanced welfare states are all, to a greater or lesser degree, grounded on the institutional and doctrinal premise that people of working age have no need for transfers and that they cannot legitimately claim such transfers, unless they are incapacitated for work or involuntarily unemployed. The assumption, by and large, is that redistribution is only required and, indeed, appropriate, to alleviate risk-induced and, as a general rule, temporary need. It seems that precisely this crucial assumption is becoming increasingly untenable.

This is what I would call the generic problem. The demand shift against the less-skilled is, however, leading to deficiencies and pathologies that manifest themselves in different guises. The variety of challenges the demand shift against the less-skilled seems to pose for advanced welfare states, in the context of present-day economic and political constraints, is nicely captured in what Iversen and Wren (1998) have called the 'Service Economy Trilemma'. This trilemma suggests that welfare states today confront a choice between full employment, wage equality and fiscal sustainability. The claim is that this service sector trilemma generates quite distinctive policy problems for different welfare state models (Hemerijck 2002).

The Scandinavian welfare states have largely avoided rises in inequality, poverty and unemployment through a sustained commitment to full employment (for men and women alike), catering specifically to the needs of less-skilled women and single parents. The main difficulty confronting the Scandinavian model, it is argued, is their continued ability to finance the set of public policies that sustain high employment in the context of egalitarian wages. The Nordic countries are said to face a hard choice between liberalising private services, which would presumably entail more wage inequality, or a continued adherence to wage equality which, under conditions of tightening budgetary constraints, would probably imply more unemployment.

The problem of the Anglo-Saxon model is not one of long-term fiscal sustainability of the welfare state, since significantly fewer resources are dedicated to sustaining high employment. Instead the problem is said to be growing wage inequality and particularly deteriorating (relative) wages for the less-skilled, coupled to ever-more unequal access to social insurance and deficient skill formation. Inadequate pay, poverty in the workplace and insufficient upward mobility are perceived to be the major problems in the Anglo-Saxon cluster. In addition, these countries are said to be trapped in a low-skill equilibrium because of ineffectual industrial relations and inadequate public investment in education, especially for the disadvantaged.

Continental European welfare, finally, is said to face the double obstacle of, on the one hand, very high fixed labour costs, especially for relatively less-skilled work, and on the other hand fiscal constraints to more elaborate employment-friendly policies, let alone large-scale public employment, deriving from the need to support an already very large inactive population. The situation there is further compounded by the still-heavy reliance on social insurance (financed primarily through payroll taxes) and the sustained male breadwinner bias in social security provisions and labour market institutions. The major problem facing Continental welfare states is inadequate job creation. It is alleged that the inactivity trap in which Continental welfare states seem caught reinforces existing insider-outsider cleavages, with less-skilled youngsters and women being the most affected.

Limits to Incrementalism

But there are additional problems. The challenge facing advanced welfare states is not just a matter of finding a new optimum *in response to* changed economic conditions and *within the constraints* presented by economic and political change. There is the added constraint that policy adaptation – especially reform of existing institutions – exhibits significant path dependency. Indeed, some writers have stressed that efficient policy adjustment to changes in the economic and social environment has been hampered, first and foremost, by the fact that welfare state institutions and policies are controlled not by 'enlightened' policymakers, but by politicians and interest groups with constituencies to satisfy (Pierson 2001).

In fact, past improvements in social protection occurred by and large in what one might label an 'incremental' way, i.e., by augmenting and expanding the existing institutions and policies. It seems, however, that it is precisely this kind of incremental adaptation that has run into some very fundamental barriers which derive from profound nature of some of the changes that have occurred in the economic and social environment. Let me clarify what I mean.

The income protection model that is dominant today in the industrialised world, and particularly in Continental Europe, was created in response to the 'social question', i.e., the workers question. The social question essentially consisted of two components. First, there was the problem that many jobs did not provide a decent income. This aspect of the social question found its resolution in major part through the social (i.e., political) correction of the market, i.e., through labour market regulation. A second component of the 'original' social question was the hardship caused by such social risks as unemployment, illness or industrial accidents. It was, of course, through the development of social security – social insurance and social assistance – that this aspect was addressed.

Let us look briefly at the first component. The twentieth century marked an enormous expansion in social legislation, e.g., redundancy protection, maximum working hours legislation, minimum wages, laws protecting trade unions, state enforcement of collective labour agreements etc., be it in some countries more elaborately than in others.

The incrementalist route – that of more regulation on top of and in addition to existing laws – seems a dead-end route today. Take minimum wages, for example, be it statutory or as agreed in collective labour agreements. For decades, gradual increases in minimum wages contributed to the improvement of the living standards of low-paid workers/breadwinners and their families. In this sense, they were a particularly successful response to the social question. This was certainly the case up until the early 1970s; throughout the 1950s and 1960s minimum wages increased quite strongly without a noticeable effect on unemployment, which by and large remained at near frictional levels. This incremental approach, i.e., that of gradual increases, appears to have long reached an end, even if such increases might in theory contribute to preventing poverty among households with a low earned income.

Higher minimum wages will inevitably lead to a further decline in the demand for low-skilled labour and thus to even higher structural unemployment among the less-skilled. High minimum wages are already regarded as an important cause of structural exclusion from the labour market. Moreover, one could argue that poverty among households with a low labour income should no longer be seen as a problem of inadequate breadwinner wages. One could well argue that the problem is not the inadequacy of breadwinner wages (which was the 'old' logic), but the fact that not enough households have second incomes. Employment rates among low-skilled women remain comparatively low, and it is conceivable that this is a consequence of, among other things, high minimum wages – which were in fact intended to protect households via the breadwinner (besides ensuring 'fair wages'). More generally, one could say that social regulation that aims to protect households via the breadwinner has become outdated and hence dysfunctional. In sum, one can argue that in the present and certainly in the future socio-economic context, no social progress should be expected from an incremental expansion of the labour market institutions that emerged in response to the social question. It could even be argued, and indeed some do, that such 'old' institutions have effectively become defunct.

A similar argument can be made with respect to the second component. In most advanced welfare states, and particularly in Continental welfare states, income security rests in first instance on social insurance and in second instance on social assistance. This model is predicated on the assumption that people who are able and willing to work will, under normal circumstances, acquire an adequate income in the labour market. A social contribution is due on this earned income, which subsequently entitles the contributor to a benefit (usually proportional to the earned income) if, and only if, he or she is affected by a recognised risk. Such a benefit is a *replacement income,* i.e., as a rule it temporarily replaces the earned income. For those who slip through this safety net, there are non-time-limited, means-tested social assistance benefits.

The deficiencies of the social insurance/social assistance model in the changed social and economic context are apparent. First and foremost, new social risks have emerged that are not adequately covered within this framework, for example inadequate earnings or single earnership. Social benefits for the working population are after all intended to replace, not supplement wages, in the assumption that the labour market provides people in work with an adequate standard of living. Furthermore, certain risks that are theoretically covered have undergone a fundamental transformation, for example the risk of unemployment. Social security was designed to offer protection against frictional, i.e., temporary, unemployment. Unemployment insurance benefits are for that reason generally limited in time. However, because unemployment today is to a large extent structural in nature, long-term unemployed individuals are often inadequately protected. Moreover, many of the structurally unemployed are not even entitled to unemployment insurance benefits, since they have earned no or insufficient social entitlements, e.g., school leavers or new labour market entrants.

The failure of social security as the main tool for income protection would appear to be manifested in the strong increase in social assistance dependency in the Western world. Social assistance schemes that were intended as a residual and temporary social safety net for very small population groups have now become a quasi-permanent source of income to large sections of the population. Poverty is rampant among households on social assistance, which is scarcely surprising; social assistance benefits tend to fall well below generally applied poverty thresholds. Increases to more adequate levels are widely deemed unfeasible because of the perceived necessity of maintaining sufficient work incentives.

So, in relation to benefits, the incrementalist approach seems to have run out of steam as well. Within the logic of the existing systems of social insurance and social assistance, more generous benefits cannot be the answer, or so it can be argued. Higher and better accessible *replacement incomes*, i.e., benefits that by definition cannot be combined with an earned income, may after all result in greater dependency traps and thus aggravate the problem of structural labour market exclusion.

Beyond Incrementalism

That incrementalism – that is, augmenting the traditional pillars of income protection – offers limited prospects has become increasingly well recognised. The last decade or so has been marked by the rise to prominence of social policy doctrines which entail a radical departure from incrementalism, particularly if understood as improved benefit adequacy within the social insurance/social assistance framework.

The consensus now is that far too many healthy, able-bodied people are chronically 'trapped' in passive benefit dependency. The emphasis has shifted towards bringing down levels of chronic benefit dependency and increasing economic self-reliance. Today's social policy agendas in Europe read as follows: how to get rid of 'perverse work incentives', 'dependency traps', 'cultures of dependency' and the like, how to 're-integrate' the long-term excluded, how to 'turn social safety nets into trampolines'. Today, politicians from all over the political spectrum – many of them with their roots firmly in the traditional left – once again tout the virtues of work and economic self-reliance.

At the centre of such doctrines as 'The Third Way' or 'The Active Welfare State' sits the idea that there is and must be a strong complementarity between labour participation and poverty reduction objectives. A noticeable exponent has been the Netherlands, where a radical policy shift from passive benefit adequacy towards boosting labour market participation was initiated around the late 1980s and where it has been vigorously pursued ever since. The Dutch government itself summed up its singular purpose in the catchphrase: 'work, work, work'. The idea that employment growth and poverty reduction are natural allies is also remarkably central – be it implicitly – to European policy as it is now taking shape within the framework of the Open Method of Coordination (OMC).

Policy innovation, as it has taken place over the past decade or so, can be broadly fitted into two categories. One category includes what one might label 'restoration measures' – measures that attempt to restore the crucial full-employment conditions that are essential for the traditional paradigm to function properly. Most advanced welfare states have implemented and vastly expanded wage and employment subsidies, training and public employment programmes, etc. with the aim of boosting the employment and income security prospects of the less-skilled.

A second category of non-incremental measures comprises what one might call 'new income protection arrangements'. I am referring here in particular to tax credits for the low-paid and for households with low earned income. Such tax credits have been introduced in various OECD countries to alleviate in-work poverty and to boost employment, especially of those 'trapped' in passive benefit dependency. In the United States, for example, the Earned Income Tax Credit – a tax subsidy for households with low earnings – is now by far the most important system of direct income distribution for the working-age population.

Yet despite such efforts, the most serious problems remain unresolved. It is clear, for example, that unemployment levels (especially if measured by broader measures of involuntary or problematic labour market exclusion) have remained far above frictional levels even in countries that have put vast resources into active labour market policies. Most crucially, it is hard to find a single country where poverty rates for the working age population have fallen.

The sense of pessimism noted at the start of this introduction has not yet yielded to a belief that a new synthesis between economic and social progress is within grasp. Many seem to doubt that much can be done, even by the most voluntaristic and egalitarian-minded government, to effectively counteract rising inequality as a result of labour demand shifts. This is perhaps the biggest reason why a thorough investigation of the nature and consequences of the demand shift against the less-skilled is important.

Organisation of This Book

To recapitulate, these are what I perceive to be three key ideas shaping the current debate on welfare state reform in response to economic change, as this plays out not only in the academic literature but also in policy documents:

a. that the economic changes of the past decades – most notably: the shift from industry to services, the intensification of technology use and increased international competition – have been accompanied by a labour demand shift against the less-skilled which has profoundly changed the structure of need and which has given rise to new social risks;
b. that traditional welfare state arrangements fail to deal adequately with the new needs and risks brought by economic change, and that, more importantly, there are intrinsic limits to what gradual adaptation can achieve to redress these deficiencies;
c. that, consequently, improved income protection for the working-age population will have to come from increased use of new – non-incremental – instruments and policies, most notably from policies often referred to as 'active welfare state' policies or 'make work pay' policies.

This volume basically deals with each of these three major issues in turn. Throughout this volume there will be a cross-cutting focus on the specific problems facing the Continental European welfare states. This is useful, I think, because this is the model which is said to be facing some of the biggest problems while at the same time being the least adaptive and capable of self-transformation. The particular focus will be on the case of Belgium and, to a lesser extent, the Netherlands. Belgium is a particularly interesting case because in many respects the country epitomises the alleged deficiencies and constraints of the Continental European model. Yet its welfare state has been markedly less inert than a cursory reading might suggest.

This is how the book is organised: The first part consists of two chapters that cover the first key assumption in the debate, the idea that some segments of the population, most notably the least educated, are on an inexorable path towards structural economic redundancy. Chapter 1 starts by empirically documenting the recent declines in economic self-reliance across advanced welfare states, particularly among the less-skilled. Chapter 2 tries to gauge whether and to what extent the observed declines in self-reliance can be attributed to structural changes in the labour market.

Whereas part 1 deals with the nature of labour market change itself, part 2 looks at the consequences upon minimum income protection and poverty. Chapters 3 and 4 assess the view that the traditional instruments of income protection are intrinsically incapable of offering adequate relief to those afflicted by, respectively, low pay and structural unemployment – two of the most significant 'new' social risks associated with the demand shift against less-skilled labour.

Part 3 focuses on the question of whether so-called active welfare state and active labour market policies are delivering on their promise to compensate for the alleged deficiencies of the conventional instruments. Chapter 5 brings together empirical evidence relating to the key notion that labour market participation and poverty reduction are natural complements. Chapter 6 assesses in more detail the effectiveness of a) employers' subsidies for the hiring of less-skilled workers, and b) benefits for workers or households on low earnings.

The final section offers a conclusion.

Acknowledgements

I incurred many debts while writing this book. Bea Cantillon provided me with the time and resources to finish first my doctoral thesis and then this book. Her encouragement and incisive comments also proved crucial to both projects. I benefited from the insights and comments of many people but I owe a special debt to Anton Hemerijck. Working at the Centre for Social Policy – Herman Deleeck at Antwerp University remains a privilege and I wish to thank my colleagues for their support, advice and friendship. I thank Ingrid Van Zele and staff at Amsterdam University Press for their excellent copy-editing support. Finally, I wish to acknowledge Stichting Instituut GAK for their financial support.

PART 1

THE DECLINE OF SELF-RELIANCE AND THE LABOUR DEMAND SHIFT AGAINST THE LESS-SKILLED: CONJECTURES, FACTS AND EXPLANATIONS

1 The Decline of Self-Reliance in Advanced Welfare States

1 Introduction

Over the past decade or so, the idea has gained ground that, as Rosanvallon (1995) has put it in his *La Nouvelle Question Sociale*, 'economic redundancy' is on the rise in the advanced economies. The idea here is that there is less and less need in advanced economies for people who lack appropriate schooling or intellectual, creative or social talents.

To quote Esping-Andersen: 'As servicing becomes the life-blood of our existence, privilege is bestowed upon the knowledge strata. Yet, there are huge areas of servicing which are labour intensive and low-skilled. The lower end of servicing society is where we must pin our hopes for mass-employment. Unfortunately, because of their sluggish productivity, low-end service jobs are threatened by a long-term 'cost-disease' problem. Tertiary employment is therefore likely to stagnate unless wages slide downwards. *Taken together, globalisation, new technologies and the service economy seem to herald one inescapable necessity: less equality*' (Esping-Andersen 1999: 96; emphasis added).

In effect, this has become the conventional wisdom in much of the social policy literature and in parts of economics literature (see for example Esping-Andersen 1996, 1999; Ferrera et al. 2000; Howell 1999; Huber and Stephens 2000; Iversen and Wren 1998; Murmane et al. 1995; Piketty 1999; Pryor and Schaffer 1999; Sandmo 2002; Snower 1996, 1998). The idea that merely possessing a pair of strong hands and a healthy appetite for work will get you nowhere (except possibly in low-paid, precarious work) is also a vision that often recurs in the press and in economics/public policy literature aimed at a wider audience (Fitoussi and Rosanvallon 1996; Galbraith 1992, 1998; Kaus 1992; Reich 1991; Rifkin 1995). The idea is not new though; as long ago as 1958, Michael Young alleged the *The Rise of Meritocracy: 1870-2033*.

In addition, there are believed to be limits to upskilling. According to some, providing more schooling for people with limited intrinsic talents, be they intellectual, creative or social, will improve their employability only to a limited extent. According to this view, observed returns that are attributed to human capital are nothing more than returns to ability, as schooling does little more than sort individuals according to intrinsic qualities such as intelligence and capacity for work. This idea was expressed at its most extreme in Herrnstein and Murray's controversial book *The Bell Curve* (1996), which prompted an enormous amount of public as well as academic debate and research, e.g., Arrow et al. (2000), Ashenfelter and Rouse (2000), Bowles and Gintis (2000), Bowles et al., (2002), Fischer et al. (1998), Roemer et al. (2003).

All this is believed to be a major factor in the impasse of persistent poverty in which contemporary welfare states seem caught. The declining demand for less-educated labour appears to be making it increasingly hard for a growing number of work-eligible people to acquire an adequate income in the labour market, even if they do everything they reasonably can to achieve their full earning potential.

This is potentially highly problematic. Minimum income protection regimes in the advanced welfare states are after all grounded on the institutional and doctrinal premise that people of working age have no need for cash transfers and that they cannot legitimately claim such benefits unless they are incapacitated for work or involuntarily unemployed. The assumption, by and large, is that cash transfers for the working-age population are only required and, indeed, appropriate, to alleviate risk-induced and, as a general rule, temporary need. It seems that this crucial assumption has become untenable.

The main purpose of this first chapter is to present and discuss empirical evidence pertaining to this issue. Using the Luxembourg Income Study (LIS) data for a selection of OECD countries and Socio-Economic Panel (SEP) data for Belgium, we gauge the rises in 'market income' poverty that have occurred during the past decades. The principal focus here is on Belgium because of the availability of time series data that allows us to look at how the less-skilled have fared over the past couple of decades. In addition, Belgium is, for a number of reasons which I will set out below, a particularly interesting case.

2 A Note on the Relevance of Self-Reliance in Social Policy

The notion of full-employment

The development of the modern post-war welfare state, and particularly social security, rested on the assumption that healthy people of working age generally had no need for or right to redistribution, unless they were affected by a recognised social risk causing incapacitation. This assumption was incorporated into the idea of full employment – understood as the adequate availability of stable breadwinner jobs that could support a family. The belief in full employment was prompted partly by the situation at the time; the modern European welfare states reached maturity under relatively favourable economic circumstances. The idea that full employment was attainable and sustainable also had a theoretical or at least intellectual foundation, namely Keynes's influential General Theory (1935) which postulated that government could assure full employment through competent macroeconomic management, particularly of aggregate demand. This implied pursuing a contra-cyclical demand-stimulating policy when aggregate demand was declining, e.g., through investment in public works. Keynesianism constituted the widely shared intellectual basis for the belief in full employment, not only in Europe, but across the Atlantic world.

The British welfare state, which probably had more of an explicit intellectual foundation than other welfare regimes, was based explicitly on the assumption of full employment, defined by Beveridge (1945: 18) as a situation in which there are more vacant jobs than unemployed men. In Beveridge's eyes, vacant jobs were 'jobs at fair wages of such a kind, and so located that the unemployed men could reasonably be expected to take them'. He took into account an element of frictional unemployment caused by mobility between jobs and the (desirable) destruction of superfluous jobs. He foresaw an unemployment rate of 3 per cent that would consist in 'a shifting body of short-term unemployed who could be maintained without hardship by unemployment insurance' (Beveridge 1945: 128). Beveridge's words reflected accepted opinion throughout most of the industrialised world.

Of course, one may ask whether this assumption was ever realistic, even in the so-called 'golden years' of welfare capitalism. Unemployment at the time may have been low, but that is not to say that all breadwinners had a job that allowed them to adequately support a family. However, the first decades after World War II, when the welfare state reached maturity, were characterised by low unemployment and very strong wage growth (including for the lowest paid). Full employment, in the sense of enough properly paid jobs for all willing and able breadwinners, was perhaps not a reasonable assumption even then but it was assumed to be an achievable condition during this crucial period in the development of the contemporary welfare state.

The potential limits to solidarity

Full employment enabled the development of a social security system that essentially rested on horizontal solidarity – the kind of pseudo-solidarity that emanates from shared exposure to insurable risks. People's willingness to pay contributions is here not motivated by compassion for those who are affected by illness, unemployment, etc., but by their need/necessity to cover themselves in a comparatively cheap and reliable manner against the same risks. The binding agent is, essentially, uncertainty about who will be affected by a certain risk and might consequently suffer loss of income. Such well-understood self-interest is thought to be the main driver behind the successful development and expansion of social security in Western welfare states (Baldwin 1990; Heidenheimer et al. 1990). According to Baldwin, it was the relative cost-effectiveness of mandatory, universal social insurance which forged a durable alliance between population segments whose relationship was otherwise unstable or even adversary.

Chronic deprivation deriving from an inadequate earnings potential is evidently not an insurable risk. It is not even a risk. It necessitates 'pure' and sustained solidarity between rich/high-skilled/very talented individuals on the one hand and poor/low-skilled/less-talented individuals on the other. Many commentators fear that high earners will simply refuse to share their wealth, and that they will either support political parties that advocate minimal or limited redistribution, or that they will simply vote with their feet, i.e., by moving to countries or regions with more favourable taxation systems. Countries that are intent on retaining their most productive citizens will have little choice but to limit the extent of redistribution.

A counter argument here is that welfare state support is not adequately grasped in a simplistic model in which the 'utility maximising' *homo economicus* balances costs (that is taxes and social contributions paid) against expected personal financial gains. People are evidently prepared to show real solidarity, but they do not do so indiscriminately and unconditionally. Research has brought to light considerable preparedness to show solidarity towards people who are sick, old or disabled; people who are manifestly unable to acquire an adequate income in the labour market for reasons beyond their own will (Boeri et al. 2000; Hemerijck 1999; Van Oorschot 1999). However, and this is perhaps of crucial importance, the preparedness to show solidarity with needy but healthy people of active age who are able to work tends to be considerably smaller. They tend to be held personally responsible for their inability to find a decent-paying job. They are universally perceived to be 'undeserving'.

This distinction between the so-called 'deserving' and 'undeserving' poor seems to have remarkably old historic roots, as De Swaan (1988), Goodin (1988) and others have sought to demonstrate (Goodin's discussion of the English Poor Law is a particularly good example). It clearly predates the modern welfare state and appears to emanate from seemingly deep-rooted conceptions of social justice and solidarity. In other words, the principle that people of working age have no need for cash transfers and that they cannot legitimately claim such benefits is probably not just an 'accidental' institutional assumption stemming from the fact that modern welfare states reached full maturity in the so-called golden years of welfare capitalism, when 'full employment' prevailed or seemed within grasp.

The perception that societies are becoming increasingly meritocratic may, for that matter and perhaps somewhat paradoxically, reinforce the distinction between the deserving and the undeserving poor. If acquiring a degree is considered to be a question of merit and if the individual is made responsible for her educational level, then the likelihood increases that unemployment or low-paid employment, too, will be regarded as a matter of personal responsibility. Perhaps the hierarchy of diplomas and degrees is already to a large extent regarded as a legitimate meritocratic hierarchy, which is rightly taken into account in processes of selection and recruitment in the labour market. According to this logic, the traditional social risk of unemployment is, in fact, no longer regarded as a real risk, but as a status for which people should be held personally responsible.

There may be other complicating factors. It would appear that people's willingness to show compassion and solidarity is to a degree determined by the physical presence and visibility of deprivation. There is evidence, from some countries at least, that shows a growing spatial segregation between winners and losers, be it at urban (inner city vs. periphery), regional (technological growth poles or 'valleys' vs. backward industrial regions) or even on the global level. If willingness to show solidarity is indeed a function of spatial proximity and visibility, then it may well be undermined by growing mobility and the resulting geographical separation of rich and poor.

One other reason why spatial segregation might undermine people's willingness to show solidarity is that it reduces the need to contribute to collective care arrangements that restrict the negative externalities of poverty and deprivation (see De Swaan 1988). It is not unimaginable that people are prepared to contribute to the welfare state partly because they do not want to be confronted with the consequences of poverty and deprivation (e.g., crime, people sleeping rough or begging in the streets). It is quite conceivable, however, that high earners will be increasingly able to distance themselves geographically from the needy, so that, in their eyes, there is no longer a necessity to contribute to collective arrangements that neutralise the threats and discomforts associated with poverty and exclusion.

Potential economic constraints to structural redistribution

In addition, there are thought to be limits to redistribution to the chronically needy at working age that are of an economic rather than political, sociological or psychological nature. In the modern welfare state, there is both direct and indirect distribution. Minimum wages and collective wage-setting procedures are important instruments of indirect redistribution. Minimum wages, for example, benefit low-wage workers at the cost of consumers (Freeman 1996). This often involves a degree of vertical redistribution since low-wage intensive services like cleaning, catering, etc. are typically consumed by higher-income consumers. Collective wage bargaining agreements generally imply some degree of solidarity between people with high earnings potential and those with lower earnings potential (Wallerstein 1999). This is largely due to the fact that group and not individual productivity increases constitute the basis for collective wage negotiations, be it at the national, industry or company level. The extent of actual redistribution (or solidarity) obviously depends on the extent to which workers contribute equally to productivity growth.

As I will illustrate in chapter 2, there have been sharp increases in the schooling premium in some countries with decentralised wage formation – the schooling premium being the additional income associated with an additional year of schooling or a degree. By contrast, in countries with corporatist wage formation, particularly in Northern and Central European countries, this has generally not been the case. Hence, there is a real possibility that wage compression is being kept artificially low in much of Europe. A classic textbook argument holds that an artificially high degree of wage compression will result in unemployment and hence a bigger demand for income transfers (Barr 1998, 2001). The resulting economic welfare loss (production foregone) combined with the increased tax burden on those who do work will also mean that there is less to redistribute than would otherwise be the case. Indeed, the extent of unemployment and non-employment in many parts of Europe is routinely attributed to what is perceived to be an artificially compressed wage distribution. At the same time, high taxes are believed to discourage highly productive (or highly talented) individuals from undertaking long and demanding studies, to be creative, to take risks and hence to create income.

Direct redistribution for income protection purposes in the welfare state is achieved mainly through social security. Income security for people of active age is still predominantly ensured through social insurance. Under such a system, one 'earns' the right to a benefit by paying contributions. The more substantial the contribution and the longer it has been paid, the higher the benefits to which one is entitled. In social insurance, there is, in other words, a direct link between 'productive contributions' and the level of social protection enjoyed, via wages and social contributions paid on these wages. Benefits are either a contingent (i.e., they are risk-dependent) or, as in the case of pensions, a deferred 'wage'. Thus, the extent of real (i.e., vertical as opposed to risk-induced horizontal) redistribution from poor to rich is, theoretically, limited. The real distribution is from groups with a relatively low risk of income loss to groups with a relatively high risk. Social insurance that predominantly redistributes horizontally is generally considered not to carry an economic welfare cost. On the contrary, some economic models predict that, under plausible circumstances, a substantial welfare gain will be achieved (Barr 2001).

By contrast, financial hardship that stems from economic redundancy (i.e., an excessively low earnings potential or structural exclusion from the labour market) requires real (i.e., vertical), structural redistribution from people with a high earnings potential to individuals whose earning potential is low. This is generally thought to give rise to potential moral hazard problems and associated economic welfare costs (Barr 1998). First, taxation to fund permanent transfers to the needy is thought to have a negative impact on the willingness of the potentially most productive members of society to work, be creative, to take risks etc. Secondly, the availability of social income is thought to have a negative effect on people's willingness to acquire schooling, look for work, accept employment, etc. Thirdly, an additional hazard may derive from the obvious difficulties of distinguishing between the 'genuinely' needy (i.e., those with a low earning potential) and those who choose not to use their full earning potential.

3 The Decline of Self-Reliance: General Evidence

Benefit dependency among the working-age population

Gauging from various indicators, economic self-reliance among the working-age population has declined substantially over the past couple of decades, not just in a few countries but in the OECD area as a whole.

Table 1.1 succinctly summarises the state of affairs in a number of major OECD countries. It contains benefit dependency rates as calculated by the Dutch Ministry of Social Affairs and Employment (Ministerie Sociale Zaken 2002). These dependency rates express the total volume of working-age benefit dependency in full-time equivalents (FTE) as a ratio of the total working-age population. It is based on the number of people on unemployment benefits, sickness and invalidity benefits, early retirement benefits as well as people on social assistance. Account is also taken of the degree of dependence since not everyone who is dependent receives full benefits.

Table 1.1 Benefit dependency: benefit recipients at working age as a percentage of the working-age population (15-64 years), 1980-1999 (in FTE)

	1980	1990	1999
Belgium	17.4	24.4	23.6
Netherlands	15.9	19.9	17.8
Germany	15.2	18.1	22.4
France	13.9	20.2	24.2
Denmark	20.1	23.2	23.1
Sweden	16.1	17.0	20.0
UK	15.2	18.5	18.9
Spain	8.3	12.3	11.2

Source: OECD 2003, based on National Economic Institute (NEI)/the Netherlands) figures.

As the table shows, the volume of benefit dependence among the working-age population as a share of the total working-age population varies in Europe between 30 and 50 per cent. The table only documents the rises in benefit dependency that occurred during the post-1980 period. But we know from national data sources that the strong increases in benefit dependency occurred during the second half of the 1970s. The strong rises during the 1970s and 1980s come as no great surprise against the background of the economic conditions prevailing at the time: weak and episodic negative economic growth, mass job loss in industry, weak aggregate job growth (in the context of rising female participation rates), high unemployment. More remarkable and interesting, however, is the persistence of mass benefit dependency during the 1990s – a period marked by far stronger economic and employment growth, less job loss in industry and elsewhere, and significantly lower unemployment than previously. In fact, some parts of the OECD area experienced the longest period of sustained economic expansion since the Second World War during this period. In 1999, the last year for which data is presented, a number of countries were on the verge of attaining their lowest unemployment rate in three decades. That dependency rates remained high during the 1990s can be interpreted as evidence that something has changed structurally. The picture here is in fact consistent with the view that important sections of the working-age population have become in effect 'economically redundant'.

Pre-transfer/tax poverty rates

The decline of economic self-reliance is also evident from the well-documented rises in pre-transfer poverty throughout the OECD area. In Cantillon, Marx and Van den Bosch (1997) we already documented substantial rises in pre-transfer poverty, particularly among the working-age population, during the 1970s and the 1980s, using LIS data. For a full description of the data sets and the standardisation procedure we refer to Atkinson, Rainwater and Smeeding (1995) and to the LIS information packages (http://lissy.ceps.lu). For an assessment of data quality, I refer to Atkinson et al. (1995; appendix 4) and to Cantillon et al. (1997). Although LIS remains the most comprehensive source of income data available, there are only a few countries for which good time series data is available for the whole period of interest. What we have is a hotchpotch of partial time series, often spanning rather short periods of time. But even if these partial time series are nothing more than clips from a longer film, they all suggest a similar plot line: rising pre-transfer poverty and transfer dependency.

Using LIS data, I have looked in more detail at five countries for which relatively longer trend data is available. The aim here was to gauge pre-transfer/tax poverty trends, that is to say, poverty rates calculated on the basis of market income rather than actual disposable household income. The adjustment made is purely an arithmetical one; social security transfers are deducted from measured household income and direct taxes and employee social security contributions are added again.

A note on poverty measurement first. The definition of poverty which appears to be widely accepted in industrialised countries refers to exclusion from the ordinary life of the community due to lack of resources. As Atkinson (1987) and Foster and Shorrocks (1988) emphasise, this still allows for a diversity of possible judgements about the specification of the poverty line and choice of poverty measure. However, the most common approach is to use relative income poverty lines, derived as proportions of mean or median household income. This is the approach employed *inter alia* in recent studies for the European Commission, Eurostat and the OECD and in cross-country comparisons based on the *Luxembourg Income Study* data. Unlike in the low-pay literature, the mean is used more often than the median, though there are arguments in favour of each: the most common practice is to use 50 per cent of mean household income, adjusted for household size and composition using equivalence scales. The equivalence scale used to make this adjustment here gives a value of 1 to the first adult in the household, 0.5 to each additional adult, and 0.3 to each child (commonly known as the 'modified OECD scale'). The precise equivalence scales employed may have a significant impact on the size and composition of the group falling below the poverty line (Buhman et al. 1988, Coulter, Cowell and Jenkins 1992), and no method of deriving such scales commands general support. The income concept used is disposable income, income of all household members from all sources minus income tax and social security contributions. Using the household as the recipient unit involves the conventional assumption that resources are shared within the household so as to equalise living standards. For a further discussion of these issues see Atkinson (1995), Atkinson, Rainwater and Smeeding (1995), Callan and Nolan (1991), Van den Bosch et al. (1993) and Van den Bosch (2001).

I initially made these calculations as part of a large-scale OECD-funded project on income distribution and further methodological details can be found in Burniaux et al. (1999) and Förster (2000). Admittedly, the most recent data sets available in the LIS are not incorporated but tables 1.2 and 1.3 do capture the period during which the strongest increases in pre-transfer poverty (and benefit dependency for that matter) occurred. These tables show a number of things.

First, there is substantial cross-country variation in the extent of pre-transfer/pre-tax poverty, but the differences between the countries included in the table are not as big as the more pronounced differences if it comes to their actual poverty rates. Sweden and the United States, for example, could not be further away from each other in terms of their actual poverty rates, but their pre-tax and transfer poverty rates are only a few percentage points apart. This holds less true, it must be said, for working-age households, the population segment we are most concerned with here.

Second, the figures indicate rises in pre-transfer poverty rates, especially among the working-age population. There appears to be considerable cross-country variation in the magnitude of these rises and exact comparisons are difficult due to the limited extent of overlap of the available time series. It is noteworthy that the strongest increases occurred among households with a head below the age of 30 and, to a lesser extent, among households with a head aged between 30 and 50. The share of both age groups in the pre-tax/transfer poor population increased substantially.

Third, it is striking that pre-tax/transfer poverty rates increased among all household types. Hence, the rises in benefit dependency and pre-transfer poverty cannot be solely attributed to socio-demographic change, particularly to the rise in single person and single parent households. While there can be no question that single-adult households, particularly single-parent households, are more vulnerable, the rises in pre-tax/transfer poverty are found across all household types, including double-adult households with and without children.

Fourth, as one would expect, pre-tax/transfer poverty rates are especially high for non-working households. But they are also significant for working households, and in countries like Canada, the United States and even Sweden, they make up a larger share of the pre-tax/transfer poor population (at working age) than the non-working households. It is also noteworthy that there are fairly substantial cross-country differences with respect to trends. (Again, exact comparisons are hampered by the fact that the data sets only partially overlap.) In several countries, pre-tax/transfer poverty rates for non-working households dropped in the periods observed, while in other countries we observe an increase.

Table 1.2 Poverty rates[1] before taxes and transfers: per cent of poor[2] individuals in each group, and changes in percentage points

		By age of the household's head				By family type						By work attachment			
	Total	Head below 30	Head between 30 and 50	Head between 50 and 65	Head above 65	Single-adult households			Two-adult households[2]			Non-working households		Working households	
						Head below 65	Head above 65		Head below 65	Head above 65		Head below 65	Head above 65	Head below 65	Head above 65
Canada, 1991	22.9	27.9	15.5	18.5	57.4	46.3	75.6		14.1	50.6		72.5	69.2	12.5	19.4
Changes, 75-91	0.3	12.4	2.8	-0.9	-10.2	10.9	-7.6		2.6	-9.5		-12.1	-15.8	0.9	-12.4
France, 1989	34.5	24.1	20.7	40.1	84.6	41.0	95.8		23.8	79.6		71.9	92.1	15.1	29.1
Changes, 84-89	1.6	6.2	2.3	-5.2	-2.8	3.0	-0.1		-0.1	-4.1		-1.0	3.7	4.0	-2.3
Germany, 1989	22.1	14.2	5.2	17.9	70.7	28.0	84.7		6.4	61.7		66.2	78.7	4.2	18.0
Changes, 78-89	1.9	4.5	1.7	0.9	0.9	-6.7	1.8		0.5	-1.4		24.1	2.3	1.0	-1.5
Sweden, 1992	33.9	37.9	14.5	21.7	90.7	40.8	97.2		12.7	85.4		90.1	95.4	13.1	30.4
Changes, 75-92	7.9	22.2	7.6	4.1	-8.4	12.6	-15.7		6.6	-3.6		27.7	-7.5	6.7	-9.1
United States, 1994	25.3	31.5	17.4	18.5	58.1	45.1	76.9		15.9	50.9		71.1	68.2	14.8	24.1
Changes, 74-94	4.5	11.9	4.8	1.2	-6.7	-7.1	-4.4		4.7	-7.9		10.1	-8.0	4.5	-1.7

	Total	Non-working households				Working households				Total households	
		With children		No children		With children		No children			
		Single adult	Two adults plus	Single adult	Two adults plus	Single adult	Two adults plus	Single adult	Two adults plus	With children	No children
Canada, 1991	22.9	96.4	67.9	75.4	62.7	44.3	12.6	20.6	8.5	19.7	26.4
Changes, 75-91	0.3	-0.4	-28.7	-11.9	-17.3	-1.3	1.1	-1.8	-1.6	4.9	-3.8
France, 1989	34.5	95.9	62.1	89.7	83.5	25.9	18.7	3.2	9.3	25.9	44.8
Changes, 84-89	1.6	0.6	-7.9	-1.7	5.7	6.0	4.9	-0.8	3.8	2.8	0.2
Germany, 1989	22.1	78.9	39.1	80.6	72.8	14.9	3.1	9.2	4.8	6.5	32.9
Changes, 78-89	1.9	1.4	14.5	-0.4	5.4	-2.7	1.0	0.9	0.1	0.8	-7.7
Sweden, 1992	33.9	93.2	88.3	95.7	92.0	27.6	9.6	26.5	9.9	16.3	48.1
Changes, 75-92	7.9	2.6	60.8	-3.9	3.8	12.2	5.5	12.4	3.4	8.9	4.2
United States, 1994	25.3	95.1	70.8	74.1	59.8	48.0	15.4	12.9	8.8	24.0	27.0
Changes, 74-94	4.5	-1.2	22.9	-5.8	-6.9	-5.6	5.7	-0.8	1.9	6.9	-0.6

1 Poverty rate by group is the number of 'poor' individuals in a group as a percentage of the total number of individuals in that group.
2 'Poor' are individuals with equivalent income below 50 per cent of median equivalent disposable income. Equivalence scale elasticity: 0.5.

Source: Analysis of LIS data.

Table 1.3 Structure of poverty[1] before taxes and transfers: per cent of all poor[2] individuals belonging to each group, and changes in percentage points

	Total	By household head's age				By family type				By work attachment			
		Head below 30	Head between 30 and 50	Head between 50 and 65	Head above 65	Single-adult households		Two-adult households[2]		Non-working households		Working households	
						Head below 65	Head above 65	Head below 65	Head above 65	Head below 65	Head above 65	Head below 65	Head above 65
Canada, 1991	100	19.6	36.2	15.6	28.7	24.5	10.3	46.8	18.4	27.9	26.4	43.4	2.3
Changes, 75-91		2.9	14.0	-3.6	-13.3	3.2	-6.3	10.1	-6.9	12.2	-9.1	1.1	-4.2
France, 1989	100	9.4	30.4	25.1	35.1	10.8	12.2	54.1	22.9	34.7	33.7	30.2	1.4
Changes, 84-89		0.7	2.8	-6.1	2.6	2.1	1.4	-4.7	1.2	-9.8	1.3	7.2	1.2
Germany, 1989	100	7.2	10.3	21.2	61.3	16.3	28.8	22.5	32.5	25.2	59.2	13.5	2.0
Changes, 78-89		3.9	1.7	0.1	-5.8	4.2	1.7	1.5	-7.5	1.5	-5.7	4.3	-0.1
Sweden, 1992	100	22.4	19.6	10.5	47.5	32.0	22.7	20.6	24.7	21.6	46.3	30.9	1.2
Changes, 75-92		9.1	8.7	-3.4	-14.3	8.2	-6.8	6.1	-7.5	2.4	-13.9	11.9	-0.4
United States, 1994	100	19.4	36.2	13.3	31.0	22.5	11.3	46.5	19.8	23.4	28.1	45.6	3.0
Changes, 74-94		0.0	8.1	-4.9	-3.2	-0.1	-0.1	3.4	-3.2	-2.8	-3.1	6.0	-0.1

	Total	Non-working households				Working households				Total households	
		With children		No children		With children		No children		With children	No children
		Single adult	Two adults	Single adult	Two adults	Single adult	Two adults	Single adults	Two adults		
Canada, 1991	100	8.0	7.7	16.8	21.7	4.7	25.4	5.2	10.4	45.8	54.2
Changes, 75-91		4.6	4.7	-4.8	-1.4	2.4	1.8	-5.3	-2.0	13.6	-13.6
France, 1989	100	3.3	11.9	18.0	35.2	1.4	24.4	0.3	5.5	41.1	58.9
Changes, 84-89		1.3	-4.7	1.8	-6.8	0.5	5.6	-0.1	2.4	2.7	-2.7
Germany, 1989	100	3.6	2.3	37.3	41.3	1.0	5.1	3.2	6.2	12.0	88.0
Changes, 78-89		0.5	-5.0	3.6	-3.4	0.0	0.0	1.9	2.4	-4.5	4.5
Sweden, 1992	100	3.3	3.4	34.8	26.4	4.5	10.4	12.1	5.2	21.6	78.4
Changes, 75-92		0.2	1.6	-5.8	-7.5	2.1	3.6	5.0	0.9	7.5	-7.5
United States, 1994	100	8.3	8.7	14.4	20.1	8.7	29.0	2.3	8.5	54.7	45.3
Changes, 74-94		-1.5	-1.2	0.1	-3.3	0.7	3.3	0.4	1.5	1.4	-1.4

1 The structure of poverty is the number of 'poor' individuals in each group as a percentage of all 'poor' individuals.
2 'Poor' are individuals with equivalent income below 50 per cent of median equivalent disposable income.

Source: Analysis of LIS data.

4 Evidence for Belgium, with a Particular Focus on the Less-Skilled

Why Belgium constitutes an interesting case

There are few countries for which time series data is available that would allow us to gauge how the less-skilled have fared over the past few decades. Fortunately, we have such data for Belgium, be it only for the Flanders region. In what follows we look in more detail at how the economic fortunes of the less-skilled have changed in the period 1976-1997, two decades marked by momentous changes.

The broad hypothesis is that ability of the less-skilled to be economically self-reliant has deteriorated in advanced economies, and that it is deteriorating further. There is a general line of reasoning behind this hypothesis and there is also a line of reasoning that applies particularly to so-called conservative welfare states.

In the general argument, global and essentially uncontrollable economic forces such as globalisation, deindustrialisation and technological change play a central role. Belgium is an interesting case because of the comparatively rapid pace of deindustrialisation during the 1970s and 1980s (from a comparatively high initial share of manufacturing industry output in total output), which had a tremendous impact on low-skilled employment.

The second line of reasoning applies specifically to the so-called conservative welfare states and is in essence a (social) policy-failure argument. 'Conservative' Western welfare states are in the classic Esping-Andersen scheme welfare states where the breadwinner is the central medium through which social progress is achieved. Now, the core idea behind the hypothesis is that in modern-day societies, the traditional breadwinner-bias in labour market institutions and social security arrangements perversely favours the highly skilled and impairs the less-skilled, particularly less-skilled women. The argument, as spelled out by Esping-Andersen (1996), runs as follows. For decades, higher minimum wages, better employment protection and more generous social income entitlements *for male breadwinners* contributed to society-wide social progress. The classic two-adult, sole (male) breadwinner household was dominant and hence it was correctly assumed that if the breadwinners were made better off, everybody would be better off.

In response to the economic crisis of the early 1970s, the post-industrial transition and the secular rise in female labour participation, the Continental European countries have, so the argument continues, by and large mistakenly opted to preserve, first and foremost, the privileged position of the male breadwinner in the labour market/social security nexus, i.e., the breadwinner model. This was done in major part through a massive expansion of early retirement in order to absorb the excess labour supply created by the economic crisis and the post-industrial transition. The aim was to avoid mass breadwinner unemployment and hence to safeguard the breadwinner model, i.e., high (minimum) wages, strong employment protection and labour market regulations (e.g., limits on temporary and part-time employment) and extensive social security rights, primary as well as derived.

This route, Esping-Andersen argues, has been to the detriment of the employment and hence (relative) living standard of less-skilled women and the households in which they live. They, unlike their more skilled counterparts, have been most negatively affected by the preservation of high minimum wages, job protection rules, etc. The high cost of mass early retirement has, moreover, led to the cost of labour having become excessively high, hampering job creation in services. Hence, the prediction of a widening gap between the less-skilled and more-skilled – reinforced by educational homogamy.

Belgium makes for a good case because it carries many of the hallmarks of what Esping-Andersen has called the conservative welfare state model, in which the Christian democratic 'subsidiarity principle' has institutionalised familialism in the sense of supporting the male breadwinner/female career model. It is fair to say that in Belgium the labour market and welfare state are heavily geared towards male breadwinner: minimum wages are among the highest in the advanced world, job security protection is elaborate, derived social security rights are extensive, the tax system supports the sole breadwinner model, etc.

Defining educational attainment

Thus, in what follows, we consider poverty and dependency trends from the perspective of schooling. In our analyses, we use two operationalisations: one absolute, the other relative. For the absolute definition, we rely on the educational level measured in our surveys on the basis of the question 'What is the highest degree you have obtained?' The idea behind this approach is that each educational level represents a certain package of skills and knowledge. It is reasonable to assume, at least in the case of some educational levels, that this package has remained relatively unchanged in recent decades. In primary education, for example, one still learns basic skills such as reading, writing and math in pretty much the same way as 20 or even 40 years ago. One could argue about the validity of this assumption, but it is nevertheless a defendable and, for that matter, commonly used method.

The big problem with absolute educational levels is that, over the past 20 years or so, significant shifts have occurred in the general schooling of the population. The proportion of 'highly skilled' (i.e., higher education graduates) has roughly tripled, while the proportion of people who have only had a primary education has declined from one in two to one in six (table 1.4). As I have already pointed out, level of schooling is to some extent 'absolute'. But an individual's success in the labour market does not depend solely on skills and knowledge acquired at school. Other characteristics are also important: intelligence, commitment, perseverance, etc. It is generally assumed that schooling not only adds human capital, but that it also contributes to a selection on the basis of more or less intrinsic talents or socio-environmentally related characteristics. It is undoubtedly so that there were more talented individuals among the 50 per cent or so people who had only received primary education in 1976 than among the 15 per cent in 1997. In this sense, a person's relative educational position is significant. It is therefore worthwhile also to consider the relative educational level. To this end, we divide the population of working age into quartiles. The first quartile consists of the lowest skilled, again measured in terms of degrees obtained.

Table 1.4 Educational profile Flemish population of working age, 1976-1997 (change in percentage points)

	1976	1997	1976-1997
Primary education	45.9	16.2	−29.7
Lower secondary	29.3	23.5	− 5.8
Higher secondary	15.3	31.9	+16.6
Higher education	9.5	28.4	+18.9
Total	100.0 (n = 7.514)	100.0 (n = 3.035)	

Source: Belgian Socio-Economic Panel Survey.

Living standard and poverty trends

During our observation period of 1976 to 1997, poverty and income inequality in Flanders remained strikingly stable (Cantillon et al. 1999). Likewise, we observe equally remarkable stability on the educational dimension. The low-skilled have seen their average standard of living rise as sharply as the high-skilled, and their poverty risk has not increased significantly over the past two decades (tables 1.5 and 1.6).

Table 1.5 Living standard by formal level of qualification, 1976-1997. Level in 1997 (1997 euros) and 1976-1997 percentage point difference

	25-64 years		25-44 years	
	1997	1976-1997	1997	1976-1997
Primary education	973	+ 6.7	984	+ 4.1
Lower Secondary	1117	+ 6.2	1102	+ 5.7
Higher Secondary	1268	− 2.0	1251	− 0.6
Higher Education	1536	− 0.1	1504	+ 0.6
All	1259	+17.4	1289	+16.4

Source: Belgian Socio-Economic Panel Survey.

Table 1.6 Poverty rate by formal level of qualification, 1976-1997. Level in 1997 and 1976-1997 percentage point difference

	25-64 years		25-44 years	
	1997	1976-1997	1997	1976-1997
Primary education	5.9	−1.6	6.0	+2.8
Lower Secondary	5.2	+2.0	5.3	+2.8
Higher Secondary	2.3	+1.2	1.5	+0.7
Higher Education	2.8	+1.2	2.6	+0.6
All	3.7	−1.0	3.0	+0.6

Source: Belgian Socio-Economic Panel Survey.

This is a robust observation: it is essentially valid irrespective of whether one applies an absolute or a relative definition of schooling (tables 1.7 and 1.8). Note, however, that the average standard of living of the low-skilled has increased by less than that of the active population as a whole. In other words, there is now a bigger gap between the average standard of living and the average standard of living of the lower skilled, even though the gap between the low-skilled and the high-skilled has remained stable. This is due to the fact that the standard of living has risen predominantly through upskilling. There are now considerably more highly skilled people than there were 20 years ago, and considerably fewer low-skilled.

Table 1.7   Living standard by educational quartile, 1976-1997. Level in 1997 (1997 euros) and 1976-1997 percentage point difference

	25-64 years		25-44 years	
	1997	1976-1997	1997	1976-1997
Ed. Quartile 1	1008	+11.0	1022	+9.7
Ed. Quartile 4	1550	+11.9	1516	+12.1
Ratio 4/1	1.54	+0.01	1.48	+0.03
All	1259	+17.4	1289	+16.4

Source: Belgian Socio-Economic Panel Survey.

Table 1.8   Poverty rate by educational quartile, 1976-1997. Level in 1997 and 1976-1997 percentage point difference

	25-64 years		25-44 years	
	1997	1976-1997	1997	1976-1997
Ed. Quartile 1	5.4	-2.9	5.7	+1.9
Ed. Quartile 4	2.8	+1.5	2.6	+1.2
4/1 (per. points)	2.6	-4.4	3.1	+0.7
All	3.7	-1.0	3.0	+0.6

Source: Belgian Socio-Economic Panel Survey.

One should of course keep in mind that those of working age constitute a very broad segment of the population. This is important, as the younger active generation is much more skilled than the previous generation. In other words, age plays a significant role in the observed trends. Moreover, in the present discourse, concern is focused mainly on the younger low-skilled. It is often argued that the enormous increase in schooling levels over the past decades has resulted in a deflation of the value of degrees and in the low-skilled being pushed out of the labour market. This trend is said to have been to the detriment mainly of those who have had to acquire a position on the labour market in the past 20 years.

But if one only considers the younger segment of the active population (i.e., the 25- to 45-year-olds), one also observes a striking stability in the gap between the low-skilled and the high-skilled. This is even the case if one defines the low-skilled very narrowly. The average standard of living of the 25- to 45-year-olds who only received a primary education has not fallen behind that of the higher skilled. Nevertheless, this is, by any standard, a very low level of schooling in today's society. It does however appear that the poverty risk of the young low-skilled has increased slightly, but by no means proportionally to the rise in unemployment among this group (see below).

Another way of illustrating the remarkable stability is figure 1.1, which provides an overview of how the cohort of 25- to 35-year-olds fared between 1976 and 1997, a 20-year period that does, after all, cover a large part of their active lives. The cohort perspective is also interesting because it does not require us to take into account the relative value of degrees. After all, the proportion of people with a specific type of degree remains relatively constant as the cohort ages: relatively few people succeed in improving their level of education substantially during their active lives. Again, we observe that the low-skilled in the cohort of 25- to 35-year-olds in 1976 did not fare worse than the high-skilled: they saw their standard of living increase to the same degree. In fact, the reverse is true: the high-skilled saw their real standard of living decline significantly during the crisis years from 1976 to 1985. However, they gained ground after 1985, which largely neutralised the levelling that had occurred during the previous period.

Figure 1.1   Living standard trend by level of educational attainment, 1942-1951 cohort (25-34 years old in 1976) in Flanders 1976-1997

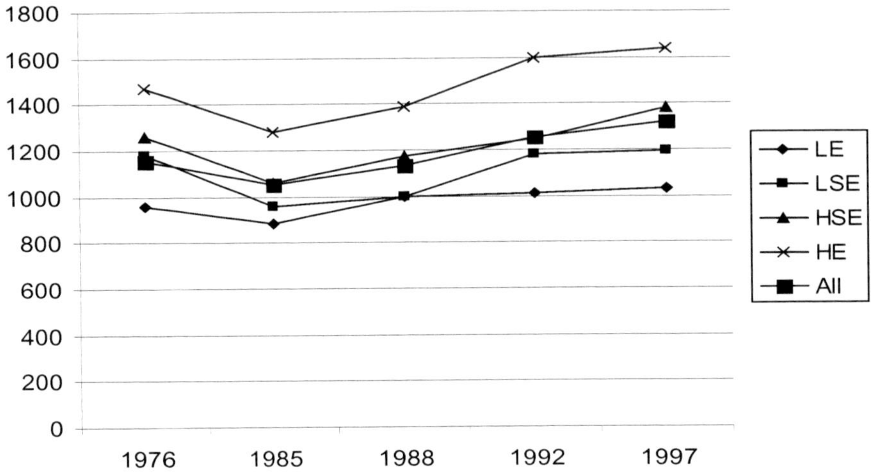

Source: Belgian Socio-Economic Panel Survey.

Employment and earnings trends

In line with general expectations, the employment rate among the less-skilled has generally gone down by a substantial margin. However, this overall decline obscures markedly dissimilar trends by age and gender.

Most of the overall decline is due to the massive drop in employment among older working-age men (that is, among those over the age of 45), the majority of whom are low-skilled by the definitions used here. In scarcely two decades, the employment rate of men with primary education dropped by 40 percentage points from a level of 70 per cent in 1976. The drop for those with an educational level one step up was almost equally spectacular (table 1.9).

However, this is only part of the story. For women, the picture is far less clear-cut. Obviously, there was a vast increase in labour market participation among women of all educational levels. In fact, the rise in participation was particularly marked among less-educated women for the simple reason that among the higher skilled, participation was already relatively high two decades ago.

Table 1.9　Indicators of employment, income and welfare state dependence, men aged 45-65 years, levels for 1997 and 1976-1997 trend, percentage point difference, except for living standard (percentage change)

	Primary education		Lower secondary education		Higher secondary education		Higher education		All	
	1997	76-97	1997	76-97	1997	76-97	1997	76-97	1997	76-97
% employed	33.3	-39.3	56.9	-26.5	71.9	-19.8	77.7	-15.3	60.2	-19.5
% unemployed	9.4	+4.6	6.4	+3.4	3.5	+2.3	1.7	+1.7	5.2	+1.8
% on benefit	78.3	+36.9	51.3	+24.3	42.7	+22.2	31.3	+19.7	50.7	+18.2
Living stand.	966	+8.3	1135	+11.9	1336	+0.9	1606	-3.7	1261	+20.8
% poor	6.1	-3.0	3.7	-0.1	1.5	-0.6	3.4	+2.5	3.6	-2.5
% pre-transfer poor	60.9	+28.8	39.6	+20.8	20.1	+10.2	16.8	+9.8	34.0	+10.3

Source: Belgian Socio-Economic Panel Survey.

Most women who entered the labour market in the past 20 years actually succeeded in finding employment, including many of the low-skilled and even the lowest-skilled. As is illustrated by table 1.10 (which relates to women aged between 25 and 45), even among women who only received a primary education, employment rates went up fairly substantially. The figures stand in marked contrast to the perception and indeed my working hypothesis that there have been far too few job opportunities for the least-skilled in the labour market, and particularly for the least-skilled women – given the presumed breadwinner bias in labour market regulation, social security and taxation. It is striking to what extent employment rates have gone up, even among the least-skilled. At the same time it should be made clear that many new entrants did end up on unemployment, frequently long-term unemployment. But the picture is less clear-cut than often thought.

This also applies to earnings. Unfortunately, our data do not allow us to draw real conclusions with regard to the evolution of earnings inequality in the strict sense. This is due to the fact that our 1976 survey data do not distinguish between full-time and part-time employment. Moreover, we only possess information about net earned income. Consequently, we are unable to distinguish between evolutions in wages (i.e., market appreciation of labour) and in taxation and social security contributions. Furthermore, there are significant differences in the manner in which labour income was measured in 1976 and in subsequent surveys.

Table 1.10　Indicators of employment, income and welfare state dependence, women aged 25-45 years, levels for 1997 and 1976-1997 trend, percentage point change, except for living standard (percentage change)

	Primary education		Lower secondary education		Higher secondary education		Higher education		All	
	1997	76-97	1997	76-97	1997	76-97	1997	76-97	1997	76-97
% employed	(44.1)	+15.9	52.0	+18.2	75.4	+25.2	85.0	+16.7	72.1	+34.6
% unemployed	(15.3)	+11.3	20.0	+16.7	4.8	+1.6	4.0	+0.6	8.3	+4.8.
% on benefit	(44.1)	+28.2	43.0	+29.8	19.5	+12.5	12.2	+4.4	23.2	+10.4
Living stand.	(986)	+5.0	1053	+1.0	1229	-5.4	1497	-5.1	1274	+16.4
% poor	(3.4)	+0.3	7.8	+5.2	1.5	+0.2	2.2	+1.1	3.1	+0.7
% pre-transfer poor	(28.8)	+14.1	31.8	+20.8	10.8	+6.8	4.4	+2.9	13.9	+3.5

( ) indicates small sample size (n<100).

Source: Belgian Socio-Economic Panel Survey.

Thus we can only provide some tentative evidence about the evolution of labour incomes in the observation period. But the data does provide a number of insights, certainly with respect to the evolution of net earned incomes – in fact, more interesting for us than earnings especially if we want to understand living standard trends. The empirical evidence that we possess suggests that the degree of inequality between the low-skilled and the high-skilled has declined rather than increased. The period 1976-1985 in particular appears to have been one of a substantial levelling of incomes, as the high-skilled saw their net earned incomes decline. This was partly due to high inflation during this period, but also to an increase in the fiscal burden. The data also suggest that the high-skilled made up ground after 1985, so that the degree of inequality is now comparable to that of 1976. In other words, the most recent trend appears to be towards more inequality, after all, albeit at a modest pace.

We can also shed some light – the same caveats still apply – on the question of whether inequality has increased more strongly at the household level than at the individual level. Our hypothesis was, after all, that the incidence of double-income households has increased predominantly among the high-skilled, so that income inequality should have become greater at household level. However, as we have seen, double earnership has also increased strongly among households with medium-skilled and low-skilled women. And the differences between the average net earned income of the low-skilled and the high-skilled have – insofar as our information is reliable – remained stable, if we compare 1976 to 1997 that is. It is therefore not surprising that we find little indication of a substantial increase in earned income inequality at the household level.

This is illustrated in table 1.11, which shows the increase in the combined earned income of couples (we have only taken into account the 25- to 45-year-olds in order to control in a rudimentary way for age). It concerns couples with at least one earned income. The effect of any differential increase in female employment should therefore become visible. The table shows that the average combined earned income of couples where the male is low-skilled increased equally strongly between 1976 and 1997 than that of couples where the male is high-skilled. Note here that roughly two-thirds of couples are educationally homogamous, i.e., the two partners have a similar level of schooling.

Table 1.11 Joint labour income, couples with head aged between 25 and 45, by level of educational attainment head, Flanders 1976-1997

	1976	1997	1976-1997
Primary and lower secondary education	1543	1583	+2.6%
Higher secondary education	2037	1915	-6.0%
Higher education	2353	2422	+2.9%
All	1780	1986	+11.6%

Benefit dependency and pre-transfer poverty trends

The two decades between 1976 and 1997 are marked by an increased reliance on social security to avoid poverty, particularly among the least-skilled. There is, in fact, a striking contrast between the stability in the actual poverty risk of the lower-skilled (illustrated in tables 1.6 and 8) and the very strong increase in pre-transfer poverty among this segment, as documented in tables 1.12 and 1.13. For clarity, a person is said to be pre-transfer poor if his or her disposable household income minus replacement benefits falls below the poverty line. Note that child benefits are taken into account in pre-transfer income as it is not a replacement benefit. The rises in pre-transfer poverty are evident for all categories of the less-skilled. As the vast drops in employment would lead one to expect, pre-transfer poverty rates surged particularly strongly for less-skilled men, particularly for those over the age of 45 (table 1.9). Particularly strong rises are also evident for women with relatively low levels of educational attainment (table 1.10). But as I indicated already, the picture for less-skilled women is more ambiguous: significant increases in employment are accompanied by equally significant increases in social security dependency and pre-transfer poverty.

Table 1.12 Pre-transfer poverty rate by formal level of qualification, 1976-1997. Level in 1997 and 1976-1997 percentage point difference

	25-64 years of age		25-44 years of age	
	1997	1976-1997	1997	1976-1997
Primary education	52.6	+24.9	26.3	+11.0
Lower secondary	32.2	+18.1	23.7	+13.4
Higher secondary	15.8	+9.8	9.8	+5.9
Higher education	8.8	+4.6	4.1	+1.3
All	23.8	+5.7	11.9	+2.1

Source: Belgian Socio-Economic Panel Survey.

Table 1.13 Pre-transfer poverty rate by educational quartile, 1976-1997. Level in 1997 and 1976-1997 percentage point difference

	25-64 years of age		25-44 years of age	
	1997	1976-1997	1997	1976-1997
Educational. quartile 1	45.4	+17.2	22.6	+6.8
Educational. quartile 4	8.5	+3.0	3.8	+0.2
4/1 difference (per. points)	36.9	+14.2	18.8	+6.6
All	23.7	+5.6	11.9	+2.1

Source: Belgian Socio-Economic Panel Survey.

The relative impact of employment, earnings and social security

How does this all add up? One way to find out is to decompose the observed living standard trends. This is what we do in figures 1.2 and 1.3, which contain the result of a decomposition analysis, in which the relative impact of each factor is gauged by keeping all other factors constant. Basically, we distinguish to what extent the labour market position of the breadwinner (by definition the male partner), the labour market position of the partner and social security have contributed to the observed changes in the average living standard of respectively the whole population and those in the first quartile in terms of educational attainment. Each component is the product of the share of the relevant population segment receiving the income component in question and the average level of that income component. For example, the component 'labour market position of the breadwinner' is the product of the employment rate of that population segment and their average earned income. The three components add up to 100, i.e., the total observed change.

It is clear that much of the observed increase in the average living standard of the less-skilled in the 1976-1997 period is due to social security. This is especially true for the less-skilled in the working aged population as whole, i.e., those between the ages of 25 and 65. Were it not for social security, their average living standard would have seriously declined, particularly as a consequence of the worsening of the labour market position of the breadwinner. This, however, is not true for those in the 25 to 45 age bracket (figure 1.3). Not surprisingly, the single most important determinant of increased living standards was the rise in double earnership. What is remarkable, however, is the extent to which this is also true for those

Figure 1.2   Determinants of living standard rise among working-age population (25-65 years), Flanders 1976-1997

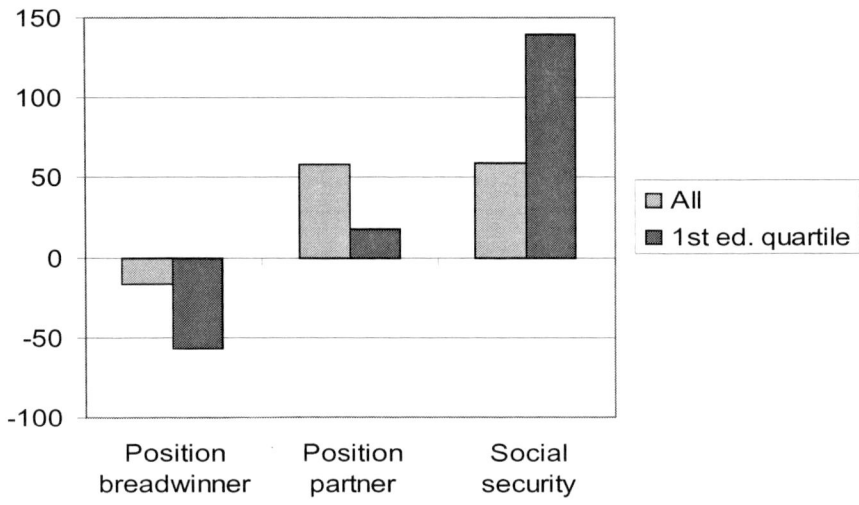

Figure 1.3   Determinants of living standard rise among working-age population (25-65 years), Flanders 1976-1997

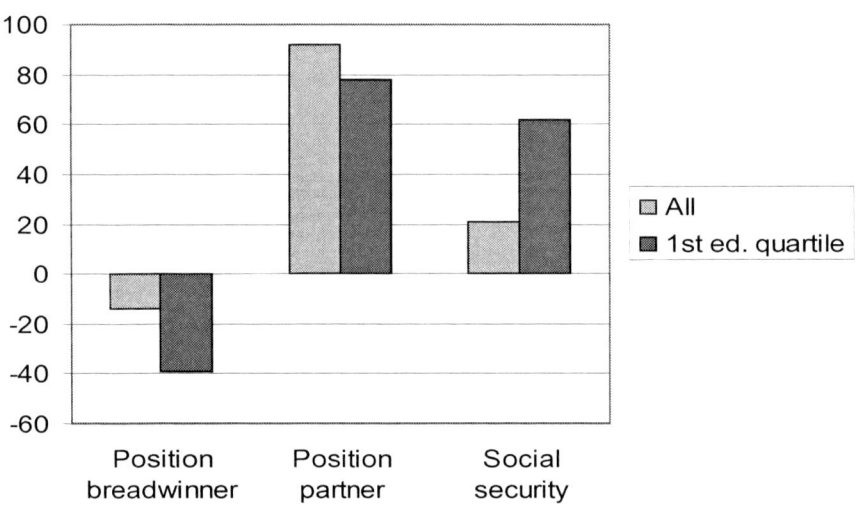

in the lowest educational attainment quartile. At the same time, however, social security played an almost equally important role in compensating for the more severe downward pressure on living standards of the low-skilled caused by deteriorated breadwinner employment rates and earnings. Hence, the story is ambiguous. On the one hand, a significant proportion of the less-skilled did remarkably well in the labour market in what were by all accounts two very tough and turbulent decades. On the other hand, social security did play a crucial role in boosting the living standards of the equally significant proportion that was less successful in the labour market. This is where we turn our focus next.

5 Difficulties of Interpretation

Direct and indirect behavioural effects

The strong increases in pre-transfer poverty, particularly among the lower skilled, appears to provide confirmation of the initial hypotheses, i.e., that the lower-skilled are finding it increasingly difficult in the labour market to attain a reasonable standard of living and that they are increasingly dependent on solidarity transfers to make ends meet.

However, such an interpretation calls for circumspection. It is, after all, based on a quite rudimentary indicator of potential self-reliance. Pre-transfer poverty is calculated on the basis of disposable household income minus replacement benefits (note that child benefits are taken into account in pre-transfer income as are not a replacement benefit). This is a simple calculation that does not take into account possible behavioural responses. If social security were non-existent, people would pay less in social contributions and taxes, which would translate into a higher pre-transfer income. The calculation also does not take into account the effect that the existence of social benefits has on the behaviour of employees (including trade unions), employers and government. The existence of benefit schemes makes it easier for employers to dismiss employees. And from the employee's perspective, social transfers may reduce, even eliminate, the economic necessity of finding a job, hanging on to a job or of finding alternative employment.

Whether or not someone decides to enter the labour market depends, at least to some extent, on the balance between the costs and benefits of remunerated labour (Atkinson and Micklewright 1991; Blundell and Macurdy 2000). Policy factors such as (secondary-earner) taxation, earnings replacement as well as work-related benefits play an important role in this context. As a consequence, the balance differs quite considerably for, say, less-skilled and highly skilled women. High-skilled women may, after all, expect a more substantial income from work than low-skilled women, and they may also expect more interesting work under better conditions. In the case of a high-skilled woman, the indirect 'income' offered by the 'marriage quotient' (this is a feature of the Belgian tax system which involves a hypothetical income transfer between partners for tax purposes) will, generally, be lower than what she can earn. Similarly, a (potential) unemployment benefit will be lower than an earned income. For low-skilled women, on the other hand, the financial difference between an income from low-paid employment (especially part-time employment) and a direct fiscal income and/or benefit is often very small, while the intrinsic job satisfaction is often much lower. These differences become even greater if the woman also has to care for children, especially young children. For low-skilled women with young children, the potential earnings from (low-paid) work often do not outweigh the additional cost of external childcare. Particularly unemployed single women with young children often have little to gain financially from a transition from unemployment benefit (plus supplementary child benefit) to low-paid work (De Lathouwer and Bogaerts 2001).

Moreover, social security benefits may have indirect effects on the availability of work. Certain institutional characteristics of the labour market may be facilitated by the existence of transfer systems that absorb resulting labour slack. Consider, just as an example, the strong and rigid tie between seniority and earnings that exists in Belgium. This makes older employees expensive, and it is generally accepted that this is one reason why people above a certain age find it very difficult to obtain a new job. It seems plausible that the development of this institutional feature has been facilitated by the existence of early retirement schemes that made it easy to remove older, less productive people from the production process. Similar hypotheses could be formulated with regard to other institutional characteristics of the labour market, e.g., limitations on temporary employment or minimum wages.

Exogenous vs. endogenous causality

The sharp increase in pre-transfer poverty among the lower skilled is consistent with the initial hypothesis. There is, however, something remarkable about the way economic self-reliance has declined. The fact that we observe such a big discrepancy between the situation at the end of the 'Golden Age' and the present situation now is not because dependency has risen steadily over the course of those thirty years. In fact, what we see is that dependency levels 'exploded' during a relatively short time period between roughly the mid-1970s and the mid-1980s. The period that follows is essentially a period of stagnation, save for fluctuations that correlate closely with macro-economic conditions (growth and unemployment rates).

This S-shaped time pattern does not appear to be consistent with the idea that the rise in dependence is driven by a secular and progressive decline in the relative demand for low-skilled labour. However, this would assume patterns of benefit dependency to accurately reflect patterns of need. In reality, however, benefit dependency levels are likely to be a reflection of changes in need as well as changes in policy. And although policy presumably reacts to changes in need, there is no reason whatsoever to expect there to be a simple, let alone linear relationship.

Let me illustrate what I mean. In Belgium, the bulk of the massive rises in benefit dependency took place during the late 1970s and 1980s. As we know, OECD economies were experiencing a recession of a magnitude not experienced in decades. The aggregate demand for labour had collapsed and the recession had intensified an already ongoing process of economic restructuring. The global recession and oil shocks had a very strong impact on the still numerous antiquated and energy-intensive companies, resulting in the loss of relatively well-paid, full-time 'breadwinner' jobs. In the early 1970s, Belgian industry was, for that matter, even more antiquated than the industries of other countries, at least according to Cassiers, De Villé and Solar (1996).

Many essentially unproductive low-skilled jobs in industry and elsewhere that had until then survived thanks to historically high levels of economic growth were destroyed in a very short period of time. And all this happened at a time when great numbers of youngsters and women were entering the labour market. A substantial rise in the supply of labour coincided with a massive drop in the demand for labour, and this amid many a mismatch – industry workers were not fit for service jobs, male breadwinner jobs were often not appropriate for women entering the labour market.

Benefit programmes (especially early retirement) were expanded (through law, collective agreement, or practice) to manage the social consequences of mass job loss and unemployment. That this expansion occurred was probably entirely justified from a social protection viewpoint, given the particularly dismal circumstances prevailing at that time. It seems probable that many of the older workers (especially those with few skills employed in manufacturing industry) who lost their jobs in the midst of the recession of the 1970s and 1980s would have been unable to secure an alternative job and hence a decent standard of living. Plant closures often resulted in large-scale, geographically concentrated redundancies. It was difficult for service employment to take up this slack. First, there was often a geographic mismatch. Many services cater locally and are thus spread relatively uniformly across the country. Secondly, there was a skills mismatch; services generally required different and usually higher skills. The result was that service unemployment was unable to absorb many of those who lost their jobs in the industrial sector. The threat of significant poverty rises was very real. Hence the vast expansion of early retirement schemes and the like. Nevertheless, the growth in dependency levels rapidly rose far and above what had been foreseen or implicitly planned – as the literature from the period demonstrates. Mass benefit dependency did not turn out to be a temporary phenomenon either, as it had been hoped it would.

However, economic conditions did improve after the mid-1980s. More importantly, the deteriorating state of public finances increasingly necessitated volume containment. But successive governments encountered great difficulties in getting rising dependency levels under control, even as economic conditions improved and labour demand rebounded. Powerful coalitions of interested parties had formed around many of the benefit schemes implemented to alleviate the social consequences of mass layoffs. Early retirement and invalidity benefits were after all a cheap and easy way for companies to make people redundant. And many workers had come to expect to get what many of their former co-workers had received: early retirement with an attractive financial package. Employees have over the past 20 years constructed fairly strong expectations regarding the possibility of early retirement. Research by Schokkaert, Verhue and Pepermans (2000) shows that workers have a very clear preference for early retirement. Successive attempts by the government and employers to scale back early retirement and to increase the effective age of retirement has encountered enormous resistance from trade unions.

In many neighbouring countries employment rates for older men have recently edged up. In Belgium, the employment rate for men aged 55-65 has remained stable at an exceptionally low level. Perhaps this can be taken as evidence that the exceptionally high rates of benefit dependency among older men in Belgium have increasingly less to do with structural job scarcity. On the other hand, an argument can be made that the economic conditions remain different in Belgium. First, the proportion of low-skilled persons among the older active population – at least in terms of formal level of education – remains significantly larger in Belgium than it is in neighbouring countries. Second, Belgium still has a relatively high degree of 'traditional' recession-prone industrial activity. And thirdly, overall unemployment has remained fairly high. One could therefore argue that there is still an economic rationale to relieve the supply pressure on the labour market through early retirement.

Successive governments were more successful in reducing the numbers on other types of benefits, such as unemployment benefits, around which collective interests were less well organised (and probably less organisable). For example, the part-time unemployment scheme, which had become a very popular form of (more or less) voluntary subsidised part-time employment during the 1980s, was scaled back (although it made something of a return in a different guise). Moreover, over the course of the 1990s, the government was successful in cutting back levels of long-term benefit dependence among certain sections of the unemployed population, particularly among cohabiting claimants – those assumed to be the least needy. Furthermore, the government was 'successful' in pushing down (by stealth) the relative value of benefits – relative, that is, to wages (Cantillon, Marx and De Maesschalck 2003). This presumably also had an effect on dependency levels because of the way the erosion of the value of benefits affected the work-dependency trade-off. However, during the same period of time (roughly the 1990s) actual poverty increased markedly, especially among the non-employed population – a sign that social policy had become less responsive to need.

This short sketch does not really prove anything. But I think there are reasons why we should not expect there to be a simple, linear relationship between the time evolution of underlying need and the time patterns of observed dependency levels. The fact that dependency levels did not rise further over the past decade or so is not in itself proof that underlying need has not increased further. Similarly, the fact that dependency levels remain high, even in the context of improved economic conditions, is not in itself proof that the underlying need for compensatory income redistribution remains high. I suspect, moreover, that in the end it may prove very difficult to untangle the role of 'exogenous' (trade, technology, deindustrialisation) and 'endogenous' factors (corporatism, path dependency) in what we are trying to understand here – the decline of economic self-reliance. It is easy to imagine there being a sequence of causality, starting with exogenous factors playing the major role in the initial expansion of benefit programmes and endogenous factors playing the major role in the further expansion and persistence of such programmes.

The interaction with socio-demographic and other factors

In addition, there is the role of non-economic factors. Non-employment trends are too easily reduced to a labour demand issue. In fact, the increased dependency rate among the low-skilled can only be understood fully if viewed as a product of a complex interaction between economic, social (socio-demographic) and policy factors. This point is perhaps best illustrated by taking the example of single mothers, a population segment with exceptionally high non-employment and dependency rates, especially among the least skilled. The proportion of single mothers has increased in most of the advanced countries. It is now widely accepted that this is essentially a socio-demographic trend that is largely detached from economic and even policy developments. Moreover, benefit policy towards single mothers has become more generous over the past decades, because of a justified concern with the high degree of poverty within this segment, which affects not only the mothers but also their children. One can see quite clearly, then, how an essentially socio-demographic trend, in the context of a benefit policy that has moved towards improved protection has contributed to the increase in non-employment among low-skilled single mothers.

6   Some Direct Evidence that the Capacity for Economic Self-Reliance Has Declined

As I have tried to show, the problem is how to interpret pre-transfer poverty trends. The convenient and indeed common interpretation is that the pre-transfer poverty rate reflects the extent of poverty that would prevail in absence of direct redistribution. Accordingly, the strong rises in pre-transfer poverty can be taken as evidence for a massive decline in the ability to be economically self-reliant. The validity of such an interpretation is, as I have just argued, highly questionable, since it effectively, and implausibly, assumes the absence of behavioural effects. So far, the only thing we can say for certain is the economic self-reliance has declined. But we remain largely in the dark as to the extent to which *the ability* to be self-reliant has actually declined.

The only direct evidence that is available is for the United States. It comes from various studies by Haveman (Garfinkel and Haveman 1977; Haveman and Bershadker 1998), using a poverty measure based on estimated capacity for economic self-reliance, that is, the ability of a family, using its own resources, to support a level of consumption in excess of the official American poverty line. (This is an absolute poverty line, i.e., a line that rises with inflation but not with general living standards, as does a relative line.) This measure of economic position is said to diverge from transitory events and phenomena, unlike current cash income and also from individual tastes for income relative to leisure. Net earnings capacity (NEC) is designed to measure the potential of a family to generate an income stream (which can then be used to support its members) were it to use its human and physical capital to capacity. Individuals living in those households with the lowest levels of NEC relative to their needs are considered to be the 'truly poor' (Garfinkel and Haveman 1977).

The NEC of a family is obtained by first estimating what each adult in the household, given his/her capabilities and characteristics, would be able to earn in the labour market if they were to work to capacity (i.e., full-time, full-year market employment), and then summing up these estimates. This value is called the household's gross earnings capacity (GEC). Then, adjustments are made to GEC for both the constraints on working capacity (e.g., due to health, disability) and the expenses (child care) that would be required if all of a household's working-age adults did work at capacity. This yields a household's NEC. If this exceeds the poverty line that household is considered to be self-reliant, if not, it is classified as 'self-reliant poor'.

Using this measure of NEC to examine the size and composition of the self-reliant-poor population from 1975 to 1995, Haveman and Bershadker (1998) find that three-fourths of those living in poverty in the United States (in 1995) would not have succeeded in pulling themselves out of poverty even if they had obtained full-time employment. One reason for this is that many of the poor could only have obtained jobs with such low wages that even if they worked at their full capacity, their incomes would have remained below the poverty line.

Individuals with low levels of education were found to have the highest levels of self-reliance poverty. More than 40 per cent of the self-reliant poor had an education level that is less than high school (which in the US context is quite a low level of education), and almost another 40 per cent had only a high-school degree. College graduates made up less than 3 per cent of self-reliant poor, half their share in the actual poor. However, it is not just low wages that caused high NEC poverty among the less-skilled. After all, the NEC poverty rate among the least educated (those with less than high school) was 'only' 28 per cent, meaning that the vast majority of the least-skilled *were* able to be economically self-reliant and actually were so. However, low earnings capacity was a problem in a single-parent context. Single parents constituted the vast majority of the NEC poor in 1995 because the necessary child care expenses reduced their net incomes.

Haveman and Bershadker's estimate that three-fourths would remain poor even if full-time employed is still on the optimistic side because it assumes that the labour market would be able to absorb all those not working at unchanged wages. More likely, a mass influx of the non-employed would bid down wages. They also found that self-reliance poverty in the United States increased more rapidly and more steadily than official poverty. Perhaps surprisingly, the growth was strongest among the better educated. But this is only true in relative terms – their NEC poverty rates came from almost negligible levels during the mid-1970s. (The NEC poverty rate for college graduates increased from 0.47 per cent to 1.22 per cent, a 5.46 per cent annual rise rate.) In percentage point terms, however, the growth was by far the strongest among the less educated. For those with less than a high-school degree, the NEC poverty rate increased from 12.6 per cent around 1975 to 28.2 per cent around 1995, 'only' a 4.59 per cent annual rise rate, but a percentage point difference of almost 16 per cent. Haveman and Bershadker suggest that the deteriorated wage rates for the less educated were an important factor in this rise.

So what we have here then is powerful direct empirical evidence that the ability of the less-skilled to be economically self-reliant has declined. But it is evidence only for the United States and as I will show in chapter 2, the US story is almost certainly not representative for the OECD as a whole, or even for most advanced economies.

7   Conclusion

This chapter has documented the decline of economic self-reliance in advanced welfare states. Economic self-reliance among the working-age population – as measured by benefit dependency and pre-transfer poverty rates – has demonstrably collapsed over the past few decades. This has been an OECD-wide trend, but there is considerable cross-country variation regarding the extent. As I have detailed for Belgium, the trend differences by level of educational attainment are marked. Chronic benefit dependency and pre-transfer poverty have become overwhelmingly concentrated among the least-skilled.

These findings are consistent with recurring claims that the least-skilled are in danger of becoming economically superfluous in advanced economies, a trend which, if true, would render invalid a key assumption upon which modern social protection rests. But the interpretation of observed pre-transfer poverty trends is beset by difficulties. The convenient and indeed conventional interpretation that pre-transfer poverty is largely reflective or at least indicative of underlying need is, as I have argued, scarcely defensible. We remain largely in the dark when it comes to the extent to which job scarcity (or insufficient job expansion) for the less-skilled is really the major factor behind the rises in pre-transfer poverty. In the next chapter we consider this issue in more detail.

2   The Demand Shift against the Less-Skilled

1   Introduction

The findings of chapter 1 appear consistent with the hypothesis that the less-skilled are finding it increasingly difficult to attain a reasonable standard of living in the labour market. But is this a valid perception? The reality is that we have remained pretty much in the dark regarding the extent to which job scarcity (or insufficient job expansion) is really the major factor behind the rises in pre-transfer poverty and benefit dependency.

In this part we look for answers in the available empirical literature, mostly in the field of labour economics. What I attempt here is to collect, interpret and critically assess what I think is some of the most relevant empirical evidence that is presently available. I think this is useful since many recent findings have not yet found their way into the social policy literature and debate.

The principal purpose of this chapter is a review of a sizeable part of the empirical evidence relating to the idea that there has been a structural and inexorable decline in the demand for less-skilled labour which has given rise to large-scale 'economic redundancy' and structural dependency on redistribution. Is it true that good jobs are becoming ever scarcer for certain sections of the population, particularly for the less-skilled? Is it therefore true that there is a growing segment of society that is becoming chronically dependent on redistribution? We look not only at the trends as they present themselves; we also weigh the empirical evidence pertaining to the alleged driving forces behind the demand shift, particularly economic globalisation and technological change.

2 Jobless Growth and the Demand for Less-Skilled labour

The golden years of welfare capitalism are often portrayed as an era during which jobs were plentiful, including for those with little or no formal education. The almost uncontested assumption is that things have changed dramatically in this respect. Full employment, arguably the single most important pillar of the modern welfare state, is believed to be one of the main casualties of the post-industrial transition. In *The End of Work* (1995), Jeremy Rifkin argues that the 'knowledge economies' in which we live today by nature require an elite workforce. This is a thesis that resonates widely.

The figures show, however, that despite the considerable slowdown in the rate of economic growth after 1973, the rate of per capita employment growth, in the OECD area as a whole, was actually somewhat higher in the decades following the 'golden' 1960s than during this period. Employment growth in the post-1973 period was definitely higher relative to the rate of economic growth than was the case in the 1960s. As Standing (1999: 154) puts it: 'There is no evidence of "jobless growth". It has been more like an expansion of "growth-less jobs", in that, despite low rates of economic growth, employment has expanded.' The first part of Standing's statement is consistent with all the available empirical evidence. The second part needs qualification in the sense that the rates of economic growth in the post-crisis period have, generally speaking, been more in line with historic averages than the atypically strong growth rates of the late 1950s and 1960s.

The relatively favourable picture in terms of aggregate employment creation does mask massive shifts in the relative demand for different types of labour. Throughout the OECD, the share of industrial employment has been declining fast. The fastest decline has been in the EU, from just over 40 per cent of total employment in 1973 to under 30 per cent towards the end of the 1990s. As Fuchs (1968) has argued and Baumol et al. (1989) have demonstrated, industrial productivity typically grows faster than the average for the whole of the economy because of relatively weak technical changes in services. Thus a constant share of industrial employment requires that industrial output also grows faster than the GDP as a whole. After 1973, however, industrial output grew slower than GDP, as consumer spending shifted towards services, the share of investment declined and there was an increase in the imports of the most labour intensive manufactures of low wage economies (Glyn and Rowthorn 1988; Rowthorn and Ramaswamy 1999). Combined with the faster growth of labour productivity in industry, the result of the slow growth of industrial output was a declining share of industrial employment. Many of the EU (then EC) countries, particularly in the early 1980s, experienced a collapse of industrial employment.

The loss of industrial employment greatly increased the demands on the welfare state. Manufacturing traditionally provided relatively well-paid, stable employment to male breadwinners. Many of them had no more than a basic education. Often, this was all that was required, in addition to good health, physical strength and skills specific to industrial work. The major declines in industrial employment resulted in large-scale, geographically concentrated redundancies, which (potentially) flooded local labour markets with less-educated labour. It was difficult for the service sector to take up this slack. Firstly, many services (for example wholesale distribution, retail, personal services, etc.) supply a local population and are thus spread relatively uniformly across the country. Secondly, and more importantly, services generally required different and frequently higher skills than manufacturing. Work practices, the culture and the schedules are often completely different. The result was that the service sector was unable to absorb many of those who lost their jobs in the industrial sector. To put it simply, a steel worker found it difficult to get a job as a computer programmer or to adapt to a job as a security guard (see for example Haskel 1996; Glyn and Machin 1997).

Service employment is now approaching three-quarters of all available jobs in several of the OECD countries (OECD 2001). Over the past two decades, employment growth was the most rapid in production and social services. Employment in personal services increased less, comparatively speaking, while the employment share of distributive services remained almost unchanged. However, in most OECD countries, distributive and social services still represent the largest shares of total employment. Only in the US has the producer services sub-sector become as large as the distributive services sub-sector. Within distributive services, the largest share of jobs is in retail trade, while health-related activities are the largest component of social services in most countries. Business and professional services account for the largest share of jobs in producer services, while hotels and restaurants are the largest component of personal services.

While manufacturing industry is often associated with stable, well-paid, breadwinner-type employment, the service sector is associated with job instability, poor working conditions and low pay. Temporary, part-time and low-paid employment have grown in a number of OECD countries during the past two decades, but the pattern is far from universal – while the growth of service sector employment is.

Comparisons of job quality based on measures of working conditions, job satisfaction and pay, reveal no simple dichotomy between the goods-producing sector and the service sector (OECD 2001). Good jobs are not primarily located in the former and bad jobs in the latter. Jobs in hotels and restaurants generally rank poorly across a range of job quality measures, including remuneration. On the other hand, jobs in the goods-producing sector are more likely to be associated with poor working conditions than is the case in many service sector jobs. Also, job satisfaction measures tend to be more favourable for the service industry.

Consistent with general perception, educational levels are generally considerably higher in the service than in the goods sector (OECD 2001). Generally speaking, the services sector is about three times as skill-intensive as the goods sector. But there is also an enormous variation among the services sub-sectors. Educational attainment is highest in producer and social services and lowest in personal and distributive services. There can be no doubt that the service sub-sectors where employment has expanded most over the past two decades – producer and social services – are 'skill-intensive' sectors (table 2.1).

Table 2.1 Skill composition by economic sector, OECD average 1998

Sector	Ratio low-skill to medium/high skill	Ratio of university to non-university workers
Goods-producing – total	1.25	0.07
– agriculture, forestry	2.79	0.04
– mining	1.46	0.14
– manufacturing	1.03	0.09
– electricity/gas/water supply	0.41	0.15
– construction	1.47	0.05
Service sector – total	0.45	0.24
– producer services	0.24	0.45
– distributive services	0.67	0.09
– personal services	1.00	0.08
– social services	0.26	0.46

Note: 'Low-skill' denotes ISCED 0-2; 'medium-/high-skill': ISCED 3-7; 'university': ISCED 6-7; 'non-university': ISCED 0-5.

Source: OECD (2001).

A host of studies and data support the view that job opportunities have expanded most for those with good educational qualifications and that there has been a contraction for those with no or few qualifications. For example, detailed studies for the UK (Ashton et al. 1999; Gallie 1991; Green 1998; Green, Felstead and Gallie 1998; Gallie 2000; Machin 1996a) show that skill demands have gone up at quite a rapid pace. Even more detailed analysis for the United States has shown that the demands for work skills, education and functional literacy have slowly but substantially increased over the past century (Pryor and Schaffer 1999). The evidence for Continental European countries is almost equally conclusive. Research performed in the context of the 'Newskills' TSER project (McIntosh and Steedman 2002) suggests that in Europe, demand for the ISCED 0-2 group has continued to fall relative to the average for higher skill levels. There are, however, exceptions. In Portugal, a rapidly industrialising country, the demand for less-skilled workers, again defined as workers whose educational levels fall within the ISCED 0-2 range (which is a comparatively sizeable group in Portugal), appears to have weakened only moderately. But such evidence goes against the general trend in the majority of OECD countries. The next section looks in more detail at how the less-skilled have fared.

3   Is There Evidence of a Universal and Structural Deterioration of the Labour Market Position of the Less-Skilled?

Underlying the idea that the less-skilled are losing out is something like a unified theory which basically says that low pay and unemployment (and consequently structural need for redistribution) are inexorably on the rise in advanced economies on account of technical change biased against unskilled workers or because of international trade liberalisation and increased competition from newly industrialising countries.

Europe vs. the United States

The classic example given in support of the unified theory is the Europe/US divergence with respect to wages and employment. Persistent high unemployment and weak (service) employment growth in highly regulated Europe has often been presented as the flip side of weak real wage growth and rampant low pay in the United States. The shared driving factor, it is thought, is the OECD-wide decline in the demand for low-skilled labour.

It is a fact that throughout the 1960s and the early 1970s about 67 per cent of the active population was employed in both Europe (EU15) and the US. The US even had higher unemployment rates during this period. By the late 1990s, this had risen to 80 per cent in the US and to only 70 per cent in Europe. (In reality, the difference is even bigger because Americans tend to work significantly more hours). However, feeble job growth in Europe went accompanied by strong increases in real wages, which occurred in a majority of countries on the European continent fairly much across the board. In the United States real wages remained virtually stagnant and fell for significant segments of the population, especially those at or near the bottom. US men at the tenth percentile experienced a *decline* on the order of 16 per cent in their real wages between the late 1970s and the mid-1990s, while workers at the tenth percentile in six other OECD countries (Australia, Austria, Canada, West Germany, Sweden and the UK) saw an *increase* of 18 per cent (Bertola and Ichino 1995; Bertola et al. 2002).

It is often claimed that a less dynamic creation of low-paid service jobs is the main reason for the relatively sluggish growth of European employment as compared to the United States. However, the difference between Europe and the United States is rather smaller than generally presumed, at least in this respect. Since 1973, service jobs in Europe have increased, but by some 5 per cent less than in the United States (9.2 vs. 14.5 per cent for the period 1973-1997). However, in Europe the number of jobs in both agriculture and industry have also fallen 4 per cent more than in the United States. The faster decline in the number of jobs in agriculture and industry has been nearly as important as slower growth of services in accounting for Europe's comparatively poor employment performance.

An analysis by the OECD (2000) for the more recent period 1990-1998 confirms and even reinforces this picture. During this period the EU/US employment gap grew by 3 percentage points. About 80 per cent of this was due to a more rapid contraction in EU goods-production employment, rather than to stronger US gains in service employment.

Still, service sector employment is more extensive in the US. In 1998, 55 per cent of the American working-age population was employed in the service sector, as compared with an average of 40 per cent in the EU area. A disaggregation shows that this is mainly due to higher employment shares for producer, and to a lesser extent social services (which are generally highly skill intensive and well paid), and also to higher employer shares for personal services (which are not skill intensive and often badly paid), like hotel and restaurant work.

It turns out, in other words, that the US has a job surplus relative to most countries not just in low-paid service jobs but equally in highly paid service jobs. This is confirmed by an OECD (2001) study in which, for the purpose of comparison, jobs are classed into three broad wage groups. Jobs (i.e., industry/occupation cells) in every country are assigned to the same wage group as the equivalent job in the US based on its wage and employment structure for 1999. Thus, the comparison becomes one of looking at jobs that are low-, medium- or high-paying by American standards and seeing whether employment in these jobs relative to the working-age population is higher or lower in the EU countries than in the US.

It transpires that the US/EU employment gap cannot be solely or even principally attributed to a surplus of low-paying service jobs. In 1999, the overall employment rate gap between the US and the EU countries was 13.7 percentage points. Around 7.5 percentage points can indeed be accounted for by higher US employment in relatively low-paying jobs. This is consistent with the US employment surplus in personal services: hotels, bars, restaurants, recreation, domestic services, etc. However, the other half can be accounted for by higher US employment in relatively well-paid jobs. This is consistent with the US surplus in social (mainly health) and producer services: business and professional services, financial, insurance and real estate services, etc.

Although the broad pattern generally holds for each EU country, there are important differences within the EU. The jobs deficit relative to the US is particularly large in countries like Italy and Spain, while it is small in countries like Denmark, Sweden, the Netherlands and the UK. For these countries, too, the thesis holds that superior employment performance is not solely related to a proportional surplus of low-paid jobs.

How the less-skilled have fared across the OECD

How, then, does the idea that the labour market position of the less-skilled has deteriorated everywhere stand up to the evidence? There is, as we have seen, a good deal of evidence that job destruction in manufacturing has mainly hurt less-skilled (male) workers and that job creation in services has mainly, though not exclusively, favoured skilled workers. There are certainly good grounds to suspect that the labour market position of the less-skilled may have deteriorated in advanced economies. Yet, contrary to widespread perception, there is no uniform pattern across countries.

The main reason why the perception is so prevalent is probably due to the fact that at least some countries where the labour market position of the less-skilled has deteriorated markedly. Without a doubt the most remarkable example is the US. American men with low levels of educational attainment have seen a dramatic drop in real hourly wages over the past 25 years: the real hourly wages of male high school drop-outs (those without at least higher secondary education) have fallen by almost 30 per cent since the early 1970s. The pay of the average high-school graduate (roughly equivalent to upper secondary education) has fallen by 17 per cent during the 1973-1999 period. By contrast, hourly earnings of workers with a college degree (first university degree level education) earned about 5 per cent more and those with an advanced university degree 20 per cent more (Krueger 2002).

Interestingly, however, the trend has no linear character. Most of the increase occurred during the 1980s. The 1990s were a period of relative stability. This seems inconsistent with the view that global forces like globalisation and technological change are behind the increase. After all, technological progress did not slow down during the 1990s and globalisation intensified (for example if measured by international trade-flows and investments). Furthermore, the decline of the earnings of the less-skilled has occurred in the context of a general increase in wage dispersion in the US. The increase of inequality between skill groups provides only part of the explanation. The within-group rise in inequality has been as impressive, suggesting that other forces than skilled-biased change must have been at work (Juhn et al. 1993).

The US is not the only country where the less-skilled have fared less well than the rest of the population. In the United Kingdom, too, the less-skilled have fared less well than the better-skilled. Using micro data from the New Earnings Survey (NES) Prasad (2002) shows that wage inequality in the UK rose quite sharply in the 1980s and continued to rise moderately through the mid-1990s (see also Dickens 1996; Machin 1996b). In contrast to the US, earnings inequality in the United Kingdom increased mostly at the top of the distribution. It has remained essentially unchanged since the latter half of the 1990s. Shifts in the structure of employment – including changes in the occupational and industrial composition of aggregate employment – are shown to have had important effects on the evolution of wage inequality. The biggest change is in the inequality among occupational groups which, by the measure used, doubled between 1975 and 1999, with most of the increase taking place during the 1980s. (Occupation is taken as a proxy for skill since education is not available as a variable in the NES.) However, as in the US, changes in within-group inequality are shown to account for a substantial fraction of the rise in wage dispersion that has occurred over the last 25 years. (In addition, there has been a significant convergence of the wage distributions for men and women; this has had a stabilising effect on the overall wage distribution.)

Such evidence for the US and the UK has often been extrapolated to the industrialised world as a whole. The reality, however, is that the United States and the United Kingdom are not representative for what has happened elsewhere in the OECD area. There are some other countries where earnings inequality has increased markedly. Barrett, Callan and Nolan (1997) find, for example, a large growth in earnings dispersion in Ireland in 1987-1994, much of which is accounted for by increasing returns to education. New Zealand too has seen a marked increase in earnings inequality (Martin 1995; Borland 1999).

But in most Continental European countries, earnings dispersion appears to have remained fairly stable. The available data series are generally less comprehensive and perhaps even less reliable than those for the United States or the UK. The principal data source is the OECD data base on earnings, which has its limits. Only full-time workers are included and earnings data is for a number of countries derived from administrative sources, such as social security records. This means that part-time workers and often also temporary workers are inadequately covered. Also, non-wage benefits, which are an important form of remuneration in high tax Europe, are not included. Nevertheless, income dispersion time series for Continental European countries covering the 1980s and 1990s show a really remarkable degree of stability on the earnings inequality front (OECD 1996).

This picture of stability is confirmed by more detailed country-specific studies like the ones for Germany (Becker 1998; Hauser and Becker 2001), or for Austria by Gusenleitner et al. (1996). For France, there is even evidence of a sustained decline in earnings inequality during the 1980s – continuing a trend measured since the late 1960s (Friez and Julhès 1998). The bottom decile in particular has continued to move towards the median, with, as Atkinson (1999a;c) notes, the time pattern much in line with the rise of the SMIC. For the Scandinavian countries as well the evidence points to relative stability (Aaberge et al. 1997; Gustafson et al. 1999; Gustafson and Uusitalo 1999; Statistics Finland 1999). In Sweden, earnings inequality did increase somewhat, be it from an extremely low base level.

Using LIS data, Acemoglou (1999b) has attempted to estimate the evolution of male skill premiums in a number of OECD countries, including a fair number of European countries for which these types of information are difficult to find in the literature (e.g., Belgium, Denmark, Finland, Germany, the Netherlands, Norway, Sweden). The use of LIS data for this kind of exercise is fraught with difficulties but the broad picture that emerges is nevertheless indicative. Acemoglou's (1999b) estimates suggest that, during the 1980s and 1990s, skill premiums have remained fairly stable in most European countries. In some countries the tendency was even more towards a decline rather than an increase.

The familiar objection, of course, is that the comparative stability of wage dispersion in Continental Europe is due to labour market and particularly wage setting rigidities and that wage dispersion stability has come at the cost of worsened unemployment and non-employment among the less-skilled.

While it is well documented that both unemployment and non-employment are far more prevalent among the less-skilled, there is much less clear evidence that, during the past couple of decades, unemployment and non-employment rates for the less-skilled have risen more strongly as compared to those for other skill groups. This is in part due to a lack of data. While there now is rather extensive data available on current employment and unemployment rates by level of educational attainment (see OECD publications 'Employment Outlook' and 'Education at a Glance'), time series that cover more than 10 years or so remain quite scarce.

The time series data that is available offers a picture that is far less clear-cut than is often suggested. Nickell and Bell (1995) bring together data on male unemployment rates by education from 15 OECD countries. For most countries, the data cover the period from the mid-1970s to the late 1980s or early 1990s. For some countries (Norway, Sweden, the UK and the US) there is even data spanning a wider time frame. They find that, in line with general perception, unemployment rates for the less-skilled increased substantially over this period in just about every country included in the study. However, if one looks at relative unemployment rates for the less-skilled the picture becomes more complicated. Relative unemployment rates for the less-skilled can be seen to have increased in some countries, but not everywhere. In some countries, unemployment rates for the less-skilled actually rose less in proportionate terms than for the more-skilled. Moreover, the time patterns of these relative unemployment rates are rather erratic for most countries, i.e., measurement year and the economic circumstances at that point matter a great deal. Interestingly, there is also no evidence that the unemployment situation of the less-skilled deteriorated less in countries where wage inequality increased. In the United States, the unemployment rate for the less-skilled doubled between the early 1970s and early 1990s, a period of vast wage deterioration for the less-skilled. In the UK, too, an impressive increase in wage inequality during the 1980s did not prevent the unemployment rate for the less-skilled rising fourfold. In both countries, however, the relative unemployment rate for the less-skilled remained stable, with only a temporary rise in the US during the mid-1980s. Data gathered by the OECD for both men and women for the period 1981-1994 confirm a general increase in unemployment rates for the less-skilled in 9 OECD countries (Canada, Denmark, France, New Zealand, Norway, Spain, Sweden, UK and US). But the OECD study finds, much in line with Nickell and Bell, that the rises for the less-skilled were in most countries roughly proportional to those for the highly-skilled.

There are several points to be made here. First, one can argue that the percentage-point increases are more relevant (especially from a social policy standpoint) than the relative unemployment rate increases. A tripling of the unemployment rate for the highly skilled from 1 to 3 per cent is arguably less dramatic in its impact than a tripling of the unemployment rate for the less-skilled from 4 to 12 per cent. Comparisons of the ratio of unemployment rates do not convey an accurate picture of differences in the probability of having work. This is true, but part of what we are doing is trying to establish whether increased unemployment (in Europe) is the flip side of increased earnings inequality (in the US) and whether advanced economies are faced with a worsening trade-off between unemployment and low pay among the low-skilled. A second point is that the overrepresentation of the less-skilled is more likely to show up if one looks at long-term unemployment rates. Time series evidence on this is even scarcer, but it is undisputable that long-term unemployment has increased right across the OECD, that it remains quite persistent, even in countries that are doing well in economic terms and that the less-skilled are heavily overrepresented among the long-term unemployed. A third point is that 'unemployment' is too strict a measure of involuntary or at least problematic labour market exclusion of the less-skilled. A good argument can be made that less-skilled workers are more prone to discouragement and hence labour force withdrawal.

For the latter reason, it may be more appropriate to look at what has happened with (non-)employment rates. Again, data is not abundantly available. The OECD now provides time series data on employment rates by educational attainment, but this data series only starts in 1995. Glyn and Salverda (2000b) have compiled what is probably the most comprehensive set of data on employment rate trends by educational attainment, at least for a wide range of OECD countries. These rates were derived from Labour Force Surveys data.

Unlike the above cited studies by Nickell and Bell and the OECD, Glyn and Salverda (2000) do provide employment rates by relative level of educational attainment, i.e., by educational quartile. As they rightly point out, the cross-temporal comparison of employment rates by actual level of educational attainment is troublesome because the proportion of the population with a certain level of educational attainment has changed over time. For example, in Belgium the proportion of the working-age population with a low level of education (ISCED 1 or 2) has halved in scarcely two decades, while the proportion of the highly educated tripled. 'Hence the deteriorating employment position of the less-skilled (defined in this way) may reflect a process of sorting, whereby the shrinking membership of the bottom educational category is increasingly confined to those with other disadvantages in the labour market (in terms of intellectual capacity, attitude and so forth). Plausibly, the distribution of talents among the population remained the same but the mapping over the range of formalised educational categories changed' (Glyn and Salverda 2000: 37). This argument is legitimate but it is nevertheless unfortunate that they only present employment rates by educational quartile and not by formal level of educational attainment, upon which the former are calculated. The raw figures would be better comparable with those contained in other studies and national statistics. Also, educational quartile is a rather abstract and broad category which may be internally heterogeneous. This is probably especially true as far as the crucial first and fourth quartiles are concerned.

Employment and wage inequality trends for men have been compiled in table 2.2 and figure 2.1, adapted from Glyn and Salverda 2000. This table contains the earnings and employment inequality trends which we have discussed. In addition, the table contains an inequality index, which is a kind of summary index reflecting both employment and wage inequality trends. One might raise all kinds of objections against simply adding up an absolute employment rate difference and a ratio measure of wage dispersion. But this inequality index nevertheless offers a convenient, albeit rough, summary measure. This table leaves little doubt that the general tendency is towards rising labour market inequality. But three things are striking. First, the deterioration, where it has occurred in substantial measure, has not been linear and progressive. The 1990s in many countries were a period of stability compared to the period before (e.g., United Kingdom and the United States) or even of declining inequality (e.g., Canada and France). Second, the extent of cross-national diversity is striking. In some countries, labour market inequality has increased quite strongly (in Ireland, the US, the UK and New Zealand), while in other countries the increases have been moderate at most (France, Germany, the Nordic countries). This extent of cross-national diversity does not appear to be consistent with the idea that universal, global forces such as increased competition from low-wage countries and technical change are driving up inequality. Third, there is little evidence that increased wage inequality is the flip side of increased employment inequality. There is, as we will further demonstrate below, simply no cross-country correlation between employment inequality trends and wage inequality trends. It is, in fact, striking, that in some countries, like the UK, earnings and employment inequality increased at the same time.

Table 2.2 Employment, wage and labour-market inequality trends, men 1970s-1990s

	Employment differences Q4-Q1, % point annual change			Wage dispersion D9/D1, % point annual change			Inequality index (Q4-Q1) + d9/d1		
	1970s	1980s	1990s	1970s	1980s	1990s	1970s	1980s	1990s
US	0.9	0	-0.2	0.2	2.1	0.9	1.1	2.1	0.8
Canada		0.4	-0.1		1.5	-1.4		1.8	-1.5
Australia		-0.1	0.8		0.3	0.9		0.2	1.7
New Zealand		1.4	0.6		2.1	2.1		3.5	2.7
UK	0.4	1.3	0.3	0.2	2.2	0.7	0.6	3.5	1.0
Denmark		0.6	0.6		0.1			0.7	
Finland		0.5	0.9		0.8	-1.3		1.3	-0.4
France		1.3	0.4		0.3	-0.8		1.6	-0.4
Germany (W)	0.2	0.6	0.6	0	-0.6	0.9		0	1.5
Ireland			0.6			3.5			4.1
Italy		0.9	1.1		-0.1	1.1		0.8	2.2
Netherlands		0.4	-0.6		1.3	1.6		1.7	1.0
Norway		0.5	0.5			-0.4			0.1
Spain		0.5	0.9						
Sweden	0.4	-0.1	0.6	0.5	0.3	1.3	0.9	0.5	1.5
Switzerland			0.8			1.1			1.9
Japan			0.1		0.9	-0.3			1.0

Source: Glyn and Salverda (2000).

So far, much of the above discussion has focused on men. This is simply because most of the available empirical inequality-trend studies focus exclusively on men. One naturally wonders whether patterns are different for women. Less is known about employment and earnings differentials trends for women. This relative lack of data is unfortunate because the proportion of households where women are the principal if not sole breadwinners has increased significantly over the past decades. In addition, the differential proliferation of double earnership has had a significant impact on poverty and income inequality.

Figure 2.1 Changes in male employment and earnings inequality (1970s, 1980s, 1990s), OECD countries

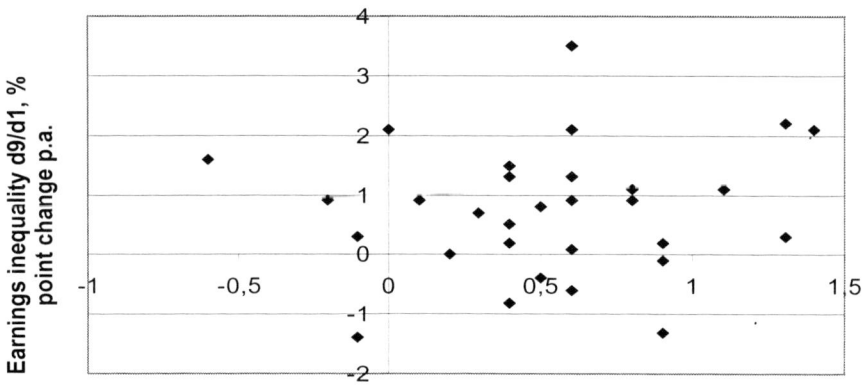

Note: Each point represents the annualised rate of change during a 10-year time period.

Source: Based on Glyn and Salverda (2000).

There are reasons to expect differences between trends for men and women. The two major trends of the past two decades, the fast decline in agricultural and industrial employment on the one hand and the growth of service employment on the other may have affected men and women differently. Particularly with respect to Europe, one might think that low-skilled men lost out because the fast decline in industrial employment, whereas low-skilled women missed out because of the slow increase of service employment. It is known that in most advanced economies substantial employment rate gaps exist between less and more highly educated women, but less is known how differences have evolved over time. In a paper that follows up on previous work and uses much of the same methodology, Glyn (2001) shows that employment rates for women in the first educational quartile have generally remained stable in Europe over the past two decades, in contrast to the substantial drops in employment for less-skilled men. In fact, there are quite a number of countries where less-skilled female employment has gone up substantially, most notably the Netherlands and Ireland – be it from comparatively low base levels.

Finally, research (see most notably OECD 2002b) suggests that less-skilled workers are overrepresented in temporary jobs, and that mobility into permanent (and generally better-paid) employment is lower for less-educated workers. Also, significant numbers seem to cycle among temporary jobs, unemployment and non-employment for extended periods of time. Again, while such evidence exists for some countries (most notably the US and the UK), less is known about the situation in other countries.

On the worsened 'trade-off' between unemployment and low-paid employment

Which brings us to the whole issue of the trade-off between unemployment and low-wage employment. The unified theory predicts that in the context of a structural and irreversible decline in the demand for low-skilled labour, countries are forced to choose between either more low-paying jobs or more unemployment among the less-skilled. Similarly, it is argued that Europe's high minimum wages are becoming increasingly detrimental to less-skilled employment, especially in the service industries (Iversen and Wren 1998). The idea that welfare states increasingly face a trade-off between employment and wage equality is recurring theme in the contemporary welfare state literature (see, for example, Esping-Andersen 2002; Hemerijck 1999; Scharpf and Schmidt 2000).

But is it necessarily the case that a reduction in unemployment has a price tag of more low-paid work attached to it? It is easy to demonstrate that there is no simple correlation between wage dispersion trends and either employment and unemployment trends (figure 2.1). Similarly, a high level of wage dispersion – a high incidence of low pay – is not systematically associated with less unemployment or higher employment among the less-skilled.

A number of studies have looked in more detail and with more sophistication at the relationship between earnings dispersion and employment performance (Blank 1995; 1997a). The OECD (1996) found no significant relationships between employment rates for the low-skilled and the incidence of low pay. The OECD study remarkably (for contrary to OECD policy doctrine) concludes 'that unemployment rates for the most vulnerable groups in the labour market – women, youngsters and the low-skilled – do *not* tend to be consistently higher in countries where low-wage work is more prevalent.' Similarly, the OECD finds that employment rates for the less-skilled are not systematically higher in countries where low-paid work is more prevalent.

Nickell and Bell (1995), too, did not find evidence that the employment effects of the drop in the demand for less-skilled labour were any more severe in countries where increases in wage dispersion were small. Card et al. (1999), in a study comparing France and the US to Canada, concluded 'consistent with the view that labour market institutions are more rigid in France, and more flexible in the US, we find that relative wages of less-skilled workers fell most in the US, fell somewhat less in Canada and did not fall at all in France. Contrary to expectations, however, we find little evidence that wage inflexibilities generated divergent patterns of relative employment growth across these countries'.

The finding that there is no simple relationship between wage compression and employment is confirmed by more detailed cross-country comparative studies. Freeman and Schettkat (2000) have looked in more detail at the question of whether the expansion of jobs in low-wage services in Europe is restricted by high wages. With services now the main sector source of employment growth this question is indeed crucial. They examine this through a detailed comparison of the role of low-wage services in the US and Germany. They find a clear low-wage service jobs deficit in Germany – much in line with general perception and with recent OECD studies (2000 and 2001). But they also show that this is not due to excessively high German wages. Surprisingly, relative wages in low-wage sectors are extremely similar in the two countries. This is a striking finding given the much wider overall wage distribution in the US. The explanation for this phenomenon is, according to Freeman and Schettkat (2000b), the much greater intra-industry wage dispersion in the US, producing similar industry mean wages as the much narrower German distribution (see also Beaudry and Green 2000).

Other studies, however, do point towards a link between earnings dispersion and employment performance. Blau and Kahn (1996) conclude that the greater wage dispersion in the US is associated with smaller differences in employment rates than in the six Continental European countries included in their study. In a follow-up study Bertola, Blau and Kahn (2002) find that, controlling for country – and time-specific effects, high employment is associated with low wage levels and high levels of wage inequality. However, it is crucial to emphasise that this is a result that only turns up in the residuals as country and period fixed effects account for a very large proportion of labour market performance variation. These country effects reflect, among other many factors, the impact of education systems and institutions – on which more below.

Thus, there is no unequivocal confirmation or rejection of the view that rising wage dispersion is the necessary price to pay for maintaining employment at the bottom end of the labour market. More refined models do suggest that wage levels and wage dispersion affect employment to some extent. Indeed, the evidence in support of the sophisticated models developed Blanchard and Wolfers (2000) and Bertola, Blau and Kahn (2002) is compelling. But this is not the point. What is important is that, contrary to what is often widely assumed in the policy discussion, wage dispersion is not the dominant factor that explains why the less qualified are more employed in some countries than in others.

Moreover, a very high degree of wage flexibility does not guarantee high employment and low unemployment among the most vulnerable. In other words, a high degree of wage dispersion is neither a necessary nor a sufficient condition to achieve a high employment rate, especially among the less-skilled. Richard Freeman (1995) has drawn attention to what he has called 'the limits of wage flexibility to curing unemployment.' The US, for instance, has one of the most flexible labour markets in the OECD area, if not the most flexible, and people have, generally speaking, every incentive to work. Long-term benefit dependence is for many Americans, especially men at working age, not an option, let alone a comfortable one. However, unemployment and non-employment rates for less-educated Americans – those who have not completed upper secondary education – are as high as elsewhere in the OECD area, including many of the European countries where low-wage work is far less prevalent and the less educated command far higher real wages (Murphy and Topel 1997; Mishel and Bernstein 2003). Those without a upper-secondary education diploma make up a substantially smaller proportion of the work force than in most European countries but an essentially similar picture emerges if one compares unemployment and non-employment rates for the bottom 25 per cent of the labour force ranked by educational attainment (OECD 1997; Glyn and Salverda 2000).

4 The Role of Trade and Technological Change Empirically Assessed

To recapitulate, our main findings thus far are as follows: First, there is clear and consistent evidence that skill demands have gone up in advanced economies; second, the labour market position of the less-skilled has deteriorated in many countries, but not everywhere to the same extent; third, while there is evidence that earnings levels and earnings dispersion affect employment outcomes to some extent, there is no evidence of a severely worsened trade-off between low pay and unemployment.

Let us now look at the empirical evidence from an entirely different angle, not from the viewpoint of observed outcomes, but from the viewpoint of theory. Two lines of argumentation feature prominently in the literature. First, the expansion of trade and economic globalisation is said to hurt employment and earnings of less-skilled workers in advanced economies and hence, their ability to be economically self-reliant. Second, technological change is said to make much of the less-skilled work redundant while at the same time increasing the demand for highly skilled workers.

Trade and globalisation

The claim that trade hurts less-skilled workers in advanced economies is both straightforward and plausible. In the global economy (i.e., an economy with more international trade because of fewer trade barriers and lower costs associated with trade) more developed countries are increasingly open to trade with less developed countries where low-skilled labour is both cheap and abundant, and where, as a result, goods of a labour-intensive kind can be produced at a lower price. The result is that unskilled workers in more advanced countries are inevitably disadvantaged in one way or another. Either they must accept lower wages or, if their wages are maintained by union power or by protective legislation, then they must face an increase in their risk of unemployment.

Robert Reich (1991) is arguably the writer who most eloquently and influentially set out the claim. In *The Work of Nations* he argues that the future lies with high-skilled, creative 'symbolic analysts'. The claim is that people with few talents and qualifications will increasingly have to settle for low-paid, precarious service jobs, or find no employment at all.

He points to the changing nature of production among the highly competitive advanced industrialised nations. Standardised mass production, he argues, has given way to custom-tailored products. Reich calls this a shift from 'high volume to high value' production. Specialty factories are replacing mammoth plants and the result is that large corporations are breaking up into independent, specialised units. This calls for creative specialists with extensive skills and education. It does not require, as in the past, a large work force with only general skills.

Second, companies are said to have lost their national character. It is increasingly common to find a company headquartered in Europe or the US, but with research, design, and production facilities spread over Western Europe, Japan and North America; additional production facilities in Eastern Europe, Southeast Asia and Latin America; marketing and distribution centres on every continent; and lenders and investors in Europe and North America. As production and services move freely across borders, the decision to locate a facility depends on where a company can find the most talented and experienced workers.

The underlying reasoning here is partly based on the well-known Heckscher-Ohlin theorem which states that, in an international economy, it is in a country's interest to focus on activities in which it enjoys a comparative advantage. In the case of advanced economies, these are mainly technology and knowledge-intensive activities. Growing free trade and increasingly cheap transportation and communications allow an economically more efficient geographical distribution of the production process: research and development mainly in advanced economies with many high-skilled workers and a technological advantage, and mass production mainly in developing economies with an abundance of cheap low-skilled labour. Thus, the low-skilled in the Western world would eventually only be able to find work in location-bound, non-exportable services requiring few qualifications.

Reich divides post-industrial employment into three broad categories: 'symbolic-analytic' services, 'routine production' services, and 'in-person' services. The first of these are carried out by engineers, scientists, consultants and other 'mind workers' who engage in processing information and symbols for a living. These individuals, who make up roughly 20 per cent of the labour force, occupy a privileged position in that they can sell their services in the global economy. They are well-educated and will occupy an even more advantageous position in society in the future.

Routine production workers and in-person service workers will fare much worse in the new economy, according to Reich. Routine production workers include those who perform repetitive tasks – assembly line workers, data processors, foremen, and supervisors. Examples of in-person service workers are waitresses, nurses, and child care workers. These two categories of workers do not compete on the global level and are at a considerable economic disadvantage. This is especially true of routine producers. The future of service workers is less clear-cut since their services are in demand by symbolic analysts.

The economic fates of these segments are diverging; Reich claims, 'All used to be in the same economic boat. Most rose or fell together, as the corporations in which they were employed, the industries comprising such corporations, and the national economy as a whole became more productive – or languished. But national borders no longer define our economic fates. We are now in different boats, one sinking rapidly, one sinking more slowly, and the third rising steadily.'

As I indicated, the idea that global trade hurts the less-skilled has a theoretical basis in the Heckscher-Ohlin and Stolpher-Samuelson models (Dixit and Norman 1980; Kanbur 2000; Krugman 1995b; Richardson 1995). The reasoning contained in these models is somewhat more complex than the popular claim as espoused by Reich, but the predictions following from these models are essentially the same: less-skilled labour in advanced economies is destined to suffer from enhanced global trade. In the basic Heckscher-Ohlin model a country that is well endowed with skilled labour can produce skill-intensive goods at a lower *relative* cost than economies that are less well endowed. These countries therefore focus their production activities on skill-intensive goods, exporting these in exchange of goods whose production makes intensive use of the scarce factor, unskilled labour. Trade in the skill-intensive goods will occur when their world price exceeds the price that would prevail in the absence of trade. Consequently, the export of these goods increases the demand for it. The increase in demand through exports raises the relative price of the abundant factor. Moreover, any increase in the price of the exported good will increase the wage return to the factor used intensively in its production – skilled labour in the case of advanced economies – and thereby decrease the relative wage return to their scarce factor, low-skilled labour. Hence, in the Heckscher-Ohlin framework, the relative wages for scarce (unskilled labour) and abundant (skilled labour) are determined through product prices on world markets. Note that relative factor abundance or scarcity are the key factors that shape world trade, and prices of traded goods and returns to the factors used.

The Heckscher-Ohlin and Stolper-Samuelson models predict relative wage changes, where wages for skilled and unskilled workers adjust to absorb the changes in demand for their services. If the wage for low-skilled workers is not downwardly adjustable, either through institutional constraints, such as the minimum wage, because of a reservation wage floor set by benefits, then the result will be falling employment rates for the less-skilled in the advanced world.

It is well documented that international trade has expanded. Interestingly, though, the expansion has not been continuous over time. World trade in relation to output grew from the mid-1800s to 1913, fell from 1913 to 1950 because of two world wars and protectionist policies implemented during the great depression of the 1930s, and then surged after 1950. Only in the 1970s did trade flows reach the same proportion of output as at the turn of the previous century, a result of the easing of tariffs and quota's (through the various rounds of negotiations under GATT and the WTO), more efficient and cheaper communications, and falling transportation costs.

One common objection is that trade with less developed countries remains rather marginal in GDP terms. But as Slaughter and Swagel (1997) point out, the ratio of exports to total output likely understates the degree of product market globalisation. More and more output in the advanced economies consists of largely non-tradable services: education, government, finance, insurance, real estate, wholesale and retail trade. A more accurate measure of the importance of trade, according to Slaughter and Swagel (1997), is merchandise exports as a share of tradable goods only. This alternative measure shows a much larger role for trade.

Moreover, from a theoretical viewpoint it is not necessary that trade be intensive. The threat in itself is enough to undermine the bargaining position of the less-skilled. And there can be no doubt that with falling communication and transportation costs, and with diminished institutional (free trade agreements) and technological (communication) barriers the threat is very real.

Let us now turn to the empirical evidence on the impact of trade on the labour market position of the less-skilled. Arguably the most influential study until roughly the mid-1990s was the one by Wood (1994 1995) which asserted that increasing competition from 'the South' was having a major impact on wages and employment of the less-skilled in the North. Wood's study was for the 1970s and 1980s, a period when rising wage inequality in the US and rising unemployment in Europe coincided with increased competition from the Asian rim countries. Wood implied, rather than demonstrated, a causal link. His claim, however, falls apart for the 1990s. The 1990s, when the expansion of trade accelerated, were after all characterised by stability and even improvement of the labour market position of the less-skilled on both sides of the Atlantic.

During the 1990s there developed a quite extensive body of economic literature, some of it quite sophisticated in terms of the econometric techniques used (Alderson and Nielsen 2002; Baldwin 1995; Borjas and Ramey 1995; Borjas et al. 1997; Burtless 1995; Cornia 1999; Davis 1998; Dewatripont et al. 1999; Feenstra and Hanson 1999; Gaston and Trefler 1994; Hahn 1998; Hanson and Harrison 1995; Lang 1998; Lattimore and Wooding 1996; Lawrence and Slaughter 1993; Leamer 1996; Lindert and Williamson 2001; Sachs and Shatz 1996; Strauss-Kahn 2001). The findings from these studies show a large degree of consistency, despite sharp differences and debates over methodology. The broad consensus of the research is that import competition accounts for only a modest part of increased income inequality. Estimates of the share of increase in inequality accounted for by trade range from zero to one-third, with nearly all indications falling in the lower part of the range. What is particularly noteworthy is that several very different methodologies have been used to estimate the contribution of trade, but almost all of the approaches found that the contribution is small. The studies that exist for the other advanced economies suggest similarly small effects of imports on wages and employment.

In Desjonqueres, Machin and Van Reenen (1999), for example, a range of empirical tests of the orthodox trade hypothesis is presented. These tests vary from looking at cross-country patterns (involving seven countries) of changes in wages and employment structure, to disaggregated analysis of what has happened in specific industries. They find that, in contradiction to the predictions of the Heckscher-Ohlin model, the within-industry (trade vs. non-trade sectors) shift towards the increased use of skilled workers makes up by far the largest component of the overall increase in the use of skills. Similarly, Berman, Bound and Griliches (1994) found for the US that approximately 70 per cent of the overall shift in labour demand was due to a within-industry demand shift towards highly skilled labour.

These studies are not necessarily inconsistent with the widespread view that expanding global trade is shaping economies and labour markets, but they do suggest that the implications are less straightforward than those suggested by the simple Heckscher-Ohlin framework. This framework which is so central to many an argument is after all a highly abstract one that only holds under a range of assumptions. Atkinson (1999c), for example, argues that a simple two-bloc model is scarcely defensible. He argues that at least a distinction within the developed OECD countries between the US and Europe is required. But once such a distinction is made, the predictions of the Heckscher-Ohlin model alter and become less straightforward than those flowing from the standard model. More elaborate and (usually less accessible) theoretical refinements of the basic Heckscher-Ohlin model come to similar conclusions (Johnson and Stafford 1999).

That the impact of globalisation on wages remains limited is most tellingly illustrated in a study by Freeman and Oostendorp (2000). Using ILO wages survey data they construct a consistent data file on pay in 161 occupations in over 150 countries from 1983 to 1998 to examine the pattern of pay across occupations and countries. They find that wages in the same occupation vary greatly across countries measured by common currency exchange rates and measured by purchasing power parity. They also find that cross-country differences in pay for comparable work *increased*, despite increased world trade. They suggest that rather than globalisation, the principal forces that affect the occupational wage structure around the world are the level of gross domestic product per capita and unionisation/wage-setting institutions.

In conclusion, the growing importance of international trade is undisputed, as is the fact that there is a tendency towards economic globalisation. But the empirical research available to date suggests a rather limited impact on the overall labour market position of the less-skilled.

Skill-biased technological change

Technological change is widely seen as the single most important and ubiquitous force (since it quickly diffuses across international borders) increasing the relative demand for better-educated, more highly skilled workers and reducing the demand for less educated workers. Low-skilled, routine jobs, done by clerical and production workers, can be automated and replaced by computers more easily than professional or managerial jobs. At the same time, computers complement skilled workers, increasing the return on the creative use of information (Levy 1996).

There is overwhelming anecdotal evidence of technological advances working against the less-educated. Robots have replaced large numbers of low-skilled workers in manufacturing and computers and other office automation technologies are replacing low-skilled workers in the service industries. The idea that computers complement highly skilled workers is supported by the key fact that highly skilled workers –particularly university-educated workers – are much more likely to use computers at work

As some authors have argued, the impact probably goes beyond direct substitution. Lindbeck and Snower (1996) and Snower (1998) have argued that advances in computer and telecommunication technologies are the main source of an 'organisational revolution' that has encompassed changes to the organisation of authority within firms, to the organisation of design, production and marketing activities, and the breakdown of traditional occupational barriers. Similarly, Bresnahan (1999) suggests that the main impact of computers has been through 'organisational complementarity' between computer systems, changes in work organisation, and high-skilled workers. He argues that because of computers and technology, a wide range of managerial functions now call for more complex cognitive and analytical skills (see also Bartel and Lichtenberg 1997).

Contrary to the outright and almost universal rejection of the (rudimentary) globalisation thesis, quite a lot of empirical evidence has sided with the technology argument (Acemoglou 1998, 2002; Allen 1996; Autor and Katz 1998, 1999; Berman and Machin 2000; Cappelli 2000; Doms et al. 1997; Haskel and Heden 1998; Haskel and Slaughter 1998; Haskel 1999; Krueger 1993; Loyd-Ellis 1999; Machin and Van Reenen 1998; Manacorda and Manning 1999). A host of other studies have attributed the much-studied rise in US wage inequality to 'skill-biased change' across industries and firms (Bound and Johnson 1992; Berman, Bound and Griliches 1994; Krueger 1993; Johnson 1997). Katz and Autor (2000), for example; find that in the United States the relative demand for college graduates grew more rapidly on average during the past decades (1970-1995) than during the previous three decades (1940-1970). They also find that the acceleration in demand shifts for more-skilled workers in the 1970s and 1980s relative to the 1960s is entirely accounted for by an increase in within-industry changes in skill use rather than between – industry employment shifts. Industries with large increases in the rate of skill upgrading in the 1970s and 1980s versus the 1960s are those with greater growth in employee computer usage, more computer capital per worker and larger investment as a share of total investment. They suggest that the spread of computer technology may 'explain' as much as 30-50 per cent of the increase in the rate of growth of the relative demand for more-skilled workers since 1970.

In a similar vein, Berman, Bound and Machin (1998) show that substitution towards skilled labour has generally taken place within industries across a range of OECD economies (Denmark, France, Germany, Japan, Sweden and the United Kingdom) rather than reflecting the decline of less-skill-intensive industries, and it has been strongest in industries producing machinery, including computers, electrical components, etc.

While there is considerable agreement among economists that skill-biased technical change has been an important factor in the rises in inequality in the United States and elsewhere, this consensus is not universally shared. Card and DiNardo (2002) point out that a fundamental problem for the 'skill-biased technological change' hypothesis is that wage inequality stabilised in the 1990s, despite continuing advances in computer technology.

I already made short reference to Dennis Snower's argument that organisational change may account for the rise in earnings inequality in the United States and the United Kingdom, particularly the puzzling rise of within-education group inequality. His argument is that the transition from an industrial, Tayloristic economy to a post-industrial, customer-oriented economy has brought fundamental change in the division and organisation of work. Specifically, he argues that in the Tayloristic era, workers' tasks used to be defined by the rigid operation of single-purpose machines, that tasks were simple and repetitive, and that little training was needed to perform them. Under those circumstances, workers, performance at any particular task tended to be quite homogenous and this was reflected in the dispersion of pay. Increasingly, he argues, workers have had to interact with flexible machines and computerised equipment and they have been given the discretion to perform different sets of complementary tasks. In addition, social competence, the ability to interact directly with customers, has become more important. As a consequence, their performance has become more idiosyncratic and employees' dispersion of productivity has grown. After all, people differ enormously in their versatility across tasks and their personal interaction skills. Whereas previous technologies and organisational structures hid these differences, the new economic environment allows these differences to manifest themselves in job performance. Consequently, inequality may be expected to rise within any one particular education group.

Although interesting and plausible, Snower's theory suffers from the same weaknesses as the other 'technological change' explanations. The timing does not seem to fit (it assumes that there was a torrent of organisational change in the 1980s and early 1990s – when inequality soared – which was proceeded and followed by periods of organisational inertia) and it seems difficult to square with the fact that wage inequality only increased in several of the advanced economies. It is hard to imagine that organisational changes were confined to the United States and the United Kingdom, although they may have been more pronounced there.

5 Accounting for Divergent Country Trajectories: The Role of Education, Institutions and Social Norms

Empirical support for the two most popular theories predicting an inexorable rise in inequality is inconclusive to say the least. In addition, there remains the empirical fact of the important cross-national differences in inequality trends. The dominant picture is one of enormous cross-national diversity, not one of rising inequality across the board.

In a similar vein, there is the fact that the low-pay/unemployment trade-off does not hold. There is no consistent relationship between wage compression – the extent of low-wage employment in particular – on the one hand and employment outcomes on the other. Some countries manage (or have done so for extended periods of time) to combine fairly compressed wage structures with comparatively high employment rates and low unemployment rates, including among the less-skilled (even if controlled for the extent of government employment and such factors). Conversely, high levels of wage dispersion are not always associated with comparatively favourable employment outcomes for the less-skilled.

The role of education

New technologies and production methods have virtually always reduced the demand for less-skilled labour. In nineteenth-century Britain, skilled artisans destroyed weaving, spinning and threshing machines during the Luddite riots, in the (correct) belief that the new machines would make their skills redundant. The artisan shop was replaced by factories where standard parts were used and later by assembly lines where standard parts were at least in part automatically assembled (Mok 1999). Since then we have had two centuries of tremendous technological progress with millions of jobs destroyed in its wake. But employment has risen almost continuously (see e.g., Gordon 2000).

Education policy features as a key variable in a number of studies which have sought to explain why the rises in inequality in some countries appear to be a relatively recent phenomenon. Evidence for the US shows that the pay gap today is still considerably narrower than at the beginning of the twentieth century (Goldin and Katz 1998). Between 1900 and 1939, US wage differentials by educational level remained fairly compressed despite the fact that factory electrification eliminated many unskilled manual jobs and increased the demand for skills. But during this period the rise in the demand for more-skilled workers was more than offset by a huge increase in the supply of educated workers. In 1910, fewer than 10 per cent of Americans had high-school diplomas; by the mid-1930s, the figure had risen to 40 per cent.

Education also features as a key variable in studies that ask why inequality has not increased everywhere to the same extent. During the 1980s and 1990s the ratio between the earnings of university graduates and high-school graduates rose sharply in America, but it fell in Canada. Katz and Murphy (1992) and Murphy, Riddell and Romer (1998) suggest that in both countries the demand for skills rose by similar margins (mostly technology driven), but the supply of educated workers rose much more rapidly in Canada than in the US. This suggests that the real factor behind rising inequality in the US is not simply technology, but the government's failure to improve education and training (Beaudry and Green 1998).

In a study of the growth of earnings inequality in the UK in the 1980s, Gregg and Manning (1997) come to a similar conclusion. They, too, show that the shift in labour demand from less educated to the more educated are nothing new: indeed, that this has been synonymous with the process of industrialisation. But the general trend has been that the supply of better-educated workers kept up with demand. During the 1980s, when earnings inequality started to rise, supply growth started to lag demand. Gregg and Manning see rising inequality as a result of the UK government's failure to ensure that the supply of the highly skilled kept up with rising demand.

Looking at a wider range of countries, Katz and Autor (2000) find that where wage differentials between skilled and unskilled workers have widened most, growth in the supply of better-educated workers has generally slowed down. In contrast, in France, Germany and the Netherlands, where wage differentials have not increased over the past two decades, the supply of educated workers has grown rapidly. It must be added, however, that Acemoglou (2002) has tested this hypothesis for a larger set of OECD economies, using LIS data –arguably not the best data source for this type of analysis – and his results, while confirmative, suggest that the differential expansion in the supply of highly skilled labour can only provide a partial explanation.

In an alternative but interesting and rather sophisticated view, it is precisely the surge in the supply of highly educated workers which may have prompted, at least partially, the increase in the demand for less-skilled labour (Kiley 1999). What has happened, according to Kiley, is that firms engaged in research and development (R&D) have become much more oriented towards creating innovations that have a large customer base, i.e., highly skilled workers and consumers. R&D activities, Kiley argues, have become increasingly more geared toward innovations that benefit skilled workers and this is still the case. As a result, economies where there was a rapidly growing supply of university graduates, such as either the US or the UK in the early 1970s, underwent several changes. The wages of university graduates initially fell as their increasing supply faced a fixed demand in the short run. In response to the increased supply of university graduates, R&D activities were redirected toward skill-intensive technologies – such as computers – resulting in a preponderance of new technologies being implemented by skilled workers and a large increase in the wages of university graduates. The technology adjustments to R&D induced by the increased supply of university graduates took time and resources, and hence the adjustments initially led to a slowdown in productivity growth. Following the adjustments, productivity growth picked up again. Kiley argues that the dramatic rise in wage inequality since the 1970s in the US and the UK has been broadly similar. Kiley argues that his model generates swings in inequality and productivity growth that are broadly consistent with the rising gap between the skilled and unskilled wages, and the slowdown of output growth that followed the surge in skilled labour's share of the labour force during the 1970s.

Education also plays a key role in a set of recent studies that have sought to explain why such enormous cross-country differences prevail if it comes to wage dispersion and why there seems to be a virtually non-existent relationship between wage dispersion and employment outcomes.

In an influential paper, Nickell and Bell (1996) ask why it is that German men (or their counterparts in most Continental European countries for that matter) in the bottom wage decile earn more than twice as much as American men in a similar position, while they are only a little more likely to end up unemployed. (Their paper refers to the situation up till the mid-1990s. Meanwhile, German unemployment has risen, but the immense structural difference between the two countries roughly remains.)

They suggested that the answer may lie in the fact that the German education system produces a much more compressed distribution of human capital than the education systems in Britain or the United States. In support of this thesis, they present evidence from international surveys which measure mathematical abilities and literacy. According to such tests, the variation in mathematics ability is far smaller in Germany, with the lower part of the ability range being vastly superior compared to the equivalent in the US and UK. This is also mirrored in literacy tests covering all employees. According to their figures, the group with zero or minimal literacy is three times larger in the US than it is in Germany, meaning significantly more compression of ability in the latter country.

Furthermore, they cite evidence that the German school system, as the educational systems in countries like the Netherlands of Sweden, is much more geared to maintaining high standards for the bottom half of the ability range. One reason is that basic standards in language and arithmetic are set for *all* to attain and instructional time and resources are used to bring all pupils to a certain level of achievement. In addition, the vocational training system ensures that a far greater proportion of early school drop-outs in Germany receive additional training and education.

The picture they sketch is of a German education and training system that trains a far higher proportion of the workforce up to a certain skill level than the US or UK system. Nickell and Bell claim that because of this, lower ability workers are far more productive in Germany than in the US or the UK. This, they argue, explains, at least in part why the patterns of relative wages in Germany, Britain and the US can be so different without corresponding unemployment patterns. A strong emphasis in the school system on sustaining a high level of performance on the part of the bottom half of the ability range, plus a comprehensive system of vocational training, allegedly mitigates many of the adverse consequences of a shift in demand away from the less-skilled.

In subsequent papers, they and others (Glyn and Salverda 2000) show that both the distribution of earnings and the distribution of measured skills – as measured by the International Adult Literacy Survey – vary widely among advanced countries, with the major Anglo-Saxon countries — the US, UK, and Canada — showing far greater inequality in *both* earnings and measured skills than Continental European Union countries in general.

However, the Nickell and Bell thesis that cross-national differences in earnings inequality are to a large extent determined by skill compression differences has also been challenged. Using the same IALS data (International Adult Literacy Survey – see Blum and Guerin-Pace 2000) for the United States, Sweden, Germany and the Netherlands, Devroye and Freeman (2001) find that skill inequality explains only about seven per cent of the cross-country difference in inequality. A much greater part, around 36 per cent, is explained by the higher skill premium in the United States. By far the biggest difference in dispersion across countries occurs in the residuals from earnings equations, is, for instance, attributable to other factors. Interestingly, they find that literacy tests in the home country language understate the labour market skills of immigrants who speak a different language. Inequality of skills in the US, the country with the highest level of inequality by far, falls markedly when immigrants are excluded, while the dispersion of earnings does not. Most strikingly, the dispersion of earnings in the US is larger in narrowly defined skill groups than the dispersion of earnings for European workers overall. The bulk of cross-country differences in earnings inequalities occur within skill groups, not between them.

The findings by Devroye and Freeman are confirmed by an almost identical study by Blau and Kahn (2001). Using micro-data from the 1994-1996 IALS, they examine the role of cognitive skills in explaining higher wage inequality in the US. They find that while the greater dispersion of cognitive test scores in the US plays a part in explaining higher US wage inequality, higher labour market prices (i.e., higher returns to measured human capital and cognitive performance) and greater residual inequality still play important roles for both men and women. And they also find that, on average, prices are quantitatively considerably more important than differences in the distribution of test scores in explaining the relatively high level of US wage inequality. This finding holds up when they exclude immigrants from the sample and they correct for sample selection.

The role of wage-setting institutions and social norms

This leads us to the question: why is the price for human capital not similar across the advanced economies? A lot of new evidence has accumulated over the past decade or so which points in the direction of wage-setting institutions. There is a well-documented difference in earnings between workers employed in industries or firms (or countries, see below) where unions have a substantial impact on wage formation and workers in firms and industries where unions are weak or absent. Analyses – mostly but not exclusively for the United States – have invariably found that years of schooling, age and other determinants of earnings have a significantly smaller effect on unionised workers than on non-union workers, and that unions have a larger impact on the wages of low-paid and low-skilled workers than on the wages of high-paid and high-skilled workers. That the empirical relationship is strong and robust is undisputed, but there has been some debate and disagreement as to the effects of unionism on outcomes. Some have attributed the strong differences to differences in unobservable characteristics and sorting effects. The idea is that firm and industries where unions are strong and where wages are consequently higher – especially for less-skilled workers – are able to select and attract the more productive and able workers. Longitudinal studies do show that the wages of workers who move from union jobs to non-union jobs (and the other way around) differ somewhat less than do the wages of union and non-union workers in cross-sectional studies. There is, in other words, some evidence for selectivity (although the greater impact of union membership measurement error in longitudinal studies may also be a factor). Nevertheless, the union effect on wages, with everything else being equal, remains quite strong (Freeman 1991; Devroye and Freeman 2002).

More importantly, a similarly strong and arguably even more impressive relationship prevails at the cross-country level; in countries with strong unions and collective bargaining wages tend to be more compressed than in countries where unions are weak and wage bargaining decentralised. Also, there tends to be more wage compression across industries in countries where centralised bargaining takes place; workers with a nominally similar level of educational attainment are more likely to be paid similar wages in Northern or Continental Europe than in the US.

In a seminal and influential paper, Blau and Kahn (1996) ask why wage inequality is so much higher in the US than in most other OECD countries. Their study analyses male wage inequality in the US and in nine other OECD countries (Germany, Britain, Austria, Switzerland, Sweden, Australia, Hungary, Italy and Norway). They find that while differences in the distribution of measured characteristics help to explain some aspects of the cross-national differences, higher US prices – rewards to skills and rents – are a more important factor. They argue and demonstrate to some extent that labour market institutions, principally the comparatively decentralised wage-setting mechanisms in the United States provide the most persuasive explanation for these patterns.

Moreover, studies have tried to demonstrate that changes in wage-setting institutions are associated with changes in the distribution of pay (Gottschalk and Joyce 1998; Kahn 2000; Lucifora 2000). The huge increase in wage inequality in Italy during the 1990s coincides with the waning of the Scala Mobile wage-setting system (Erikson and Ichino 1995; Manacorda 1999). The rise in US wage inequality during the 1980s has been linked to the fall in union density (Card 1992, 1998; DiNardo and Lemieux 1997; Di Nardo, Fortin and Lemieux 1996; Fortin and Lemieux 1997; Freeman 1991; Freeman and Katz 1994; Gosling and Machin 1994; Lee 1999), as has the rise in wage inequality in the UK, although less convincingly (Gosling, Machin and Meghir 1994; Bell and Pitt 1995; Gosling and Lemieux 2001).

For Sweden, too, there is evidence that the weakening of centralised bargaining has gone accompanied with a rise in wage inequality and the skills premium (Bjorklund and Freeman 1997; Edin and Holmlund 1995; Edin and Topel 1997). Similarly, in a comparative study of the United States, Canada and the UK (chosen because the institutional arrangements governing unionisation and collective bargaining are relatively similar in these three countries), Card, Lemieux and Ridell (2003) find that unionisation helps explain a sizeable share of cross-country differences in male (but not female) wage inequality among the three countries. They also conclude that de-unionisation explains a substantial part of the growth in male wage inequality in the UK and the US since the early 1980s.

In addition, there may be an indirect link between institutional characteristics of the labour market and inequality. Acemoglu (2002), for example, conjectures that inequality did not increase everywhere to the same extent because the relative demand for skills may have increased differentially. It is possible, he argues, that labour market institutions creating wage compression in Continental Europe may have encouraged more investment in technologies increasing the productivity of less-skilled workers, thus implying *less* skill-biased change in Europe than in the US.

Atkinson (1999b) adds in another element: social norms. His argument is that wage inequality might be affected by ideas and norms about what constitute fair/justifiable pay differentials, and that, consequently, inequality trends might reflect value shifts. His argument has considerable intuitive appeal and more importantly, internationally comparative value studies show marked differences between countries when it comes to judgements of what constitute fair income differentials (Austen 2000).

Particularly interesting is Atkinson's suggestion that multiple equilibria may exist in a country. Suppose, Atkinson argues, that there is a social code, or pay norm, that limits the extent to which individual earnings increase with earnings potential. Where this code is followed, people are paid only a fraction of their productivity plus a uniform amount. Such a policy involves a degree of redistribution. Less productive workers can be expected to subscribe to the pay norm. But other workers will also accept it, Atkinson argues, even when they could be paid more if they broke the norm, since by breaking it they would suffer a loss of reputation and societal integration. Now, the extent of the loss increases with the proportion of the population that adheres to the norm.

Crucial in the argument is the idea that multiple equilibria may exist. Depending on the initial conditions, a society converges to a high level of conformity with the social code, or to the virtual absence of conformity.

In this kind of situation, an exogenous shock may switch the society from equilibrium with conformity to the pay norm, and hence relatively low wage differentials, to an equilibrium where everyone is paid on the basis of their productivity.

I suspect Atkinson's hypothesis makes sense and that it may help explain the episodic nature of the inequality rises that have been observed in some rich countries. Take for example the British case. We know that the astonishingly sudden and exceptionally strong rise in wage inequality in the UK during the 1980s remains largely unexplained by 'external' factors such as trade and technology. Even the widely cited explanation that institutional change – the abolishment of minimum wages, the introduction of tighter legal constraints on trade union power – has been the main driving factor fits uneasily with the facts. Changes in the tax and benefit system can also be ruled out. The timing does not match and the institutional changes themselves do not seem anywhere big enough to have caused such an increase. The rise does coincide, however, with the rise of Thatcherism; a profoundly anti-egalitarian economic doctrine. Conceivably, wage inequality exploded because vast wage differentials came to be seen as not only socially acceptable but even desirable and entirely justified. The dramatic change in the political and even cultural climate during the 1980s may have shattered the social constraints on pay inequality that used to exist. The time pattern of the rise in inequality is wholly consistent with the idea of the sudden evolution to a new equilibrium.

6   Conclusion

In much of the social policy literature, the decline of self-reliance, as documented in chapter 1, is often attributed to what are seen to be structural changes in production systems. Less-skilled workers and people with fewer cognitive, analytical and social abilities are said to be inexorably losing ground in advanced economies. In addition, many believe that there are limits to what education and upskilling can do to counteract this.

This chapter has tried to piece together the voluminous empirical evidence as it presents itself today. This review is inevitably incomplete and probably does not do justice to the sophistication of some of the studies. Essentially, the empirical evidence leaves little doubt as to the reality of the increased demand for skilled labour. However, this shift appears part of a secular trend and it remains uncertain whether structural acceleration in that demand shift has actually taken place over the past decades. The labour market position of the less-skilled – as measured by their relative employment chances and their relative earnings – has generally deteriorated but the extent of cross-country variation is quite substantial. Some countries have clearly managed to avoid significant rises in labour market inequality, even in absence of large scale government intervention in the form of public or subsidised employment. Hence, the idea that economic inequality is inexorably on the rise in advanced economies does not appear to be supported by the evidence as it presents itself today, a conclusion echoed in a similar recent review by Pontuson (2005). A score of recent studies suggest that education and upskilling can still make a significant difference if it comes to countering the consequences of changing skill requirements.

Yet the practical barriers to effective upskilling seem far from trivial. Changing the skills profile of the working-age population cannot be done overnight. Traditional educational policy, for example, can only have an effect on the schooling of cohorts that have yet to enter into the labour market. Moreover, the younger, better-educated cohorts are becoming increasingly small, so that the upskilling of the working population as a whole will proceed a lot more slowly over the next decades than was the case until very recently. An even bigger problem from a policy perspective is that it remains rather unclear why certain educational systems are more effective in providing marketable skills to the least talented than others. As studies show, some countries are evidently more successful in providing the less-talented segments of their populations with skills, knowledge and credentials that are worth something in the labour market. But much less remains known about which traits of the educational system are most important in producing these outcomes. Furthermore, even if one were perfectly capable of identifying all of the factors that distinguish a good educational system from a less adequate system, it is unlikely that the necessary organisational and cultural changes could be made quickly (see e.g., Vrieze, Mok and Smit 2003).

PART 2

NEW SOCIAL RISKS, POVERTY AND THE ADEQUACY OF SOCIAL PROTECTION

3   Low Pay and Poverty: Anatomy of a 'New' Social Risk

1   Introduction

The next two chapters are about the poverty and social policy consequences of the labour demand shifts documented in the previous chapters. The demand shift against the less-skilled is thought to have given rise to two major 'new' social risks: structural unemployment and low-paid employment. This first chapter of the second part looks at the poverty consequences of low pay.[1]

There is widespread concern that 'poverty in work' has worsened in countries that have seen a rise in earnings inequality and as a direct consequence of this an increase in the incidence of relatively low-paid work. To compensate for the perceived inadequacies and limits of the traditional minimum income protection provisions, in-work benefits and/or tax credits are being introduced or expanded, with the aim of alleviating or preventing in-work poverty. In Continental Europe, where most countries have seen little or no increase in earnings inequality and where low-wage employment remains less widespread than in the Anglo-Saxon countries, the policy debate is somewhat different. Here, enhanced wage flexibility is being debated as a cure for persistent high unemployment. But there the concern is that an expansion of low wage employment could lead to

---

[1]   This chapter draws extensively on work I have done together with Brian Nolan and Gerre Verbist. The present chapter is a revised and expanded version of a paper written with Brian Nolan and published as Nolan, B. and I. Marx (2000), 'Low pay and household poverty', in: M. Gregory, W. Salverda and S. Bazen (eds.), *Low-Wage Employment: A European Perspective*. Oxford: Oxford University Press. This chapter also draws on Marx, I. and G. Verbist (1998), 'Low wage employment and poverty: an cross-country perspective?', in: S. Bazen, M. Gregory and W. Salverda (eds.), *Low-Wage Employment in Europe*. London: Edward Elgar.

a proliferation of the working poor. Invariably reference is made to the US, where poverty in work is alleged to be rampant among the many occupants of so-called 'McDonalds jobs' –low-paid, menial service jobs.

It is in this context that this chapter attempts to shed some light on the empirical relationship between low pay and poverty. Much of the debate revolves around the question of whether and to what extent low-paid workers live in low-income households, and hence whether minimum wages or in-work benefits are effective as a poverty alleviation device. This chapter draws on data from the Luxembourg Income Survey (IS) database and the European Community Household Panel to show what that relationship looks like empirically in industrialised countries. While most of the results are for full-time employees, the position of part-time employees is also considered. The extent of overlap between low pay and poverty is found to be rather more limited at an aggregate level than might generally be expected, but there is also a good deal of variation across countries. This chapter discusses how this arises, and the factors influencing the extent to which the low-paid are to be found in poor households. While these results are based on snapshots from cross-section data, the importance of a dynamic perspective in this context is then discussed. In the concluding section, some of the policy implications are explored.

2   What Is Low Pay?

A variety of approaches can be used to define and measure low pay (see, for example, CERC 1991, OECD 1996). Significant choices have to be made first about the earnings measure to be employed – should it be weekly or hourly; should it be only basic pay or should auxiliary payments such as overtime be included? The population of workers to be covered must also be decided upon – should it include part-time as well as full-time employees, and should it include those who work only part of the year? Finally, how shall the low-pay benchmark itself be derived – should some external standard be used or just a purely relative benchmark based on a point in the earnings distribution itself? Without rehearsing these issues in detail, probably the most commonly used approach has been to set the low-pay cut-off as a proportion of median gross earnings, most often two-thirds of the median. This has been the benchmark used by, for example, the OECD in recent comparative studies of low pay across countries. By this definition, the proportion of low-wage workers in the OECD area ranges from around one in 20 in countries like Belgium and Sweden to around one in four in the United States. In order to avoid the complications of untangling the impact of differences in wage rates from those of differences in hours worked in the week or weeks worked in the year, that OECD analysis has also concentrated on full-time full-year workers.

The poverty status of the household is, as elsewhere in this book, measured against an income poverty line set at half average disposable income, adjusted for household size and composition using the modified OECD scale. Household poverty is measured on the basis of disposable income over a whole year, since that is the accounting period for income used in most of the LIS and ECHP surveys.

3 Low Pay and Poverty

The overlap between low pay and poverty

The relevance of the issue is tellingly illustrated in figure 3.1, which shows that there exists a remarkably strong and consistent cross-country correlation between the incidence of low-wage employment, as defined and measured by the OECD, and relative poverty at working age. The poverty rates here are drawn from Förster (2000).

Figure 3.1 Incidence of low pay and poverty

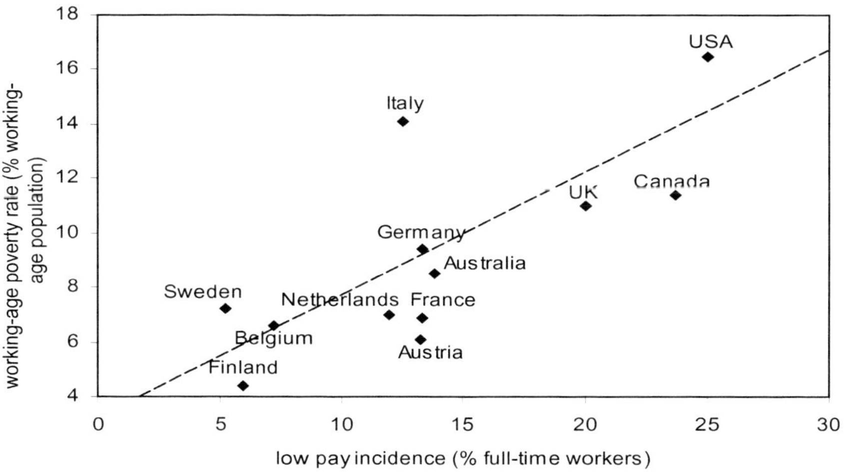

Source: Low pay: OECD (1996) Employment Outlook; poverty: Förster (2000); data for mid-1990s.

The strong cross-country correlation between the incidence of low-paid work and poverty seems consistent with the idea that 'poverty in work' is more widespread in countries where low-paid employment is more prevalent. In order to gauge the validity of that perception, we now look at the relationship between low pay and household poverty in a cross-section perspective, using data from the LIS. Table 3.1 first shows the poverty rates for the working age population in each of the countries investigated. Poverty is highest in the US, by a considerable margin, at 19 per cent. Australia, Canada and the UK have the next-highest rates, at 12-15 per cent, while the remaining countries have rates of between 5-8 per cent.

Given that income is being measured on an annual basis, it is necessary to define low pay in a manner consistent with that accounting period. The coverage of the analysis is therefore limited to full-year, full-time workers, and low-paid workers are then defined as those earning less than two-thirds of the median gross wage of all full-year, full-time workers in that particular country. This means that low-paid temporary and part-time workers are not included in the analysis, and countries in the database for which there is no or insufficient data available on weeks and hours worked – namely Denmark, France, Italy, Norway and Spain – had to be excluded. The incidence of low-wage employment this produces is shown in the second column of table 3.1.

Table 3.1 The extent of poverty, low pay, and poverty among the low-paid, based on LIS data, late 1980s/early 1990s

	% of working-age population in poverty (below ½ mean)	% of employees who are low-paid (below ⅔ median)	% of low-paid employees who are in poor households
Australia	12.5	14.5	7.6
Belgium	4.7	10.8	6.2
Canada	12.3	21.4	11.5
Finland	5.0	6.7	4.3
Germany	7.9	12.7	5.6
Netherlands	6.9	12.4	9.5
Sweden	6.6	11.2	5.5
United Kingdom	14.5	19.9	8.8
United States	19.1	26.4	24.0

Source: LIS.

We see that the US again has the highest rate, with 26 per cent low paid, while Canada and the UK are next with about 20 per cent. Most of the other countries have approximately 11-14 per cent in the low-pay category, with Finland being an exception with only 7 per cent. Because some countries with relatively high poverty rates for those of working age generally have relatively high low-pay percentages, the correspondence is by no means exact. These estimates of the extent of low pay are basically similar to those produced by the OECD (1996) and Keese and Swaim (1997), based on a similar definition of low pay.

The third column in table 3.1 shows the percentage of individuals categorised as low paid who themselves are living in poor households – our central focus of interest here. The overlap between low pay and poverty is greatest for the US, where about a quarter of the low-paid live in poor households. For Canada, Australia, the Netherlands and the UK poverty rates for low-paid workers are about 10 per cent. For Belgium, Finland, Germany and Sweden only about 5 per cent of low-paid full-time (full-year) employees live in poor households. These results suggest that for most countries there is only a limited – and often extremely limited – overlap between low pay and poverty.

We can see how robust this result is by turning to an alternative source of data on the relationship between low pay and poverty, the European Community Household Panel survey (ECHP). The ECHP is a harmonised longitudinal survey of households and individuals carried out in the European Union member states for Eurostat, the Statistical Office of the European Community. The first wave of the ECHP was conducted in 1994 in the then-12 member states. Income data in the survey refer to receipts in the previous calendar year. Eurostat has recently published summary results (Eurostat 1998) of an analysis of low pay and household income based on data from the first wave, carried out in collaboration with the OECD, which has presented some related results (OECD 1998). The OECD also includes results for the US based on the Current Population Survey for 1996, which we draw on to provide another set of 'observations' on the relationship between low pay at the level of the individual and poverty at the level of the household.

The Eurostat/OECD analysis also focuses on full-time, full-year wage and salary earners, once again to avoid the complications of disentangling the impact of differences in wage rates from those of differences in hours worked in the week or weeks worked in the year. Low-paid individuals are again defined as those earning less than two-thirds of the median for full-time full-year employees. However, it appears that the earnings measure employed is net of tax and social security contributions rather than the more usual gross earnings concept generally employed in analysing low pay. Household poverty is again measured in terms of annual disposable household income adjusted for differences in size and composition.[2] However two differences between this and the LIS-based poverty measure now arise: the equivalence scale calculates the number of equivalent adults as the square root of household size, and the poverty line is set at half the median rather than half the mean income.

Table 3.2 first shows the percentage of all full-time, full-year employees who are low paid in these results. Only five countries are included in both the LIS-based results reported earlier and in this Eurostat/OECD analysis – Belgium, Germany, the Netherlands, the UK and the US. For these, the incidence of low pay is generally similar to that shown by the earlier LIS-based results, though it is now somewhat higher in Germany, presumably because of the inclusion of former East Germany.

Table 3.2 The overlap between poverty and low pay, based on ECHP data, 1993

	% of employees who are low paid	% of low paid who are in households	
		Below 50% median income	below 2/3 median income
Belgium	9.1	7.3	17.2
Denmark	9.6	3.1	18.1
France	14.3	7.7	22.6
Germany	18.3	9.7	20.6
Greece	11.9	11.5	21.2
Ireland	18.9	3.3	7.1
Italy	11.7	18.4	28.8
Luxembourg	19.2	9.2	32.7
Netherlands	14.3	11.2	21.0
Portugal	15.4	13.7	23.2
Spain	16.8	10.6	21.8
United Kingdom	21.0	9.1	19.9
United States	26.3	22.1	38.4

Source: OECD (1998) Tables 2.7 and 2.8.

---

2   However, the data for France relates to gross rather than disposable earnings and incomes.

The table shows the extent to which low-paid employees defined in this way are in poor households, that is, below half the median equivalent income. The US again has the highest proportion of its low-paid living in poor households, at over 20 per cent. For most of the other countries, the proportion of the low-paid in poor households is much lower. To assess the sensitivity of these results using the location of the household poverty line, the percentage in households falling below two-thirds of the median is also shown. The degree of overlap is now somewhat higher, but in most countries it is still means that less than one-quarter of the low paid are in these, what one might term 'poor or near-poor', households. The exception is again the US, where 38 per cent of the low-paid live in these households.

These results on the limited overlap between low pay and household poverty are consistent with earlier studies. For example, Layard, Piachaud and Stewart (1978) and Bazen (1988) found that between 10-22 per cent of low-paid workers were in families below conventionally used poverty lines in the UK, while Burkhauser and Finnegan (1989) reported about 8-18 per cent for the US. However such results have to be interpreted carefully. While most low-paid workers do not live in poor households, most workers in poor households are themselves low paid. Table 3.3 shows that, in the results presented by the OECD, generally two-thirds or more of the workers living in households below the half-median income poverty line are in low pay households. For many countries, then, only 10 per cent or less of the (full-time, full-year) employees in poor households are not low paid.

Table 3.3   The probability of being low paid for employees in poor households, based on ECHP data, 1993

	% of employees in households below 50% median income who are low paid
Belgium	64.9
Denmark	54.3
France	65.5
Germany	85.0
Greece	86.7
Ireland	89.9
Italy	73.4
Luxembourg	68.9
Netherlands	90.3
Portugal	61.6
Spain	88.0
United Kingdom	92.5
United States	87.2

Source: OECD (1998) Table 2.7.

The position of low-paid workers in the income distribution

What could explain this – at first sight curious – pattern whereby most low-paid employees are not in poor households but most employees in poor households are low-paid? The crucial factor underlying it is the location in the household income distribution of all employees – whether low paid or not. Table 3.4, drawn from the results presented by Eurostat, shows that very few employees are in fact in households in the bottom part of the income distribution. In most countries, rather less than one in ten of all employees are in households located in the bottom quintile of the income distribution. If the 12 EU countries are taken together, only 5 per cent of all employees are in this type of household. Indeed, less than 20 per cent of all employees in the 12 countries are in households in the bottom two quintiles – 80 per cent are in the top 60 per cent of the household income distribution. In other words, employees are mostly not found in households in poverty or towards the bottom of the income distribution, in which there is generally no one employed.

Table 3.4 Location of employees in the household income distribution, based on ECHP data, 1993

	% of employees in households located in		
	Bottom quintile	Second quintile	3rd - 5th quintiles
Belgium	3	11	86
Denmark	4	13	83
France	6	15	79
Germany	7	16	77
Greece	3	11	86
Ireland	1	8	91
Italy	5	13	82
Luxembourg	12	14	73
Netherlands	6	12	82
Portugal	4	14	82
Spain	4	12	83
United Kingdom	3	11	86

Source: Eurostat (1998) Table 9.

It is then not so surprising that low pay is prevalent among employees in low income households, but that these employees account for only a minority of the low-paid total. Again drawing upon the results presented by Eurostat, table 3.5 shows where low-paid employees are located in the household income distribution.

Table 3.5   Location of low-paid employees in household income distribution, based on ECHP data, 1993

	% of low-paid employees who are in households located in		
	Bottom quintile	Second quintile	3rd - 5th quintiles
Belgium	10	17	73
Denmark	15	27	58
France	18	27	55
Germany	22	27	50
Greece	10	18	72
Ireland	5	11	84
Italy	18	17	65
Luxembourg	32	21	47
Netherlands	16	13	71
Portugal	13	23	63
Spain	16	18	66
United Kingdom	14	22	65

Source: Eurostat (1998) Table 10.

We see that generally about 60 per cent of the low-paid are in the top 60 per cent of the income distribution, and another one-quarter are in the second and not the bottom quintile. Less than one in five low-paid employees are in a household located in the bottom quintile of the income distribution. There is a good deal of variation across countries. Ireland is a striking exception in terms of very limited overlap, having only 5 per cent of all low-paid employees in the bottom quintile. At the other extreme, Luxembourg has the most pronounced overlap of the EU countries, with 32 per cent of the low-paid in the bottom quintile of the household distribution. The results presented by the OECD for the US and shown in table 3.2, in terms of proportions below poverty lines rather than in different quintiles, suggest that the overlap is even greater in that case. For most of the countries covered, though, 10-15 per cent of the low-paid are in households in the bottom quintile.

4 Why the Overlap between Low Pay and Poverty Is Limited

The overlap between low pay and poverty is thus rather more limited than often assumed in policy debates, and this is primarily because in most countries most poor households do not contain an employee – low paid or otherwise. In order to understand the observed pattern and tease out its implications, however, we want to know what distinguishes the minority of the low-paid who are in poor households from the majority who are not. With the same data and definitions as table 3.1 above, table 3.6 now looks at how the percentage in poverty varies among the low-paid by gender and age.

Table 3.6 Poverty rates for low-paid individuals by age and sex, based on LIS data

	% of low-paid in poverty by sex		% of low-paid in poverty by age		
	Men	Women	Under 25	25-54	+55
Australia	10.2	5.3	4.6	12.2	7.7
Belgium	16.1	1.6	1.5	8.6	0.0
Canada	13.7	9.8	8.9	12.5	9.3
Finland	7.4	3.0	3.6	4.9	0.0
Germany	7.5	4.3	3.6	6.7	0.0
Netherlands	12.8	6.0	4.8	17.7	0.0
Sweden	10.8	2.2	12.4	3.7	1.8
United Kingdom	13.0	5.6	4.2	13.3	6.8
United States	32.2	18.3	21.7	25.4	17.8

Source: LIS.

Household composition and the household income package

We see that, as one would expect, the association between low pay and poverty is stronger for men than for women. Poverty rates for low-paid men are much higher than those for low-paid women in all the countries included in the analysis. In some, notably Belgium and Sweden, low-paid women are very unlikely indeed to be in poor households. As far as age is concerned, it is again in line with expectations that poverty rates for low-paid workers in their prime tend to be higher than those for young people, although Sweden is an exception. (It should be noted that these poverty estimates by age and gender are based on relatively small numbers in some countries).

A crucial influence on the poverty status of households with a low-paid employee is the extent to which the household relies on those earnings. Analysis of the LIS data reported in table 3.7 shows that most low-paid workers in fact live in households with more than one earner, and that this is particularly the case for low-paid women. The proportion of low-wage workers living in single-earner households varies from slightly over one in five in Canada and the UK to around one in three in Belgium and Germany. For the remainder, in a significant number of cases there are not two but three earners in the household.

Table 3.7 The distribution of low-paid workers by number of earners in the household, based on LIS data

	One earner	Two earners	Three or more earners
Australia	24.3	39.3	36.4
Belgium	34.8	53.5	11.7
Canada	21.7	48.8	29.5
Finland	27.0	54.3	18.7
Germany	33.8	42.7	23.5
Netherlands	24.6	52.5	22.8
Sweden	28.5	67.7	3.8
United Kingdom	22.1	43.6	34.3
United States	28.1	49.5	22.4

Source: LIS.

These low-paid individuals in multi-earner households are often married women or younger workers still living in the parental home. As a consequence, among low-paid workers the percentage in poverty is particularly low for married women. Analysis of the LIS data suggests that only about 5 per cent of low-paid married women were in poor households in the UK and Canada and the figure was even lower in the other countries covered, except in the case of the US. There the figure was 13 per cent – much higher than elsewhere but still low relative to other low-paid employees in the US. Poverty rates for low-paid men with a partner but no dependent children are also relatively low in most countries, though in the UK about 10 per cent were in poor households and for the United States the figure was 20 per cent.

It is low-paid married men who are 'household heads' and have dependent children for whom the percentage in poverty is generally highest. The extent of cross-national variation here is striking, as shown in table 3.8. The poverty rate for low-paid household heads with children was over 50 per cent in the US, around 40-45 per cent for the United Kingdom, the Netherlands and Belgium, around 30 per cent in Australia and Canada, and as low as 15 per cent for Germany, 10 per cent for Finland and 5 per cent for Sweden. Households having to make ends meet on low pay constitute a minority but the financial hardship facing such households should not be neglected. A factor contributing to their poverty is that in many countries low-paid household heads are more likely to have a non-employed spouse, or one in temporary or part-time work, than heads in work who are not low-paid. This presumably reflects the fact that, among other things, partners tend to have similar levels of education; it could in some instances also be affected by disincentives in tax/welfare systems.

Table 3.8 Poverty rates and the impact of social transfers and taxes for low-paid household heads of household, couples with dependent children

	% In poor households	% In poor households before transfers and direct tax
Australia	33.3	38.5
Belgium	39.4	61.1
Canada	27.2	36.0
Germany	15.7	37.4
Sweden	5.7	34.7
United Kingdom	45.6	57.3
United States	55.5	57.1

Source: LIS.

The impact of taxes and transfers

Table 3.8 also shows that the impact of social transfers and personal taxes on poverty rates may be a key factor explaining these differences. On a purely static basis, this shows, for example, that Australia, Canada, Germany and Sweden would all have had poverty rates of about 35 per cent before transfers and direct tax. Hence, the fact that they had such different poverty rates is largely due to the differential impact of transfer and tax policies. For the UK and the US, on the other hand, it is seen that their very high poverty rates reflect both very high pre-tax and transfer poverty rates and the limited – in the US case minimal – impact of transfers and taxes. (Note, however, that social security contributions, which are particularly important in Continental Europe, are not taken into account in this analysis.)

Both the tax and transfer systems, and the role which low–pay earnings play in the income of the households in which the low-paid live, will differ from country to country. To explain more comprehensively the variation in the degree of overlap between low pay and poverty across countries, other factors obviously come into play. In general, one might expect those countries with relatively high poverty rates, and with a relatively high proportion of low-paid employees, to have a greater overlap than others. This does seem to be the case more often that not, and the US is, of course, the extreme case of a country with both high poverty and low-pay rates and the greatest degree of overlap. However, the data from the both the LIS and ECHP do not themselves give an entirely consistent picture of the way the degree of overlap actually varies across countries, and there are in any case counter-examples to the general rule just advanced. The most obvious is Ireland, which has high poverty and low-pay rates but, as the OECD highlights, a very limited overlap between low pay and poverty.

The reasons for this are instructive. Ireland (until the mid-1990s) had both a very high rate of unemployment (especially long-term unemployment), a large farming sector, and a level of support for the unemployed and pensioners that, compared to most richer EU member states, was relatively ungenerous. This meant that the – relatively large – population below relative income poverty lines was dominated by the unemployed, farm households, and those relying on state pensions. Since household poverty is measured vis-à-vis relative income lines, then, the position of the low-paid will depend not only on the income of their own households and how low-paid earnings contribute, but also on the position of other types of households relative to the average or median income. To understand the overlap between low pay and poverty fully, indeed, an in-depth analysis of the overall poverty profile in each country would be required.

5 Further Considerations

The results described thus far show that in most EU countries only minorities of low-paid full-time employees are found in poor households, and that among the low-paid it is those who are household heads with dependent children who are most likely to be poor. Before concluding that low pay is mostly not associated with poverty, however, a number of features of these analyses have to be emphasised, notably their limited coverage and focus and their cross-section perspective.

Part-time low-paid workers

As far as coverage is concerned, both the LIS- and ECHP-based analyses were confined to those employees who worked full-time, full-year. We know that those who work part-time are more likely to be low paid than those working full-time, and also those who worked only part of the year are probably more likely to be low-paid when employed than those working the full year. We might also expect that these sub-groups among the low-paid are more likely to be in poor households than low-paid full-time full-year workers. An analysis of the survey data for Ireland mentioned above shows that when part-time employees are also included among the low-paid (using an hourly earnings low-pay threshold), a substantially higher proportion of the part-timers are found to be in households below half average income (Nolan and Watson 1998). The same point is shown by results presented by the OECD (1998) for three countries only, separately for the low-paid among full-time full-year workers and among all workers, shown in table 3.9. We see that when all low-paid employees, rather than just full-time full-year ones, are included the proportion in households below half the median is again considerably higher in all three countries.

Table 3.9 Poverty for low-paid full-time full-year workers versus all low-paid, the Netherlands, the UK and the US, 1993

	% of low-paid in households below poverty line	
	Full-time, full-year workers	All workers
Netherlands	9.9	15.0
UK	3.9	9.7
US	23.2	33.0

Source: OECD (1998) Table 2.10.

The role of low earnings in keeping households out of poverty

The focus of the analysis of the overlap between low pay and poverty is also limited in the sense that no account is taken of the role of the earnings of low-paid individuals in lifting and keeping their households out of poverty. The Irish data already mentioned can be used to illustrate the impact of the earnings of low-paid workers on the position of their households vis-à-vis the income poverty lines by a crude but revealing exercise. This involves simply deducting the net pay of the low-paid individual from the disposable income of the household, and then comparing that reduced income with the relative poverty lines. Table 3.10 shows how often this would bring the households with low-paid individuals (below two-thirds of the median) below the 50 per cent income poverty line. We see that over one-third of all low-paid men and 22 per cent of all low-paid women are in households which are above the poverty line, but would be poor if the 'low pay' was not going into the household. For low-paid women who are widowed, separated or divorced, about half are in households that would fall below the income lines without their earnings. Table 5.7 in chapter 5 illustrates something similar for Belgium, namely that a small additional household income can be sufficient to lift a single-earner household out of poverty if the sole earner is low-paid.

Table 3.10   Poverty rates for households of low-paid employees in the absence of their earnings, Ireland 1994

	% In households below poverty line without the earnings of the low-paid individual
Men	37.8
Women	22.2
Married	13.6
Widowed/separated/divorced	50.5
Single	24.3

Source: ECHP.

The dynamic perspective

The extent of overlap between low pay and household poverty at a point in time, as revealed by an analysis of cross-section data, is also clearly only part of the story. From a dynamic perspective, the consequences of long-term low pay interspersed with periods of unemployment are clearly much more serious than those of low pay experienced for a relatively short period, perhaps at an early stage in one's working career. Dynamic analyses of earnings mobility and the relationship between earnings, unemployment and poverty over time are becoming increasingly possible as suitable panel data become more widely available. The relationship between experiencing low pay and poverty which this reveals is a complex one, with that relationship appearing more or less pronounced than in static cross-sections depending on the perspective one adopts.

This can be illustrated by the results of analysis carried out by the OECD (OECD 1998; Keese, Gittelman and Stancanelli 1998). Panel data for Germany, the Netherlands, the UK and the US allowed individuals who are low paid in a given year, in either of two years, and in any of five years to be identified. Table 3.11 shows the percentage of full-time, full-year employees experiencing low pay who were in households below the half median income poverty line during the period in question. (In other words, for example, when the five-year window income over the five years is used to determine poverty status). The results show that most employees experiencing low pay in a given year are once again not in poor households, and that when the time period is lengthened, the degree of concentration in poor households falls. For example, in the case of Germany, about 13 per cent of those low paid in 1993 were in poor households in that year, whereas only 8 per cent of those who were low paid in at least one year between 1989-1993 were in households with income over that whole period below half the median. (The UK is an exception here, with a slightly higher percentage in poor households when the five-year rather than the one-year window is used). This pattern reflects the fact that, among other things, some of those who are low paid in a particular year will be in higher-paid employment in a subsequent year.

Table 3.11 Percentage of employees experiencing low pay who are in poor households over different periods, Germany, the Netherlands, the UK and the US

		% In households below poverty line
Germany	1993	13.4
	1992-93	10.0
	1989-93	7.7
Netherlands	1993	9.9
	1992-93	6.7
	1989-93	4.8
UK	1993	3.9
	1992-93	5.4
	1989-93	5.8
US	1993	23.2
	1992-93	22.5
	1989-93	21.3

Source: OECD (1998) Table 2.10.

While these results are illuminating, they only focus on one side of the coin: how the poverty risk varies when we count all those who experience low pay at some point during different periods. The other side of the coin is how the risk of being poor at some point varies with the duration of experience of low pay. The extent and nature of mobility over the earnings distribution and in/out of low pay has been the subject of considerable research in recent years (see, for example, Atkinson, Bourgouignon and Morrison 1992; Gittleman and Joyce 1995; OECD 1996). Again, what these studies show regarding how one reacts to the persistence/mobility with respect to low pay depends on one's prior expectations and the way one views the results. Sloane and Theodossieu (1996) report that, in the first and third waves of the British Household Panel Survey (BHPS), only 44 per cent of those who were low paid in 1991 were still low paid two years later. Stewart and Swaffield (1997) present results from the first four waves of that survey which provide a different perspective: of those who were low paid in 1991, 1992, 1993 and 1994, over two-thirds were also low paid in 1994. However, about 1.7 times as many people who experienced low pay in the first year also experienced low pay in at least one of the four subsequent years.

From the point of view of the impact on household poverty, it matters a great deal precisely which types of low-paid individuals are likely or unlikely to move up the earnings distribution ladder. Gregory and Elias (1994) show, for example, with UK New Earnings Survey data, that low pay (defined as being in the bottom quintile of the earnings distribution) is more persistent among workers in their prime age and older workers than among younger workers, and is much more marked for women. Few studies have looked directly at the relationship between persistence of low pay and household poverty, but Sloane and Theodossieu (1996) do report that when one focuses on those who remained in low-paid employment in both the first and third waves of the BHPS, less than 30 per cent were in households in the bottom three deciles of the income distribution.

A particularly important point in the context of low pay and poverty that emerges from the research on earnings mobility is that the low-paid can escape low paying employment not simply by moving up the earnings distribution ladder, but also by moving from employment via unemployment, illness or removing oneself altogether from the labour force. Stewart and Swaffield (1998) note that in the British data such exit transitions are more likely for the low-paid than the more highly paid, thus restricting one's attention throughout to employees only overstates the movement up the earnings distribution ladder. They also conclude that those entering employment from a spell of non-employment are more likely to be low paid, and those who had been low paid prior to being not employment are more likely (than other entrants) to be low paid when they subsequently return to an employment situation. Such a cycle of low pay and joblessness is also found in Jensen and Verner's (1997) analysis of longitudinal data for Danish workers over a ten-year period. It is important to stress then that among the low-paid, it is not only those who persistently fill low paying jobs over time who we expect will face a heightened risk of poverty.

Taking a life-cycle perspective, the impact on low pay, or of a cycle of low pay and joblessness, over a career is likely to have effects carrying over into retirement. As Atkinson (1973) emphasised, substantial experience of low pay and unemployment during one's working years are linked to inadequate pension entitlement and poverty when one becomes elderly. This applies both to occupational and social insurance pensions. With social insurance pension entitlement generally depending on a sustained record of contributions over one's career, a low pay or non-employment cycle may in retirement lead to a dependence on a means-tested social assistance pension safety net. In addition, of course, it minimises one's chances of building up assets such as financial savings or housing, which can play a crucial role in influencing living standards in retirement.

A longitudinal perspective, not just over a number of years but over an entire working career and beyond, adds greatly to the depth and complexity of the relationship between low pay and poverty. However, what is most important about this type of dynamic analysis is the long-term causal connections it highlights, on which policy will ultimately have to focus if it is to be successful.

The intra-household distribution of earnings

Before going on to the implications of these results and the complexities which surround them, one further complication must be mentioned. We have focused throughout on poverty measured at the level of the household, in contrast to low pay which is of course at the level of the individual. This follows the conventional practice in the poverty measurement literature, but as mentioned earlier using the household as the recipient unit involves the critical assumption that resources are shared within the household so as to equalise living standards. If this does not in fact happen, there may be differences in poverty risk between individuals within a given household, which could have particularly important implications in the context of poverty and low pay. Suppose, for example, that some married women who do not work outside the home have a lower standard of living than their husbands, because the husband controls the resources coming into the household. Even with household income above the poverty line, some of these women may have living standards as low as those in poor households. For them, working in a low-paid job might not be necessary to lift the household out of poverty, but it might allow the woman herself to escape poverty. The evidence regarding the extent of these inequalities within the household and of 'hidden poverty' is extremely limited because the 'black box' of behaviour and distribution of power and resources within the household is such a complex area of investigation (see, for example, Jenkins 1991).

6 The Impact of Traditional Policy Instruments and the Role for New Policy Instruments

The limits to targeting

The first and most obvious implication of these empirical findings on the limited overlap between low pay and poverty is that any policy aimed at improving the earnings of the low-paid as a group will directly benefit only a minority of poor households. A valid response is that the same is true of any policy aimed at helping the working poor, simply because in most countries most poor households do not include an employed household member: policies aimed at that sub-set must be judged on their effectiveness in benefiting that target group rather than their overall impact on poverty. This is only true up to a point, however because the limited (direct) impact which policies aimed at the working poor will have on poverty has to be kept in mind when considering their role in an overall anti-poverty strategy and the extent to which they can only complement other policies – notably those that focus on unemployment and pensions for the elderly. In this sense, policies aimed at the low-paid may be similar to those aimed at specific local areas with high poverty rates – commonly referred to as 'pockets of poverty' or 'black spots'. In a number of countries such area-based policies have begun playing a major part in the rhetoric and practice of anti-poverty action. The reality is, however, that most poor people do not live in these kinds of areas. An anti-poverty strategy which has as its central premises measures targeting the low-paid and specific high-poverty areas – whatever their merits and attractions – will simply not assist the majority of the poor.

Unlike area-based policies, policies aimed at the low-paid as a group will also have a very substantial spill-over as a portion of the non-poor will also benefit. This applies, for example, to a minimum wage, even one which is highly effective in increasing the gross earnings of the low-paid without having an adverse impact on employment levels. Recent US studies suggest that even there, where the overlap between low pay and household poverty is greatest, increases in the minimum wage have a relatively limited impact on poverty or income inequality and substantial spill-over to the non-poor (see, for example, Horrigan and Mincey 1993; Mishel et al. 1995; Neumark and Wascher 1997).What tends to be somewhat neglected – both by proponents and opponents of the minimum wage – is the limited direct effect one would expect a minimum wage to have on household poverty on its own . Even in the absence of negative effects on employment, most of the benefits would go to non-poor households, simply because that is where most of the low-paid are found. (See for example Gosling 1996; for the UK, Sutherland 1997; for Ireland, Nolan 1998). Where any *disemployment* effects would be felt is also important, of course, but it is far from clear whether the low-paid in poor households are likely to be more or less vulnerable than those in non-poor households.

The impact of minimum wages and effective wage floors

This limited impact on poverty is not in itself an argument against the introduction of a minimum wage or minimum wage increases. It is also important to be clear that the pattern in any one country can change substantially over time, as evidenced by the increase in the numbers of the 'working poor' in the UK in recent years. As Gosling (1996) put it in the context of the UK debate at the time, a minimum wage is not a good way to redistribute income from the rich to the poor, but it would be more distributive there now than in the past.

From the point of view of poverty and policies aimed at reducing it, though, the central role of unemployment in the case of most EU countries must be stressed. As debates about the minimum wage illustrate most sharply, the potential impact of alternative strategies on not just the low-paid but on low earnings and unemployment taken together must therefore be the focus of attention. It is important to note in that context that introducing or increasing the minimum wage may also have an indirect effect on poverty in the sense that it could help to draw people depending on benefits, particularly on social assistance, back into work. (This is particularly important if there is more upward income mobility from low-paid jobs than from long-term dependence). Also, increasing minimum wages could in some instances affect the scope for increasing benefit levels, where the latter are constrained by the level of the statutory minimum wage. This is the case, for example, in Belgium, where it is an accepted principle that the maximum unemployment benefit level should not exceed the minimum wage. Because of this link, an increase in the minimum wage could indirectly benefit the non-employed living on benefits, particularly the unemployed.

The direct and complementary role of tax and benefit systems

The interface between tax, social security and low pay is a key policy area, both in terms of the potential for the direct impact of reforms on poverty and for ensuring that dynamic behavioural responses enhance rather than erode that direct impact. The tax and welfare systems offer ways of targeting the low-paid who are in poor households, and this can look attractive as a way of minimising spill-over and concentrating on the sub-set of the low-paid who are in poor or near-poor households (Scholz 1996; Whitehouse 1996). Indeed, in several countries a minimum wage policy is now complemented with in-work benefits, with the aim of raising work incentives and alleviating in-work poverty. Since its expansion after 1993, the Earned Income Tax Credit (EITC), which supplements the incomes of low-wage working parents, has become a major anti-poverty programme in the United States. The direct impact of EITC on poverty appears to have been quite substantial, especially in terms of reducing child poverty (CEA 1998). There is also evidence that the EITC has raised the work efforts of single women – a remarkable upsurge in work activity of single mothers closely tracks the expansion of EITC after 1993 (Eissa and Liebman 1996).

However, even where such measures do reach their intended target – which may not happen due to problems of non-take-up of benefits, for example – this generally comes at a high cost in terms of disincentive effects. In-work benefits encourage labour participation because in-work benefits are made relatively higher than out-of-work incomes. Also, in the phase-in stage, marginal tax rates will tend to fall, providing increased work incentives for those already working. But the labour supply effects may not be unambiguously positive because in-work benefits are gradually reduced once a certain earnings limit is reached. If the phase-out range is wider than the phase-in region and if more people fall within the phase-out range (which may well be the case) then more people may in fact face increased marginal tax rates. In the case of the EITC, however, this effect does not seem to have dominated the positive effects for other groups (Blank, Card and Robins 1999). Chapter 6 discusses the EITC in greater detail.

In-work cash transfers aimed at the low-paid may be seen as complements rather than substitutes for the minimum wage. Indeed, a substantial minimum wage may be a prerequisite for in-work benefit programmes to be efficient in the longer run. For example, if low wage supplements are available, low-pay workers may have less of an incentive to bargain for higher wages. They might even put up with even lower pay (Freeman 1996). As the discussion in Keese, Gittelman and Stancanelli (1997) and OECD (1998) points out, whether they operate effectively as such depends on the level of the minimum wage and the extent and nature of the in-work benefits themselves. Other factors matter too, like the nature of earnings distribution, or the cost and availability of child care. And there are likely to be important interactions with other aspects of the tax/benefit system. All this makes it difficult to evaluate the net effects of a combined policy of in-work benefits and minimum wages. Simulations for the United States, which focus on the EITC, suggest that there are strong complementary effects (OECD 1998). However, Sutherland's (1997) simulation analysis for the UK points out the potential for serious disincentive effects and poverty traps is real. Indeed, withdrawal of benefits or increases in tax and social security contributions as earnings rise may mean that it is precisely the low-paid in poor households who fail to benefit from a minimum wage.

The role of broader income support provisions

This focuses attention on the broader range of policies aimed at helping families with children, including introducing or increasing universal cash transfers (e.g., child benefits). This can have a more immediate impact on poverty both among those depending on earnings and those on social welfare, without adversely affecting work incentives, but at significant budgetary cost. To give another example, availability of high quality child care may be critical in reducing the disincentive to work for lone parents and women married to low-paid men in receipt of in-work benefits. Particularly when one takes the implications of the dynamic perspective seriously, it is clear that to be effective, policies aimed at the working poor will have to fit within a broad-based anti-poverty strategy, rather than focus narrowly on a specific sub-set of the low-paid at a point in time. This also applies to policies aimed at making labour markets – and particularly wages setting – more flexible in response to persistent, and in some countries rising, female and youth unemployment. A general expansion in low wage employment is sometimes advanced as a way of tackling poverty by promoting the employment prospects of potential second earners in low-income households. However, the countries where low pay is most prevalent are also currently the ones where means testing in social protection is most important, and they in fact have relatively high poverty rates both among the low paid and among non-employed households. The context in which low-paid employment occurs is crucial for its impact on poverty, and the same is true for an expansion in low-paid employment.

7   Conclusion

Low pay has emerged as one of the major new risks facing welfare states today. There is widespread concern that (relative) poverty in employment situations has worsened in countries that have seen an increased incidence of relatively low-paid work. In Continental Europe, where enhanced wage flexibility is considered a cure for persistent high non-employment, there exists a widespread perception that an expansion of low-wage employment (mostly in the currently underdeveloped personal services sector) could lead to a proliferation of the working poor.

This chapter has attempted to shed some light on the empirical relationship between low pay and poverty, drawing on data from the Luxembourg Income Survey database and the European Community Household Panel. The main finding is that the extent of overlap between low pay and poverty is rather more limited and less clear-cut than is often assumed in policy discussions. Most low-paid workers live in multi-earner households and they frequently have living standards that exceed the poverty threshold by a very wide margin. Moreover, a small proportion of low-paid workers seem to provide the additional income needed by the household to live free from poverty. Nevertheless, in most countries there is a significant minority of low-paid workers for whom poverty is a very real problem. This is most notably the case in countries where passive benefit dependency is less of an option for those with a low earnings capacity.

Fears that there are limits to what can be achieved with the traditional instruments of minimum income protection seem well-founded in light of these results. Higher minimum wages can only have a limited impact on poverty – even among the low-paid – and the potential impact needs to be judged against the cost of potential job loss. New instruments like low-pay supplements – in the guise of tax credits or otherwise – can in theory be far more (cost-) effective in this respect, as chapter 6 will argue in more detail. However, this does not mean that 'traditional' instruments of social protection policy such as minimum wages no longer have a role to play. In-work cash transfers aimed at the low-paid can probably only be complements rather than substitutes for statutory minimum wages and other collective wage setting institutions. There is after all a real danger that effectively subsidising low-paid work might induce further wage erosion at the lower end of the wage spectrum. Moreover, in order to be effective as an anti-poverty device, low-pay supplements need to be strongly targeted. But strongly targeted benefits almost inevitably come at a high cost in terms of work and possibly household formation disincentive effects. This again highlights the continuing importance of 'traditional' instruments such as child benefits that can have an immediate impact on poverty – both among those depending on earnings and those on replacement benefits – without adversely affecting work incentives. Particularly when one takes the implications of the dynamic perspective seriously, a strong case can be made that in order to be effective, policies aimed at the working poor will have to fit within a broad-based anti-poverty strategy in which the classic instruments of income support play a crucial role.

4 On the Limits to Incrementalism in Income Protection Policy: The Case of Structural Unemployment in Belgium

1 Introduction

Structural unemployment is the second major 'new social risk' habitually associated with structural change in the labour market, particularly the demand shift against the less-skilled. As I proposed in the general introduction, it is often said that the traditional pillars of income protection – social insurance and social assistance – are not particularly well-adapted for dealing with the social risk of unemployment as it presents itself today, i.e., as a problem of structural labour market exclusion rather than as a risk-induced and typically temporary phenomenon. Basically, the claim here is that the distributional effectiveness, the economic efficiency and the political legitimacy of the social insurance/social assistance-based model crucially hinges on a state that approaches full employment, i.e., the sufficient availability of jobs that enable economic self-reliance.

The dominant thinking now is that social insurance/social assistance-based systems need to be maintained and adapted to the extent that is possible, but that augmenting the traditional pillars of social protection – I refer to this as incrementalism – cannot be considered the way forward in combating poverty in a sustainable way. Instead, attention is increasingly focused on policies that seek to restore the conditions under which the social security/ social assistance model can function properly again. Particularly, much effort (and resources) is put into measures to recreate a full employment environment: wage and employment subsidies, reductions in social security contributions, active labour market programmes. In addition, there is an expansion of income protection (anti-poverty) arrangements that are meant to be complementary to the main social insurance/social assistance pillar: earned income tax credits etc., which we return to in part 3.

Discussions about the possibilities and limits of incrementalism tend to be rather general and theoretical. This chapter examines in some depth the case of Belgian unemployment insurance (UI). This case is worth exploring because the UI system underwent a fundamental transformation in response to the changes in the economic and social environment. The system effectively evolved from a social insurance system fairly much in the classic Bismarckian mould into what effectively amounts to a minimum income protection system. In that process of gradual transformation, the objective of containing and reducing relative poverty played an explicit and central role, to some extent successfully, as I will show in this chapter. But the Belgian case also offers a good vehicle for illustrating and exploring some of the alleged limits to gradualism and incrementalism in social protection policy.

2 Unemployment Insurance in Belgium

Unemployment insurance in Belgium, as elsewhere, was implemented with a very limited purpose: to alleviate temporary need among breadwinners in a full employment environment – or at least an economic context approaching full employment. At the time it seemed to be 'a perfect system', for it simultaneously achieved several goals, or so it can be argued. First, the system enhanced economic efficiency. Unemployment insurance, as both an anti-poverty and income maintenance device, helped to limit risk-aversion and resistance to change among workers, since frictional unemployment became less of a threat to a people's livelihood. Second, in a context in which the breadwinner model prevailed, there was a natural overlap and complementarity between the income maintenance function of the system and its poverty alleviation objective. In other words: it was socially efficient. Third, the system generated its own public support. Benefit entitlements were 'earned' through work, and hence an extension of previous earnings. The system did not rest, or did not need to rest on real solidarity. Well-understood self-interest served as a sufficient binding factor and as motivation to contribute to the system.

The first oil shock marked a fundamental and dramatic change in the economic environment. There was a sudden and massive increase in the number of unemployed workers and consequently in the number of people claiming unemployment insurance benefits. But more importantly, there was the transformation of the nature of the unemployment risk: frictional unemployment increasingly became structural unemployment. By then an equally dramatic change in the socio-demographic environment was already in full swing, most notably the increase in female participation. This caused the heterogeneity of the claimant population to increase.

These factors taken together imposed considerable strains on the system. First of all, it clearly jeopardised the budgetary sustainability of the system. The massive rises in the number of claimants as well as the more long-term nature of unemployment drove up expenditure and rapidly caused an imbalance between the expenditure and income side of the system.

Second, its potential as an anti-poverty effectiveness deteriorated. In a social insurance system, the level of support given to an unemployed person is generally dependent on past contributions, previous wages and work history. This means that the risk of unemployment is adequately covered if there is no structural jobs scarcity and workers are capable of accumulating adequate benefit entitlements through work. The unemployed population of the post-oil shock period increasingly consisted of new labour market entrants who had never had the chance to accumulate entitlements – women and school leavers.

Third, the socio-demographic changes affected the redistributive efficiency of the system. The rise of secondary and tertiary earner unemployment gave rise to an increased tension between the income maintenance function of the system and its anti-poverty objective. With the rise of non-breadwinner unemployment, the automatic link that used to exist between risk occurrence and need (potential poverty) ceased to prevail. With the proliferation of secondary earner unemployment, a rising proportion of total benefit expenditure benefits ended up in households with a fairly high pre-transfer household income. The tension between this fact and the fact that many of the unemployed had no access to unemployment benefits at all became highly problematic.

3   Policy Responses to Mass Unemployment

The expansion of early retirement

The main objective of this chapter is to show how the social security system – the UI system in particular – coped with the rise in unemployment and particularly its changed nature. But first, we focus on the important and complementary role of early retirement. However, since our main focus is on the UI system proper, we will do so briefly.

The principal early retirement scheme (the so-called 'bridge-pension') was formally instituted as an extension of the unemployment insurance system. But as the name implies, the so-called 'bridge pension' was conceived from the start as a retirement scheme and not as an unemployment scheme. It is also perceived as such. The policy dynamic surrounding the system has therefore followed its own path and logic. For example, the need to maintain work incentives, a perceived constraint to benefit generosity in the regular UI system, has never been an equally important consideration with respect to early retirement benefit levels.

Let me first sketch the context in which the principal early retirement scheme was implemented and then expanded. The Belgian industrial sector, being rather old and energy intensive, was particularly hard hit by the oil shocks and the economic downturns of the 1970s and 1980s (Cassiers et al. 1996; Hemerijck et al. 2000). The share of industrial employment (including mining and construction) in total employment, which was still around 40 per cent in 1975, fell rapidly in the years thereafter, reflecting major structural adjustments in steel, coal and textile industries. During the 1980s, Belgium recorded the fourth largest percentage of manufacturing job loss in the OECD area. By 1992, employment in industry represented less than 28 per cent of total employment (OECD 1997b).

As most Continental European countries, Belgium resorted to an expansion of early retirement schemes to help alleviate the social consequences of structural economic adjustment and massive job shedding in industry. Kohli et al. (1993) and Esping-Andersen (1996, 1999) have argued that in Continental Europe early retirement policies 'became the main – if not exclusive – means to facilitate industrial restructuring' (Esping-Andersen 1999: 130). Belgium probably went further than any other Continental European country in the extent to which it resorted to early retirement. Labour force participation among men over the age of 55 dropped rapidly and massively during the late 1970s and 1980s. It is now, at 37 per cent, still at one of the lowest levels among the OECD countries. To put this figure into context: the OECD average is 65 per cent and the EU average is 53 per cent.

The main early retirement scheme that was implemented in the late 1970s to shelter the casualties of the industrial collapse, consisted of a social security benefit, which formally had the status of an unemployment benefit because it was paid out by the unemployment insurance administration, supplemented by an additional benefit paid out by an industry fund. In this way, many of the early retired accumulated a net benefit income that was only marginally below their last wage. Although instituted during the late 1970s, the scheme saw its biggest expansion during the 1980s.

Early retirement achieved two direct goals; adequate poverty relief and cost containment, and it arguably also achieved a third, indirect one: reduced competition for scarce jobs.

First, the main early retirement scheme provided adequate – many would say generous – protection to those who lost their jobs during a time when re-employment chances were low, especially in the economic prevailing circumstances. As I indicated, job loss in Belgium's industrial sector was massive after the oil shocks of the 1970s and 1980s. Many of the workers who lost their jobs were sole breadwinners with few formal qualifications or with very specific technical skills. Many of them lived in regions strongly dependent on industrial employment where alternative employment opportunities were scarce. The poverty consequences of high unemployment among traditional sole breadwinners would have been extremely grave since unsupplemented unemployment benefits would usually have been quite insufficient to protect them and their households from poverty. It is difficult to ascertain to what extent early retirement effectively prevented a rise of 'real' unemployment among older men but the unemployment rate for men between the age of 55 and 64 has remained comparatively low in Belgium. During the 1990s, it was well below 5 per cent versus an EU average of around 9 per cent.

Secondly, cost containment. The co-funded nature of the principal early retirement scheme initially helped to contain the budgetary cost of mass job shedding in the 1970s and 1980s. It would have been much more costly if the cost of providing adequate benefit packages to the many casualties of the post-industrial transition had fallen entirely on the social security system. On the other hand, one could also argue that job shedding was actually induced by the availability of financially attractive early retirement schemes. The co-funded nature of early retirement allowed and still allows employers to externalise a substantial part of the cost of laying-off redundant older workers. Because early retirement packages were so attractive, employers planning lay-offs typically encountered little resistance from trade unions and workers. Quite the contrary, older workers developed a strong preference for early retirement (Schokkaert et al. 2000). The fact that early retirement remains rampant even in today's vastly improved economic context is almost wholly due to the fact that trade unions have made continuation of early retirement one of their main demands. So far, they have been highly successful in getting this demand met, despite growing resistance from employers, who increasingly complain of labour shortages. The government too has proclaimed its intention to scale back early retirement but has weary of trade union reaction and public opinion, taken few concrete steps so far.

The massive expansion of early retirement arguably also achieved a third goal: it relieved supply pressure on the labour market and reduced competition for jobs. Indeed, employers who resorted to early retirement were and are in principle required to hire a young person to replace the person who takes early retirement. In practice, however, the replacement rule has never been adhered to. Still, unemployment rates for men of prime age remained comparatively low in Belgium even when overall unemployment reached peak levels.

More generally, the labour market position of the prime-aged male breadwinner has remained extraordinarily robust (table 4.1). The vast majority have a reasonably well-paid job and usually a stable one; OECD data on job tenure indicate comparatively high job stability with the average job tenure among Belgian workers being among the highest of OECD countries (OECD 1997a). Furthermore, OECD data show that low-wage work is less prevalent among Belgian men than in most of the other OECD countries (OECD 1995). About 4 per cent of Belgian men in full-time employment work for a wage that is below 66 per cent of the median gross wage, compared to around 10 per cent in Germany and France and 13 per cent in the United Kingdom.

Table 4.1 The robust labour market position of the male breadwinner: Labour market position of men of prime age in a European perspective

	Unemployment rate	Low pay incidence (% below 66% median)	Average job tenure, in years
Belgium	6.2	3.9	11.7
Denmark	4.1	-	8.3
France	12.9	10.6	11.0
Germany	8.0	7.6	10.6
Ireland	9.7	-	9.8
Italy	7.5	9.3	12.1
Netherlands	3.6	8.1	9.9
Portugal	5.0	-	11.1
Spain	13.6	-	9.8
UK	6.7	12.8	8.9
OECD Europe	7.4	-	-

Source: OECD.

The transformation of the UI system

Early retirement schemes relieved the pressure on the UI system proper to a considerable extent. But by doing so it effectively strengthened the need for changes to the UI system. After all, early retirement absorbed much of the classic breadwinner unemployment for which the unemployment insurance system was originally designed. This further increased the already growing heterogeneity of the claimant population and hence worsened the distributive inefficiency of the system, especially from a poverty alleviation viewpoint. During the 1970s and 1980s, an increasing proportion of the rapidly rising total benefit expenditures went to secondary earners with a relatively high (pre-transfer) living standard, while many others, most notably new labour market entrants with insufficient contribution records, found themselves increasingly exposed to poverty.

The UI system has undergone a veritable transformation over the past couple of decades. The process of change has been broadly guided by two main concerns: containing the cost of the system and maintaining goal effectiveness, primarily in terms of ensuring minimum income protection. The system has been transformed from a social insurance arrangement in the Bismarckian mould into what effectively amounts to a minimum income protection system. Benefit generosity has become much more a function of assumed need than of previous earnings and contributions, as is normally the case in a social insurance system. The strong link between contributions and benefits has in fact been all but abandoned over the past two decades.

There were a couple of major reform moments, but the transformation of the system was really achieved through a succession of piecemeal interventions or sometimes non-interventions, e.g., not adjusting benefit levels to compensate for inflation. In broad strokes, the reform of the system can be characterised as follows:
– Cost containment and the enhancement of distributive efficiency through the introduction of categorical selectivity, i.e., benefit differentiation according to assumed need rather than contribution record.
– Strengthening of the minimum income protection component of the system through selective minimum benefit increases and the widening of eligibility to minimum benefits.
– Weakening of the income insurance function on the benefit side and a strengthening of solidarity on the contributions side.

The introduction of categorical selectivity

In a social insurance regime, benefits are in theory individual entitlements that are a function of individual work history and past contributions (and hence past wages). Belgium's unemployment insurance system has never been a pure social insurance system in this sense. From its inception in 1944, the Belgian system has been characterised by a strong emphasis on minimum income protection (Clegg 2006). Until 1971, unemployment benefits were basically flat-rate, though there was an element of categorical selectivity in that men were entitled to higher benefits. There was also a degree of differentiation between rural and urban areas (De Lathouwer 1997).

However, because of the 1971 reforms, Belgium had a fairly typical social insurance system in place by the time the economic crisis struck. Unemployment benefits had become individual, non-means tested entitlements earned through work – only those with a sufficient contribution record and work histories were entitled. Benefits were also wage related, be it within certain minimum and maximum limits (the spread was in the order of 25 per cent). In addition, a distinction existed between so-called heads of household and others. This had been introduced as a substitute for the more explicit but discriminatory and hence unconstitutional differentiation between men and women.

In the years immediately after the 1973 crisis, there was a sudden and vast increase in the number of people claiming unemployment benefits (table 4.2). As a result, the cost of the system exploded and a serious financial imbalance developed between the contribution and the expenditure side. Also, a growing share of benefits started flowing to secondary earners. As a consequence, benefits were increasingly ending up in households that did not really need them to stay out of financial hardship.

Table 4.2	Evolution of the number of people entitled to unemployment insurance benefits for full-time unemployment, Belgium 1970-2000	
	Number of full-time unemployed	Full-time unemployment as a percentage of the labour force
1970	70,753	1.9
1975	174,48	4.4
1980	322,310	7.9
1985	505,944	12.3
1990	364,696	8.7
1995	555,252	12.9
2000	439,149	10.1

Source: Deleeck (2001).

The major reform moment came in April 1981 when a further distinction was introduced between three categories of claimants: heads of households (those providing for dependent persons: children or non-working spouses), single persons and so-called 'cohabitants': unemployed persons who lived together with a person who has an income above a certain threshold (possibly another unemployed person).

The first two categories of claimants remained entitled to a full benefit because they were assumed to be most needy. For cohabitants, however, the link to previous wages was only maintained for the first period of unemployment. After roughly the first year and a half of unemployment (depending on their work history) cohabitants only became entitled to a relatively low flat-rate amount, regardless of their previous earnings. Benefits for cohabitants were made increasingly more regressive throughout the 1980s and 1990s.

The time duration of unemployment benefits has also become more a function of assumed need rather than of work history and past contributions. Unlike in most other countries, unemployment insurance benefits have never been time limited in Belgium. In this respect at least the system was from the start better adapted to deal with structural unemployment than systems in which unemployment insurance benefits expire after one, two or more years.

Only cohabitants could have their benefit terminated after an 'abnormally' long spell of unemployment, and only if the total household income exceeded a certain threshold (far above the poverty thresholds for most conventional household types). Until 1993, the general rule was that benefit termination proceedings could only be initiated if a cohabitant's spell of unemployment exceeded twice the average spell of unemployment in the region of residence, also taking into account the sex and age of the person. After 1993, this period was shortened to 1.5 times the average spell.

In practice this means that benefit termination proceedings are not initiated until a spell of unemployment exceeds 3 or 4 years. In regions with unfavourable labour market conditions, this period can be as long as 8 or more years. But even then benefit termination is still not automatic. The administration has some discretion in granting exemptions. For example, it can be judged that a claimant has made 'extraordinary' efforts to find work. Yet, since the early 1990s, officials have become considerably less lenient in granting exemptions for this reason (De Lathouwer 1997; De Lathouwer and Bogaerts 2000). But even despite a tightening of rules concerning benefit termination, the Belgian system remains highly atypical in terms of average benefit duration.

Single persons and heads of households can only have their unemployment benefits suspended in cases of proven fraud. This is the main reason why at least some of the unemployed need to resort to social assistance, at least for the duration of the suspension, which is usually temporary.

Table 4.3   Distribution across benefit categories in unemployment insurance, Belgium, 2000

Head of household	36.4
– men	17.5
– women	18.8
Single persons	18.0
– men	10.9
– women	7.1
Cohabitants	45.4
– men	13.8
– women	31.7
Others	0.2
	100.0

Source: RVA (2000).

The strengthening of minimum income protection
As I have already indicated, the Belgian unemployment insurance system was from its inception characterised by a fairly strong emphasis on minimum income protection. Unemployment insurance benefits were initially flat rate. It was not until 1971 that unemployment benefits became wage related. But even at that time there existed a minimum benefit level in order to ensure a decent level of protection to those with low previous earnings.

Despite the continuous efforts over the past decades to contain the cost of the system, minimum income protection within the UI system has been strengthened substantially. In a passive sense, the concern for maintaining anti-poverty effectiveness is evident in the way categorical selectivity was introduced. But there have also been intentional reforms aimed at strengthening the adequacy of minimum income protection.

First of all, the conditions to gain access to (full) UI benefits have been relaxed over the years. Unemployment benefits are now frequently in excess of what people would be entitled to if the equivalence principle had been strictly adhered to. For example, years spent in full-time education count as time worked. Activities other than paid work have also counted. Of the unemployed in the category 'head of household' almost half receive the guaranteed minimum benefit (RVA 2000).

Second, minimum benefit levels, at least those for heads and single persons, have increased more than UI benefits in general. During the 1970s, benefits were automatically first linked to consumer prices and then, be it for a short period of time, to real wages. As a consequence, benefits increased fairly strongly across the board. The automatic link with wages was already abandoned in the late 1970s and the automatic link with consumer prices was abandoned in the early 1980s. During the mid-1980s (1984-1986) benefits and wages were not adjusted for inflation, causing a drop in the real value of both wages and benefits (De Lathouwer 1997). From then on adjustments for inflation have been made in a selective manner. Those on minimum benefits have disproportionately benefited but it is nevertheless the case that the inflation-adjusted increases have remained fairly limited over the past few decades (figure 4.1).

Figure 4.1   Minimum UI benefit levels, in 2001 prices

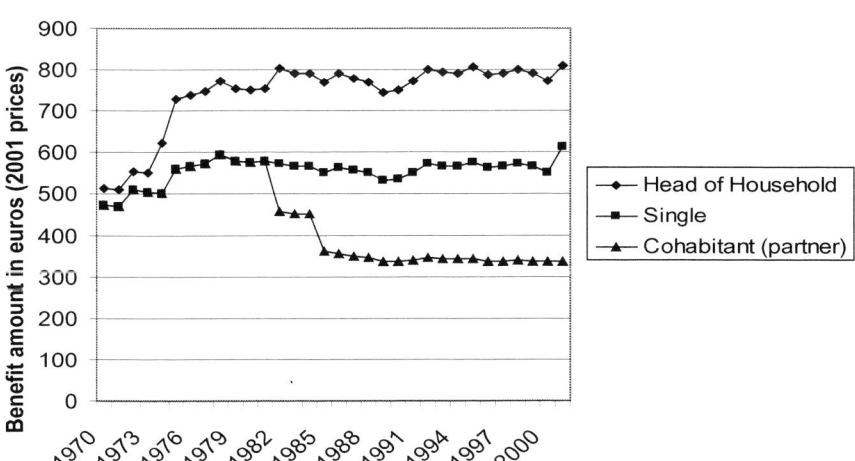

Source: Cantillon et al. (2001).

Third, supplementary benefits have been introduced for what are assumed to be particularly needy categories of beneficiaries, most notably supplementary child benefits for unemployed persons with dependent children. Such supplements were introduced partly in compensation for the general non-indexation of benefits (and wages) during the 1980s.

The weakening of the insurance function

The Belgian unemployment insurance system never amounted to a full-fledged social insurance system; the difference between minimum and maximum benefits has always been fairly limited, even during the early 1970s when the system most resembled a classic social insurance scheme most strongly. In the post-oil shock crisis decades, the insurance function was rapidly scaled back again. Clearly, the strengthening of categorical selectivity meant a weakening of the insurance principle. Furthermore, the real value of the maximum benefit levels has been allowed to decline more strongly that the real value of minimum benefits. As a result, today only a very small wedge remains between maximum and minimum benefits. To illustrate this: in 1975, the difference between the minimum and maximum benefit amounts for an unemployed head of household amounted to almost 25 per cent, by the mid-1990s this had shrunk to less than 13 per cent.

At the same time, and more importantly, high earners now contribute more to the system. Until 1982, workers only paid contributions up to a certain maximum amount – a logical compensation for the fact that maximum benefit levels were also constrained. As the cost of the system soared during the 1970s, this contributions ceiling was gradually increased, basically in order to get more money into the system. In 1982, this contribution ceiling was completely abandoned.

4   Outcomes in a Comparative Perspective

Cost containment while maintaining, even selectively improving, minimum income protection guided the initial reforms to the UI system during the 1980s. The introduction of the relatively cheap cohabitant category, for example, was a typical measure in that it was intended to reduce the cost of the system while safeguarding the level of protection offered to the neediest. What did the reforms deliver?

Cost

Overlooking the post-crisis period one is struck by the extent to which the budgetary cost of the UI system has been successfully contained and even reduced, despite the massive rises in the number of claimants. Standardised expenditure figures for the entire period studied are impossible to find, but the available figures roughly sketch the following picture. As one would expect, there was an out-and-out cost explosion after 1973. In 1970, when there were less than 71,000 people in the system, the overall cost of the unemployment insurance system (including early retirement) amounted to roughly 0.7 per cent of GDP. Ten years later, there were almost 600,000 benefit claimants and the cost had risen almost five-fold, to 3.3 per cent of GDP (Cantillon et al. 1987). The OECD estimates the cost of the UI system for that year – the first year of its standardised expenditure database – at 2.5 per cent. The cost of the system continued to rise during the early 1980s. By 1985, there were an additional 200,000 benefit claimants and the cost had risen by almost another percentage point.

After 1985 there was a radical and rather spectacular turnaround, as is evident from the figures. Despite a continuing rise in dependency levels (almost another 100,000 benefit claimants by 1990), the cost of the system in GDP terms *dropped* quite steeply during the late 1980s. This was a result of two factors. First, the changed composition of the benefit claimants population – less people claiming benefits for full-time unemployment, more people claiming benefits for part-time unemployment. But more important was the fact that over this period the inflation-adjusted value of benefits declined in the context of strong economic growth. In the five years between 1985 and 1990, the cost of the system dropped from 3.4 per cent of GDP to 2.6 per cent. Over the course of the 1990s, the cost of the system remained fairly stable, despite another significant increase in the number of claimants for full-time unemployment, especially during the mid-1990s.

According to the OECD Social Expenditure Database, Belgium in 1997 allocated 2.65 per cent of GDP to unemployment benefits, a comparatively high figure – the OECD Europe average at the time was only 1.65 per cent. But this figure needs to be seen in the context of Belgium's exceptionally high benefit dependency rate, particularly among the unemployed. Countries like Denmark or the Netherlands, where proportionally fewer working-age people received benefits, were spending significantly more on benefits for the unemployed, respectively 3.37 and 2.60 per cent.

The fact that the aggregate cost of the UI system was successfully contained arguably helped Belgium sustain the effectiveness of the system in terms of its capacity to provide adequate income protection for those most in need (single persons and heads). It is difficult to predict what would have happened if the equivalence principle (the link between individual wages, contributions and benefits) had not been abandoned to the extent that it was. The overall cost of the unemployment insurance system would undoubtedly have been higher and the distributive efficiency would probably have been much lower, that is, from a poverty protection viewpoint. A far higher share of overall benefit expenditure would have gone to comparatively affluent double income households. It seems highly unlikely that it would have been possible to maintain the unlimited time duration of benefits in a more classic social insurance context.

Social assistance dependence and poverty in comparative perspective

Turning to outcome indicators, the first notable fact is that social assistance dependence has remained far less widespread in Belgium than elsewhere. Unlike in many other European countries, the rise in structural (long-term) unemployment during the 1970s and 1980s did not cause a big influx into social assistance in Belgium. Social assistance dependence of working age Belgians has remained below 1 per cent of the total population and long-term social assistance dependence below 0.5 per cent. These are considerably lower dependency levels than in most other European countries, where, moreover, the long-term unemployed tend to make up a considerable portion of the population on social assistance (Gough et al. 1997).

The explanation lies in the extent of the coverage of Belgium's UI system. A vast proportion of the working-age population receives compensation for full-time unemployment and even many more receive some other type of UI benefit. As a consequence, the official Belgian unemployment rate, which is based on the number of UI benefit claimants, has always been much higher than the ILO unemployment rate, which is based on the number of people who register as unemployed and actively seeking work.

This is not because access thresholds to the system are especially low. People generally need a substantial employment record in order to gain access to UI entitlements. Unemployed school leavers are a major exception; they gain access to benefits on the basis of their time spent in school. But what makes the Belgian system atypical is the time duration of benefits, which is effectively unlimited for the unemployed for whom their UI benefits serve as their principal income. Recall that only 'cohabitants' with a household income (fiscal income in the previous year) that is far above the social assistance threshold can have their benefits terminated solely for duration reasons. This is in all probability the principal explanation why social assistance dependency levels have remained so low amidst persistent long-term unemployment.

Coming to what is in the present context the most important measure of policy performance, evidence suggests that the poverty consequences of mass structural unemployment (in the broadest sense of the word) have remained comparatively limited in Belgium. Belgium's comparatively low poverty rate stands in marked contrast to its international position regarding various employment indicators.

Cross-country comparative poverty studies on the basis of the LIS database have consistently shown that Belgium has one of the lowest poverty rates among OECD countries (Atkinson 1997; Gottschalk and Smeeding 1999). This is particularly true for the non-employed, as figure 4.2 shows, which is based on calculations on the basis of LIS (see chapter 5). In fact, Belgium has the lowest poverty rate for the non-employed of the 14 major OECD countries included in the analysis. This LIS-based picture was recently confirmed by an OECD study which uses alternative data sources for many countries, including Belgium. The OECD study also shows relative poverty rates for Belgium to be at the lower end among OECD countries (Förster 2000).

Figure 4.2   Relative poverty rates for the working-age population, OECD, early 1990s

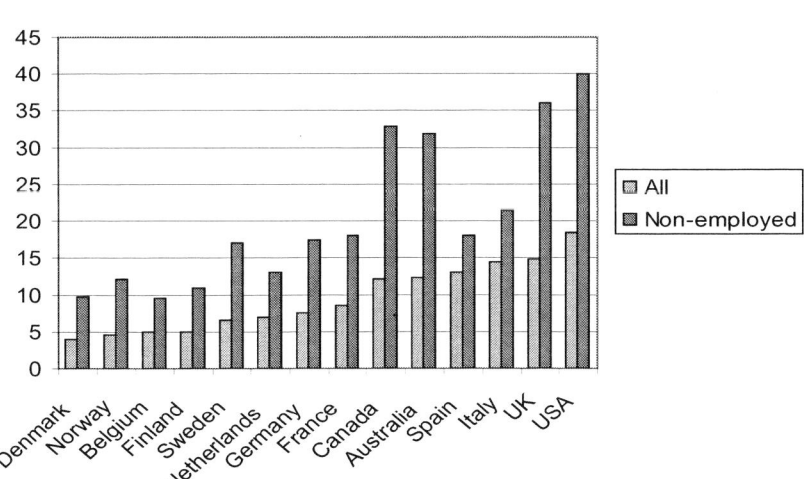

Source: LIS.

Figure 4.3 Relative poverty (50% mean equivalent household income) among the unemployed, 1994

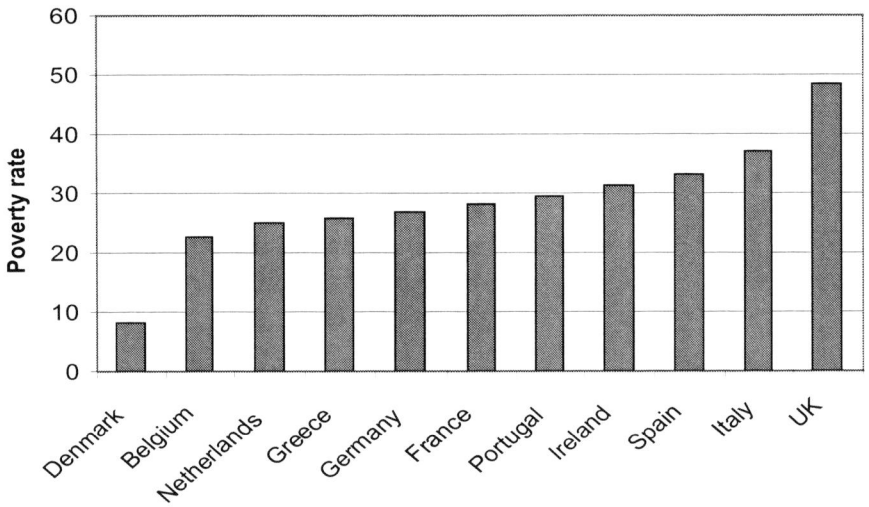

Source: ECHP, Gallie et al. (2000).

Poverty estimates on the basis of the European Community Household Panel present a somewhat different picture: ECHP poverty rates for Belgium tend to be higher than the LIS-based estimates (Eurostat 2001). This discrepancy exists for many OECD countries, and country rankings on the basis of LIS and ECHP are quite similar, but the magnitude of the difference is larger for Belgium than for most of the other countries (Van Hoorebeeck et al. 2002).

Gallie et al. (2000) present comparative data on relative poverty rates among the unemployed, drawn from the ECHP (figure 4.3). As I have just indicated, this data source is fraught with problems and consequently, the figures should be treated as being indicative more than anything else. In addition, it is generally difficult to get a good match between someone's employment status (which typically refers to someone's status at a particular point in time) and his or her poverty status (which is typically measured on the basis of yearly household income). Data for 1994, Gallie et al. (2000) reveals that 23 per cent of Belgium's unemployed lived on an income that was below 50 per cent of median equivalent household income, compared to 25 per cent for the Netherlands, 27 per cent for Germany,

28 per cent for France, 37 per cent for Italy and 48 per cent for the UK. (It is worthwhile to point out that the authors used a measure of monthly, and not, as is usually the case, annual income for this exercise because this allowed a better match with the employment status variable.)

5 How the UI System Started Failing the Most Vulnerable

Going by the evidence available, poverty rates for the working-age population are comparatively low in Belgium, including for the unemployed. But this generally favourable picture obscures a much bleaker one in so far as the most vulnerable are concerned. And what is most important, the efficacy of the system in providing minimum income protection to the most needy appears to have deteriorated quite substantially within the time frame for which we have data. The data source is the Belgian Socio-Economic Panel Survey (SEP).

In 1985, the earliest year for which we have SEP data, about one in ten (self-reported) of the unemployed were living in financial poverty, i.e., they resided in a household with a total household income that was below 50 per cent of average household income adjusted for family size (that is, in the month which preceded the one during which the interview took place). However, by 1997, the most recent year for which comparable data is available, this proportion had doubled to about one in five (table 4.4). This SEP-based poverty estimate of 20 per cent is of the same magnitude as Gallie et al.'s estimate using ECHP data. Hence, even despite the rise, poverty among the unemployed in 1997 remained comparatively low.

Table 4.4	Poverty incidence by labour market status, Belgium 1985-1997					
Labour market status	Relative poverty incidence			Share in working-age population		
	1985	1992	1997	1985	1992	1997
Non-employed	6.4	9.0	11.2	44.5	40.6	41.2
Unemployed	10.4	13.4	22.2	7.6	7.4	8.7
– with UE benefit	10.0	12.2	19.3	6.6	6.6	6.6
– no UE benefit	13.3	22.6	31.4	0.9	0.8	2.1
Working-age population	3.9	4.4	5.1	100.0	100.0	100.0
				(n = 6,598)	(n = 3,528)	(n = 4,228)

Source: Calculations on the basis of the Belgian Socio-Economic Panel Survey.

The principal reason for the limited overlap between unemployment and poverty can be found in the profile of the unemployed population in Belgium (table 4.5). The vast majority of the unemployed in Belgium live in households with at least one wage earner. In 1997, almost eight out of ten households receiving unemployment benefits also had other financial means (table 4.6). For them, the unemployment benefit was only one component in their household income package and frequently only a minor one. The majority of UI claimants in 1997 would not have been poor even if they had not received any benefit at all. This is evident if one looks at the pre-transfer poverty rates for households with an unemployment benefit – a rough measure of dependence on benefits to stay out of poverty. The 'favourable' composition of the unemployed population is probably in major part a consequence of the extent to which early retirement schemes were used to shelter the most vulnerable sections of the unemployed, particularly sole male breadwinners who became unemployed as a consequence of the economic shock and the post-industrial transition.

Table 4.5 Poverty exposure of unemployed persons by household type, 1997

	Poverty risk	Share in population of unemployed persons in poverty
Single adult	45.7	32.2
Two adults, no children	16.0	17.4
Two adults, children	22.5	28.1
Single parent	19.4	7.2
Other household type	13.9	14.1
All	22.2	100.0

Source: Belgian Socio-Economic Panel Survey.

Table 4.6 Profile of households receiving unemployment benefits (UEB), Belgium, 1997

	Households with UEB	Households that have to make ends meet on UEB	Households receiving UEB and other income
Share in the population of households receiving UEB	100.0	22.9	77.1
Share in the total population	13.0	3.0	10.0
% Pre-transfer poor	55.7	0.0	72.3
% Lifted from poverty thanks to UEB	29.1	42.1	25.2
% Poor despite UEB	15.2	57.9	2.5

Source: Belgian Socio-Economic Panel Survey.

But the fact remains that poverty among the unemployed increased substantially in the 1985-1997 period. And what is more important, the fairly modest overall rise in poverty among the unemployed obscures a far bigger rise among the minority of households who actually had to make ends meet solely on their unemployment benefit. In 1997, 60 per cent of the households depending almost entirely on UI system income (i.e., excluding regular and supplementary child benefits if applicable) were found to be living on an income below the poverty threshold, up from 30 per cent in 1985 (figures 4.4 and 4.5). Which brings us to the core focus of this chapter – why did the adequacy of the system vis-à-vis the most vulnerable deteriorate so dramatically?

Figure 4.4 Poverty rates for households receiving UI benefits, 1985-1997

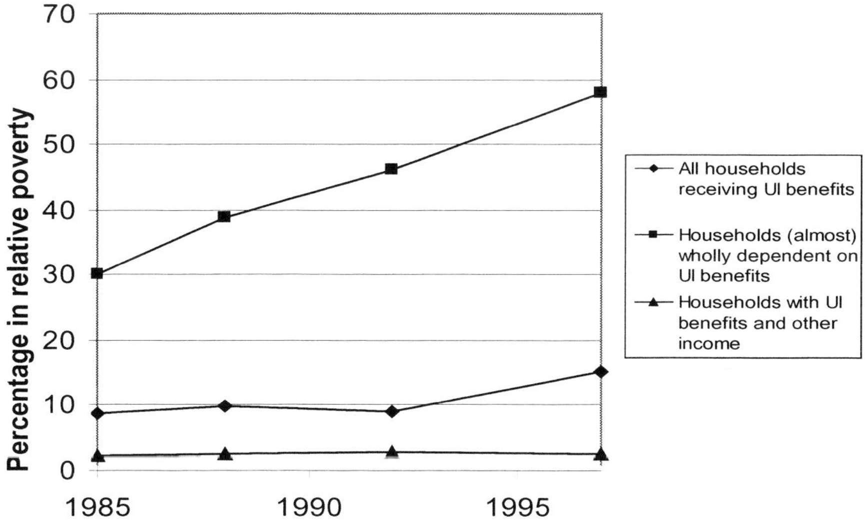

Source: Belgian Socio-Economic Panel

Figure 4.5 Households receiving UI benefits, share in total population, 1985-1997

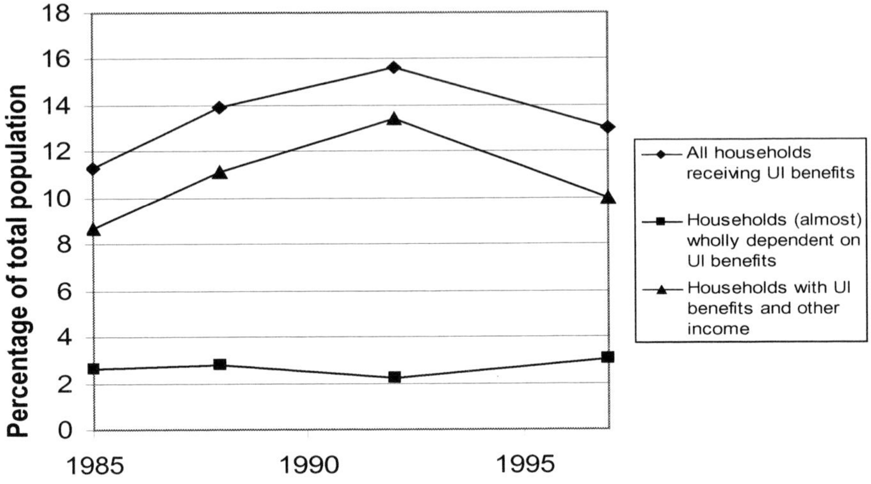

[Chart showing percentage of total population from 1985 to 1995 with three lines: All households receiving UI benefits; Households (almost) wholly dependent on UI benefits; Households with UI benefits and other income]

Source: Belgian Socio-Economic Panel

6 Why the UI System Started Failing the Most Vulnerable

The direct reason why poverty increased so dramatically is simple: benefit levels dropped below the adequate level (figure 4.6). While benefit levels almost stagnated in real purchasing power terms after the early 1980s (figure 4.1), average living standards and hence relative poverty thresholds continued to rise, leading to a severe decline in the relative value of benefits (figure 4.7). It is not surprising then that poverty levels among the unemployed surged dramatically, especially since minimum UI benefit levels were only just adequate at the start of the period we consider here.

In the social policy literature, there has been an impulse to attribute stagnant benefits and rising poverty to 'welfare state backlash' or 'welfare state retrenchment'. The core idea is that social protection arrangements became increasingly inadequate during the 1980s and 1990s because neo-liberal tendencies started to dominate social policy thinking.

Figure 4.6 Adequacy of minimum UI benefits, expressed as percentage of relative poverty threshold for relevant category

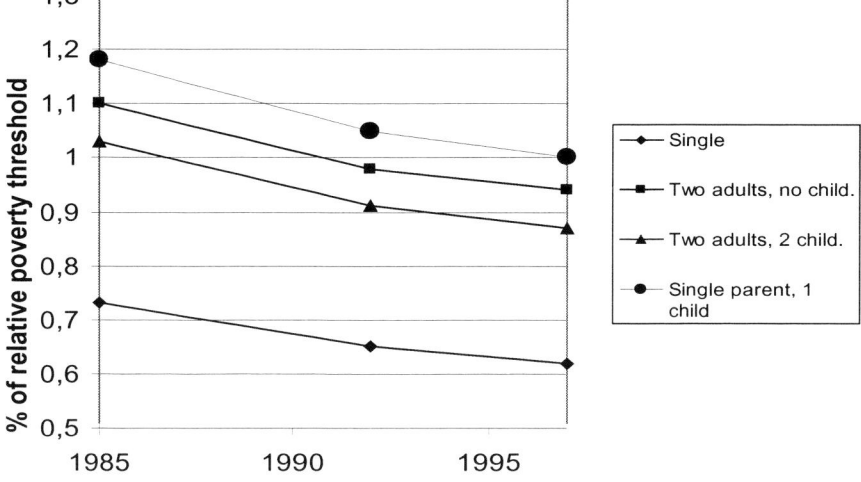

Source: Based on Cantillon et al. 1999; 2001.

However, it has also been argued that there are other, more fundamental reasons why benefits, in Belgium as elsewhere, have become more and more inadequate. The progressive decline in the adequacy of the UI for unemployed breadwinners, which was already evident by the late 1980s, led to claims that social security was approaching its limit (Cantillon 1993). One of the principal reasons, it was suggested, is that over the past few decades the general living standard and hence the relative poverty threshold have both been pushed upward, not by real wage growth (as was the case in the 1950s and 1960s) but by the proliferation of double earnership.

Figure 4.8 illustrates this point. The average living standard in the period 1985-1997 rose by just under 20 per cent, as naturally did the relative poverty threshold. In contrast, the average gross wage rise for employees, according to figures published by the Federal Ministry of Employment, remained limited to 10 per cent. For manual workers it was even less. (And on the basis of the SEP dataset, we find that the average net income from full-time work rose by 8 per cent.) Wages clearly did not keep up with average living standards in the period covered. Benefits and minimum wages have lagged even further behind (figure 4.9).

Figure 4.7   Minimum UI benefit levels relative to national income per head

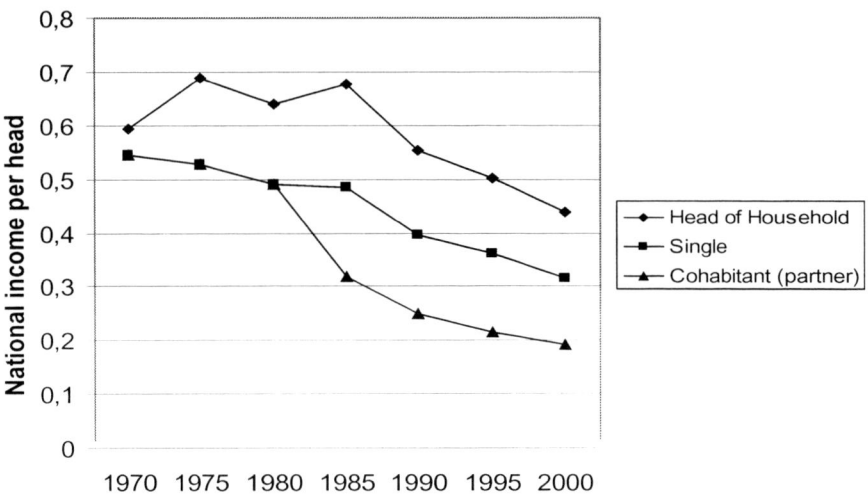

Source: Cantillon et al. (2001).

Figure 4.8   Average living standard, wages and UI benefits: real terms trend between 1985 and 1997

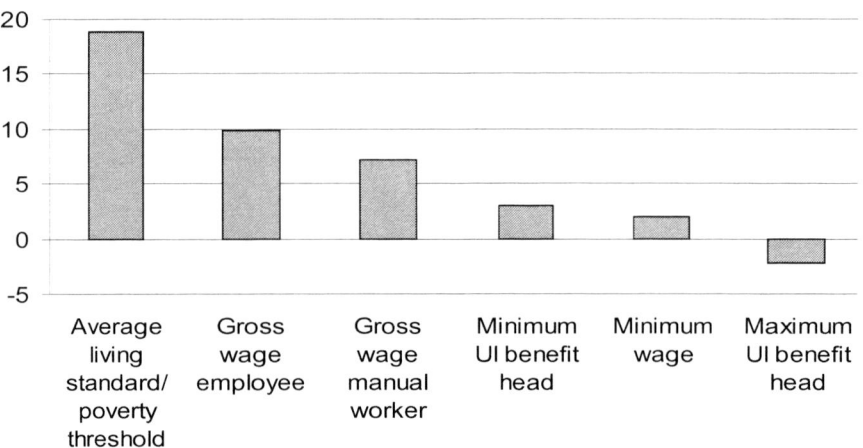

Source: Average living standard/poverty threshold: Cantillon et al. (1999); wage trends: Ministerie van Arbeid en Tewerkstelling (2000); benefits: Cantillon et al. (2001).

The implication is that relative poverty among unemployed breadwinners could only have been maintained at the 1985 level or thereabouts if UI benefits rose in line with the general living standard, which would have required a far stronger real rise in benefits than in real wages. Similarly, improving the level of minimum income protection for the unemployed within the UI system would have required benefits to have increased more strongly than average wages.

Figure 4.9 How the minimum wage and UI benefits have drifted from the average standard of living

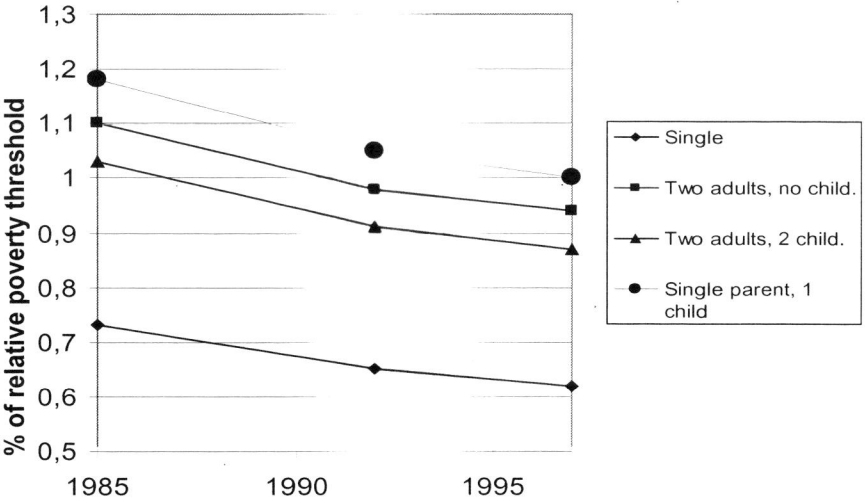

Source: Based on Cantillon et al. 1999, 2001.

This, it was argued, would have been both economically infeasible and politically unrealistic. Hence the claims that it was becoming ever more difficult and eventually impossible to achieve substantial social progress within the framework of the conventional social security system.

First of all, it was and still is assumed that a certain gap between benefits and minimum wages needs to be maintained in order to maintain sufficient work incentives. It is also claimed that there it is a moral and political imperative to do so – the legitimacy of the welfare state can only be sustained, it is argued, if a clear hierarchy exists between work and inactivity. The key problem, it is argued, is that some categories hardly gain anything from making the move from dependency to work. Lone parents, most notably, can actually suffer a substantial net income loss if they make the move from a full benefit package to a low-paid job, especially if they fully or even partially incur the extra cost of child care (De Lathouwer 2001).

An obvious, but in many eyes unrealistic, way out of this cul-de-sac would be to raise the minimum wage. This would create scope to increase benefits and improve the level of income protection offered to the most needy, i.e., chronically unemployed breadwinners. However, the problem is that a really substantial increase would be required. After all, the minimum wage has remained essentially constant in real value over the past 20 years, as have UI benefits. Over the same time period, the average living standard has risen by more than 20 per cent real terms and so has the relative poverty threshold.

Although it has remained essentially constant, the Belgian minimum wage remains among the highest in the OECD area, in absolute purchasing value terms as well as in relative terms, i.e., relative to the median wage (table 4.8). Over the past two decades, net wages have also tended to increase less than the average standard of living – living standards have been pushed up by the proliferation of multi-earnership and not, as in the past, by real wage growth. A reduction of poverty among unemployed sole breadwinners within the UI system would therefore require a stronger increase in the minimum wage than wages in general have risen in the past two decades. If this would happen, it would imply a further compression of an already comparatively compressed wage structure. This, again, is widely deemed unfeasible in a post-industrial environment where a demand shift against the less-skilled has occurred. The predominant opinion is that an even more compressed wage structure would have a detrimental effect on the employment prospects of the less-skilled and would push even more people in dependency.

The 'limits to social security' argument is compelling in many respects. But have the limits of social security really been reached? We will now consider the arguments in greater detail, starting with the alleged economic limits.

7 On the Economic Limits to Incrementalism

On the gap left between benefits and minimum wages

There is no statutory minimum wage in Belgium, but there is a nation-wide collectively agreed minimum wage. It is this minimum wage which features prominently in calculations that have to do with work incentives, unemployment traps and the like. However, the minimum wage has more of a benchmark purpose than anything else – it constitutes the absolute base of the wage building. 'Real' minimum wages (i.e., pay scales for the youngest, least qualified and least experienced workers) are negotiated at the industry level. These tend to be considerably higher than the nation-wide minimum wage. Figures published by the Belgian Ministry of Employment and Labour (2000) suggest that the industry minimum wages are on average about 10 per cent higher than the nation-wide level. Industries where the lowest pay scales are 20 to 30 per cent higher than the nation-wide minimum are not exceptional. There are even a few industries where the lowest pay scales are almost twice as high as the nation-wide minimum. All the available evidence suggests that very few people actually work – or can work – for the nation-wide minimum that features so prominently in the debate.

All this aside, even the wedge between the nation-wide minimum wage and the minimum or even maximum unemployment insurance benefit levels for the various categories of beneficiaries has remained quite substantial. However, what really matters, particularly from the perspective of labour supply incentives, is the net minimum wage, i.e., the gross minimum wage minus social security contributions and taxes. Net minimum wages do tend to be quite a bit lower than the gross minimum. Social security contributions payable by the employee are levied as a fixed percentage of the gross wage (13 per cent). Personal income taxes then have to be paid on what is called the gross taxable wage. The level of personal taxation depends on a great number of factors apart from income level. What matters in particular is household composition, specifically the number of dependents. In 1999, the year closest to 1997 for which detailed information is available, the gross/net wedge at minimum wage level for single people amounted to 29 per cent, 20 per cent for single parents and 14 per cent for heads with two children (De Lathouwer and Bogaerts 2001).

Other factors influence the net income package when someone is employed or on benefits. Unemployment insurance benefits are more favourably taxed than wages and unemployed people with children are entitled to additional child support benefits. Work, on the other hand, brings with it additional costs such as travel and possibly child care.

In 1999, the net financial gain for a single person who made the move from long-term unemployment (while receiving the maximum unemployment insurance benefit) to a minimum wage level job amounted to around 40 per cent (on the order of 250 euros). However, for a head of household the gain was much smaller: around 20 per cent (in the order of 100 euros). A single parent making the move from benefit dependence to full-time work actually suffered a small net income loss (around 40 euros), especially because of the additional cost of child care. Clearly, work disincentives were only a real issue as far as lone parents were concerned.

This is important because single people were precisely the category for whom the poverty rates were highest in 1997. As table 4.5 shows, single unemployed adults faced an almost 50 per cent chance of poverty. They also made up one-third of the total unemployed population in poverty. It is clear that this was a direct consequence of benefit inadequacy. In 1997, the minimum UI benefit for a single person was well below the poverty threshold (figure 4.6). Given the huge gap even between the maximum UI benefit and the net minimum wage for a single person, there undisputedly existed scope to increase benefit adequacy for this the most vulnerable category.

Moreover, if the government's priority had been to maximise benefit adequacy, while maintaining a substantial wedge with the net incomes of low-paid work, an obvious option would have been to reduce social contributions and personal taxes on low wages. Successive Belgian governments have sought to boost the demand for less-skilled workers by reducing the employers' social security contribution burdens on low wages. It was not until 2000 that a modest social security contribution reduction for low-paid employees was introduced. The reduction consists of a flat rate amount. Minimum wage workers get the full reduction. The reduction then gradually becomes smaller until it reaches zero at a gross wage level that is around 120 per cent of the minimum wage. This reduction has brought down the gross/net wedge for minimum-wage workers from 29 to 24 per cent for single people and from 13 to eight per cent for single parents (De Lathouwer en Bogaerts 2001). As a consequence, work has become more worthwhile for people on unemployment benefits. (Note that this reduction constitutes a further strengthening of the solidarity principle and a further move away from social insurance.) However, the net effect of the social security contribution reduction is tempered by the way personal taxation works. Thanks to the reduction low-paid workers pay less in social security, but since this raises their taxable gross wage they end up paying slightly more in taxes.

Is a strict hierarchy between minimum wages and benefits required?

What about the fundamental claim that as a general principle benefits for the unemployed need to be significantly lower than the minimum wage in order to maintain work incentives? This supposed requirement obviously imposes a very serious constraint on the level of income protection that can be offered to the most vulnerable.

The UI system was initially designed for the male breadwinner era. The implicit assumption was that the UI did not pose a threat to work incentives in any real way. Men were expected to work and the vast majority wanted to work, if only for reasons of self-esteem and social status. The econometric labour supply literature seems to support the view that financial disincentives to work have a more limited impact on working men's labour supply than on women's (Blundell and Macurdy 1999).

The concern with work incentives appears to be entirely legitimate. There is actually a good deal of evidence that an important section of the long-term unemployed in Belgium might justly be labelled 'voluntarily unemployed' – i.e., that many prefer benefits rather than a job that can reasonably deemed to be within their reach if they made serious efforts to find, secure and hold on to these jobs. An in-depth study of work attitudes among the long-term unemployed by De Witte (1992) provided direct evidence that a significant percentage of long-term unemployed women had little real interest in work and that they preferred a relatively low but steady social income to a work income. It turned out that 'voluntary' dependence was heavily concentrated among less-skilled women with children. A more recent study by De Lathouwer and Bogaerts (2000) which examined the consequences of forced exit from the UI system provides similar indications. Specifically, the study looked at the labour market and income status of a sample of long-term unemployment insurance beneficiaries who had seen their unemployment terminated, and this was done nine months after the termination. The vast majority (almost all women) were found to be non-employed and not actively seeking work several months after the benefit termination had taken effect. It is possible that many were discouraged job-seekers, but an analysis of responses to questions that gauged one's attitudes toward work strongly suggest a moderate genuine interest in work at best.

Entry into the UI system in Belgium is fairly easy provided that a person has enough of a work history and provided the claimant has been dismissed by an employer. Access is denied, however, if the dismissal was for gross dereliction or reprehensible behaviour. In theory, a person who quits voluntarily is not entitled to UI. In practice, however, employers are frequently requested to 'grant' dismissal. It is, of course, up to the employer whether or not to grant such a request, but the pressure to comply can be substantial. Moreover, the practice of 'dismissing' people on their own request in order to offer them access to UI is, though fraudulent, socially accepted. The practice appears largely tolerated as the administration seems only concerned with the formal validity of the claim not with its truthfulness.

Such practices are probably difficult to prevent. It would become very cumbersome and costly if in each dismissal case a full investigation into the validity of the reported motives of the employer had to be established. At least this is what the case of the Netherlands suggests. The UI administration there takes a more active role in controlling access to the UI system. This is because the law there is such that the applicant's conduct prior to dismissal plays an important role in determining entitlement. For example, a person is denied access to UI benefits if he or she insufficiently objected to the employer's intention to dismiss. This requirement imposes a heavy case load on the involved agencies. Annually, some 40,000 cases are pursued in court. Not surprisingly, court proceedings are conducted in a bureaucratic and run-of-the-mill manner. Given the heavy caseload, there is rarely much time or the means to conduct an in-depth investigation into the exact circumstances and events surrounding the dismissal (Knegt 2000). Of course, the question is whether a court would ever be able to stand between two colluding parties playing the formalities correctly.

Likewise, one could theoretically argue that no strict hierarchy between benefits and minimum wages is required if sufficient effort were made to make sure that claimants accepted suitable jobs; that is, if the requirement to accept a suitable job is implemented stringently and is perceived to be implemented stringently, i.e., if there are real controls on work search and job acceptance behaviour and if there are appropriate sanctions. That, one could argue, would make it possible to offer sufficient income protection to the truly needy: those genuinely unable to find a job.

It is certainly the case that in the past the work requirement condition has not been imposed very stringently by the Belgian UI administration. What is considered a 'suitable job offer' for an unemployed person has always been interpreted in a narrow way. A job offer needs to fit someone's qualifications and experience fairly strictly. Elements like geographical proximity of the job offer etc. are also taken into account. In practice, a refusal to accept a job rarely results in severe sanctions. Even repeated refusal is not generally punished. Personal autonomy in deciding which job to accept or refuse tends to be respected within fairly wide limitations. It may in fact be the case that the incidence of sanctions is so low in Belgium because the legally prescribed sanctions are so severe. The severity of the sanctions (loss of benefits for 26 to 52 weeks is the penalty for a first-time job refusal) seems to make officials reluctant to actually apply them.

Arguably, in such a context it is necessary to keep benefit levels well below minimum wages in order to maintain a sufficient work incentive. In a way, low benefit levels are the necessary price for a lax imposition of the theoretical requirement that an unemployed person is required to seek employment and accept a more or less suitable job if offered.

A theoretical alternative then is to introduce a Norwegian-like strictness. There, the unemployed must generally accept shift jobs or night jobs, must be prepared to work anywhere in Norway, must be ready to accept any job they can do without reference to their previous occupation or wage level, and cannot refuse a job on religious or ethical grounds (although administrative discretion may be invoked in such cases) (OECD 2000: 133). There is evidence from other countries that this type of strictness helps, be it to a limited extent (OECD 2000: 141).

But an eligibility enforcement regime that could sustain adequate benefits for the most vulnerable would probably require an infringement on personal freedom and autonomy beyond what people have become accustomed to and beyond what can be deemed desirable on moral grounds. As a matter of fact, Norway-like strictness may well be culturally and politically infeasible in the Belgian context. Moreover, the stricter the rules are and are applied, the greater the risk that mistakes will be made and the truly needy get hurt. Many sanctions in Belgium and elsewhere are for such details as a failure to report a change in family situation on time. These mistakes are as often the result of ignorance or bureaucratic incompetence as anything else.

As the OECD (2000) concludes from a survey on the effects of eligibility criteria and their enforcement on unemployment: '...there is considerable uncertainty about the overall effectiveness of particular methods, such as job-search reporting requirements and individual action plans, which attempt to oblige the unemployed to take initiatives to find work. While these methods are likely to be effective to some degree, they are also likely to encourage and even unfairly reward purely formal compliance...'

Or to put it differently, while the notion of a stricter job search and other such requirements is to create scope in order to offer better income protection to the most vulnerable, the risk is that as a consequence many of the most vulnerable will lose out because of their inability to 'play the system'.

Is it feasible to increase the minimum wage and hence benefits?

It would seem that in the end, when the scope for fiscal and para-fiscal relief is really exhausted, it all boils down to this question: is it really impossible to increase minimum wages and, subsequently, benefits?

Minimum wages in Belgium have remained virtually stagnant in real purchasing power terms over the past couple of decades as is the case in many but not all other European countries – France is a notable exception (figure 4.10). Relative to average wages, minimum wages have generally fallen fairly strongly. Replacement benefits have, as we have seen, roughly followed a similar path, maximum benefits more so than minimum benefit levels, and this as a direct consequence of the linkage that prevails between replacement benefits for the working-age population and the minimum wage.

Figure 4.10   Real minimum wages 1970-1995; 1975 = 100

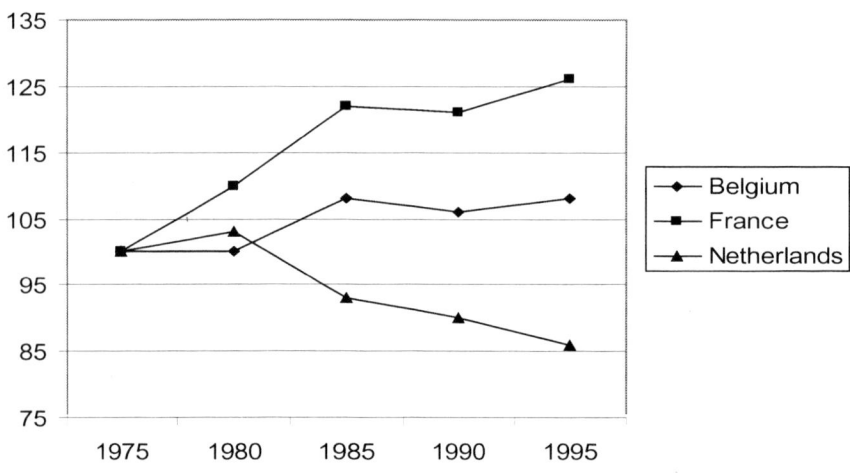

Source: OECD (1998).

The consensus is that a substantial increase in the minimum wage is neither possible nor desirable. The idea here is that significant minimum wage hikes would simply be too harmful to employment and would effectively worsen Belgium's entrapment in 'welfare without work'.

Historically speaking, the strongest increases in wages, including at the bottom end of the distribution, occurred during 1950s and 1960s – not a period marked by escalating unemployment. Of course, the 1950s and 1960s were an exceptional period. Economic growth was exceptionally strong by historical standards, the labour supply was limited, the workforce was relatively homogenous and solidaristic wage policies did not only produce wage equalisation but also low inflation (Eichengreen and Iversen 1999).

It is widely assumed that deindustrialisation, economic globalisation and technological change have made minimum wages far more harmful, also because the labour supply has become more heterogeneous (see chapter 2).

However, much of the recent econometric evidence contradicts the view that minimum wages, at prevailing levels, are particularly harmful to employment. The orthodox view has been challenged in a profound way by recent research. The wave of recent studies on the employment effects of minimum wages was prompted by Card and Krueger (1995), who claimed that they had found an instance (in the United States) where a minimum wage hike was accompanied by a slight increase rather than a decline in employment. Their well-publicised and provocative findings did not go unchallenged; some revisionist studies found an effect in the opposite direction, albeit an equally small one (see Neumark and Wascher 1995, 1996; OECD 1998).

Indeed, the overwhelming impression one gets from the body of research now available is that the overall employment effects of both minimum wage reductions and increases tend to be small or negligible, even in sectors that are considered most vulnerable to minimum wage rises. This is perhaps because the scrutinised changes tend to be equally marginal, though not always. The abolishment of the minimum wage in the United Kingdom in 1993, for example, offered an instance of a radical change. But in this instance as well, the employment effects were found to be small to non-existent (Machin and Manning 1994, 1996).

Research does suggest that the effects may be stronger for particular subgroups. The employment of young people tends to be more responsive to minimum wage levels. When significant employment effects are found, they tend to be for youngsters (Bazen and Skourias 1997; Dolado et al. 2000; OECD 1998). A study by Laroque and Salanié (1999), for example, attributes close to 15 per cent of non-employment among married women in France to the minimum wage, which is among the highest among OECD countries.

While the evidence is fairly conclusive that the effects are generally small, there can be no doubt that estimating the effect of minimum wages on employment is fraught with methodological difficulties. Much empirical work has adopted a time series approach. The empirical findings from time series models tend to be sensitive to the estimation method and to the inclusion or not of different explanatory variables such as time trends and business cycle controls. There is the problem of the possible endogeneity of the minimum wage/average wage ratio, that is: this ratio may capture not only variations in the level of the minimum wage but also the impact of labour demand or supply shocks on the level of the average wage. Minimum wage hikes may also have spill-over effects which may cause average wages to rise. Furthermore, the estimates often cover short-term effects only (OECD 1998).

And there is perhaps an even more important caveat. Most research has been done for countries where minimum wages are comparatively low, most notably the US. The US offers a rich testing ground because the extent of minimum wage variations from state to state. But the differences tend to be very small and there is not a single US state that has a minimum wage that comes anywhere near Continental European levels, at least in relative terms. On the other hand, when minimum wage hikes have occurred in the United States, they have often been quite substantial, relatively speaking. Again, the empirical evidence that minimum wages have a limited effect (either way) on employment seems abundant, but it comes overwhelmingly from countries with low minimum wages.

Belgium, on the other hand, is definitely a country where the high minimum wage is already very high (table 4.7). According to OECD data, the adult minimum wage in Belgium amounts to 61 per cent of adult full-time median earnings (excluding overtime pay and bonuses. In the US it is only 43 per cent. (For reference: in the Netherlands it is 56 per cent and in France 69 per cent.)

Table 4.7 Adult minimum wage relative to a range of average earnings measures, mid-1990s

	Full-time median earnings		Mean hourly wage in manufacturing
	Basic	Inc. overtime pay and bonuses	
Belgium	61.1	50.4	59.9
France	68.5	57.4	68.7
Netherlands	55.9	49.4	58.1
Spain	36.4	32.4	40.6
United States	43.3	38.1	36.1

Source: OECD (1998).

Research on the effects of minimum wage hikes in countries with high minimum wages is therefore more likely to be relevant. Research available for Continental Europe is however broadly in line with that for the US. Most notably, the study by Dolado et al. (1996) for a number of European countries confirms the weak relationship between minimum wage variation and employment. In a subsequent article, Dolado et al. (2000) cite studies which further substantiate this claim, as does, perhaps surprisingly, the OECD (1998). The evidence even seems to suggest that minimum wage increases may well be feasible in countries where minimum wages are already high. Real minimum wages in France continued to rise above already high levels during the 1990s and there is little direct evidence of serious negative effects on employment.

The fact that in France and elsewhere in Europe very few people work for the minimum wage or could even afford to work for the minimum wage, given their age, qualifications and experience, is cited as one of the reasons why minimum wage hikes have such a small measurable effect on employment. However, as Dolado et al. (2000) argue, the spill-over effects are likely to be more important in the European collective wage-setting context than in the more decentralised US or UK contexts. These possible spill-over effects (especially in the longer term) have received scant attention in the empirical literature. It may well be the case that serious minimum wage hikes are only feasible if embedded in effective general wage moderation.

8   On the Political Limits to Incrementalism

A well-known theoretical argument holds that a social insurance system essentially rests not on a broad-based attachment to lofty ideals of solidarity but on well-understood self-interest. The binding agent is said to be common risk exposure. Thus, the willingness to pay contributions is not primarily motivated by compassion for those who are affected by illness, unemployment, etc., but flows from a broad-based need to get cheap and reliable coverage against certain risks.

In a study of welfare state development in Western Europe, Peter Baldwin makes the case that horizontal solidarity – the type of self-interested solidarity that flows from shared exposure to a set of insurable risks – lies at the heart of the successful development of social security in Western welfare states (Baldwin 1990). It is the comparative economic efficiency of mandatory, universal social insurance which forged a durable alliance between the working classes and the middle classes and which contributed to its massive expansion. Within the context of a comprehensive, universal and therefore intrinsically complex and opaque system there exists considerable scope for departing from actuarial principles and for deploying a considerable degree of vertical solidarity to the benefit of the most vulnerable. For example, in most social insurance systems there is no contribution differentiation according to risk exposure. This may be a matter of pure economics rather than solidarity by design (Hey 1989; Barr 1998, 2001). Premium differentiation itself is, for reasons of asymmetric information, often difficult or expensive. It may be perfectly consistent with the well-understood self-interest of low-risk categories to continue to participate in universal social insurance, even if there is no premium differentiation and high-risk groups benefit significantly more from the system. This has to do with, among other things, the economies of scale associated with risk pooling – insurance becomes cheaper as more people participate (Barr 2001). Even if the univeral solidaristic system offers a less than optimal deal to low-risk groups, the alternative of private insurance may still be far more expensive.

But what is remarkable about the Belgian system is that the insurance principle has gradually become subordinate to the need principle and this for the sake of cost containment and poverty relief. In fact, the equivalence principle – the link between contributions and benefits – the defining characteristic of a social insurance system and arguably fundamental to its legitimacy, has ceased to exist.

It has been argued – most notably by Schokkaert en Spinnewyn (1995) – that the gap between what the majority of workers contribute to the system and what they may reasonably expect to gain has become so large that it has seriously undermined the legitimacy of the system and the willingness to contribute to it, especially by high-earners, who are the biggest source of income. In fact, they claim that the limits of solidarity were long ago reached and have probably since been surpassed.

The severed link between contributions and benefits

There can be no doubt that a serious discrepancy has developed between what high-earners pay into to the system and what they may expect to get out of it in the (unlikely) event that they become unemployed. While the value of maximum benefits has eroded quite substantially in real value terms, high-earners have been made to pay higher contributions, mainly through the lifting of the contribution ceilings that used to exist. (It used to be the case that social contributions – fixed percentages of gross earnings – were only levied up to a certain maximum. This was a logical compensation for the fact that benefits were also proportional to previous earnings up to a certain maximum.)

Why then has public support for the system remained so robust, as it appears it has? If Schokkaert and Spinnewyn are right, a middle and higher income revolt against the actuarial unfairness of the UI system is long overdue. In reality, the weakening of the equivalence principle has never become an issue of any real importance. Trade unions (especially the socialist union) have at various points in time demanded higher maximum benefits and a re-strengthening of the insurance function. But they have not really pushed the issue. There are plenty of other issues relating to unemployment insurance (the time duration of benefits, for example) to which trade unions have reacted much more ferociously in order to get their demands met (Kuipers 2006). In the wider political sphere, the decline of the insurance function has remained pretty much a non-issue. One would be hard pressed to name an instance when a political party or politician has tried to score points among middle and higher income voters on a promise to restore 'a fair link between contributions and benefits'.

In fact, there exists direct empirical evidence that the erosion of the insurance principle has not weakened support for the UI system significantly, including among the better paid with low risk exposure. In 1996, Verhue et al. (1997) did a survey of attitudes towards the UI system. A representative sample of workers was asked directly how they felt about the system. They found overwhelming support for the prevailing system or for an even more generous system. Only some 11 per cent were in favour of a less generous system. A slightly stronger preference for this option was found among university-educated workers. Still, 80 per cent were in favour of the existing system or a more generous one.

There are several possible explanations why, despite the erosion of the equivalence principle, the UI system has continued to enjoy what appears to be widespread support. One obvious potential reason is pure ignorance. The transformation of the system has happened more or less by stealth, which is to say by small, piecemeal reforms. Moreover, the social security system is so comprehensive and opaque that people are likely to have a very rough idea of what they pay into the system and what they get out of it. Social contributions are in theory earmarked but hardly anyone is aware of this. What workers see on their pay slip is the monthly contribution they pay for the social security package as a whole, including health insurance, sickness and invalidity insurance, pensions etc.

Verhue et al. (1997) provide evidence, however, which suggests that people are fairly well informed about the system. At the time of their survey most workers had a fairly good idea what the maximum unemployment benefit was for an unemployed head of household. Interestingly, most questioned workers grossly overestimated what they contributed towards the UI system in terms of social security contributions. The surprising implication, then, is that people, especially high-earners, tend to overestimate the actuarial unfairness of the system.

Hence, middle- to high-earners seem to be well aware that a serious unbalance exists between what they pay into the system and what they may reasonably expect to get out of it. But this is only true at the individual level. The picture is different at the household level, arguably the more appropriate unit of analysis. Contributions paid by relatively high-earners, for whom as individuals the compulsory system is indisputably a bad deal, often flow back via the unemployed secondary earner. This explains why, despite the move towards targeting the neediest, unemployment benefits still flow in significant proportion to households in the upper deciles of the income distribution, as is documented in figure 4.11. But the fact that many middle- and higher-income households benefit from the system, at least to some degree, does not explain why people are willing to put up with the flagrant actuarial unfairness of the system and its emphasis on minimum income protection.

Figure 4.11   Distribution of unemployment insurance benefits across household income deciles, 1997

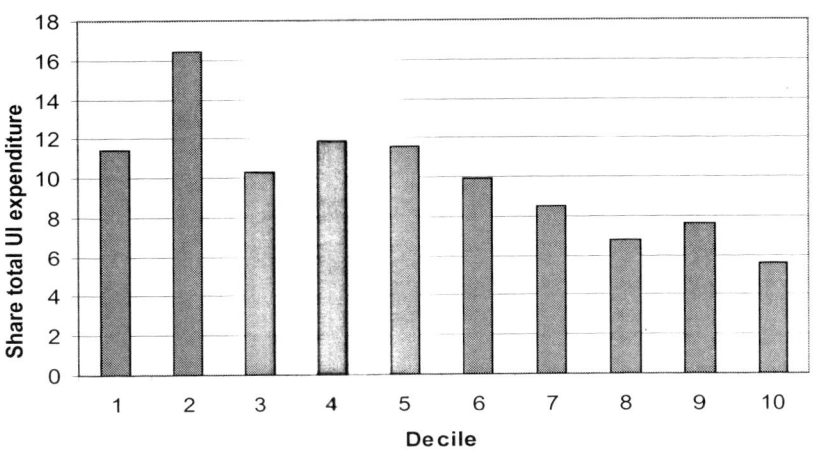

Source: Belgian Socio-Economic Panel Survey.

Perhaps then there is a more profound reason why broad-based support for the system has not crumbled. The willingness to contribute to a social security surely cannot be grasped by a simplistic model in which the *homo economicus* balances costs (that is contributions) against expected gains. This, again, is quite evident from the study by Verhue et al. (1997). Workers were explicitly asked whether, in addition to their own unemployment insurance contribution (assuming it was actuarially fair), they would be prepared to pay an extra contribution to ensure adequate coverage for less-skilled workers employed in industries with a higher dismissal probability. The vast majority (70 per cent) said they would be prepared to do so. The percentage was even higher among the better-skilled. At the same time, a similar majority was against a hypothetical non-universal system that would provide cheaper coverage for workers in low-risk industries and more expensive coverage for workers in high-risk industries.

It would appear, therefore, that although limits to solidarity are generally assumed to exist (based on sound theoretical reasons), there is little actual evidence that the shift towards basic income protection has undermined support for the system and the willingness to contribute. The implication seems to be that, contrary to what is so often tacitly assumed and in so many words suggested by, among others, Schokkaert en Spinnewyn, there is little hard evidence that a further strengthening of minimum income protection would be impossible.

Opportunistic behaviour and legitimacy

This is not to say that all is well when it comes to the legitimacy of the system. The study of Verhue et al. (1997) also demonstrates that the vast majority of workers believe most of the unemployed are capable of finding a job if they really made an effort. The widespread perception appears to be that dependence on unemployment benefits is to a large extent voluntary and opportunistic in nature.

The really surprising thing is perhaps not that there has been little reaction against the weakening of the insurance principle, but that this has happened in the context of large-scale chronic dependence among what is so often deemed to be a 'non-deserving' segment of the population. After all, it is generally assumed that people are not very inclined to 'subsidise' healthy people who are capable of working and that compassion-based solidarity, to the extent that it exists, is restricted to those who are unable to acquire adequate incomes for reasons that are manifestly beyond their own will. It appears highly paradoxical then that such a large majority remains in favour of the system as it exists (in terms of generosity) or an even more generous system.

Now, one could argue that within the Belgian context there is a very specific reason why (the perception of) rampant voluntary dependence has undermined the legitimacy less than one would be inclined to think. I think it is fair to say that the general perception is that the UI system is in fact to a large extent improperly used as a kind of career interruption scheme. 'Voluntary' dependence, where it does occur in any real sense of the word, is largely concentrated among women with young children. Perhaps this explains in part the apparent leniency. Indeed, over the last few years Belgium has seen an expansion of benefit systems that effectively *encourage* voluntary withdrawal from the labour market for reasons involving care.

And yet, somehow this ad hoc explanation does not seem wholly satisfactory. This phenomenon of a huge discrepancy between what the theory (and our intuition for that matter) would lead us to think and what the facts relating to public support tell us is not just limited to Belgium. The direct empirical evidence on public support for the welfare state tends to fly in the face of the pessimism expressed in so much of the literature. In fact, the idea that public support for the welfare state is fragile has a long history. As early as 1975, Wilensky predicted a middle-class revolt against the apparently inexorably expanding (American) welfare state. In a completely different and perhaps for us altogether more relevant context – the Dutch one during the late 1970s – Zijderveld (1979) made the case that the Dutch welfare state, which at that time was characterised by generous benefit policies and soaring dependency levels, was morally corrupting its citizens and producing a growing and inevitably fatal tension between those funding the welfare state and those living off it.

The theme of the looming 'middle class' revolt against the welfare state has run through the literature ever since. Galbraith (1992) popularised the idea of the 'contented majority' losing interest in those unable to keep up in the post-industrial economy: the unemployed and the low-paid. The concept of the 'two thirds society' became equally popular. In his seminal work *Culture Shift*, Inglehart (1990) predicted waning public support for the welfare state, because it was becoming increasingly incompatible with the growing emphasis on individualism. It would be possible to produce countless quotes from the social policy literature in which it is suggested that the legitimacy of the welfare state is under threat, that broad-based support for the welfare state is crumbling, that those with stable, well-paid jobs are becoming increasingly reluctant to support the unemployed, etc.

However, empirical studies on welfare legitimacy have generally failed to detect a substantial decline in public support, especially in Europe (see for example: Pettersen 1995; Taylor-Gooby 1998; Roller 1999; Van Oorschot 1999; Mau 2001). The evidence is perhaps not overwhelming in terms of its volume but it seems to be surprisingly robust and unequivocal.

Some have analysed this puzzling contradiction between the empirical evidence and the general sentiment in the literature as a result of an insufficient understanding of the nature of public support for the welfare state and the motives behind it. In an interesting study of motives for welfare support among the Dutch population, Van Oorschot (1999) found that several reasons simultaneously play a role; the motive of self-interest plays the most important role, followed by feelings of moral obligation and what is called 'affection and identification'.

The puzzle, then, remains far from resolved. Political science offers a possible answer as to why the system remains, or appears to remain, so robust. Basically, the idea is that costs and benefits of public reforms tend to be unequally distributed. Harsher benefit policies would directly and greatly harm a small section of society while the benefits to the rest of society would be small. In 'The New Politics of the Welfare State', Pierson (1996) argues that a simple redistributive transfer from programme beneficiaries to taxpayers (or people paying social contributions as in our case), engineered through cuts in social programmes, is generally a 'losing proposition'. 'The concentrated beneficiary groups are more likely to be cognisant of the change, are easier to mobilise, and because they are experiencing losses rather than gains are more likely to incorporate the change in their voting calculations.' Pierson here refers to studies of electoral and political behaviour which show that negative feelings are more strongly linked to a range of political behaviours than positive attitudes. He also refers to the well-known result from experimental economics that individuals exhibit a negativity bias, meaning that they are more likely to take action to prevent a worsening of their present situation than they would to improve their situation.

All this certainly seems relevant to understanding the apparent robustness of public support for the unemployment insurance system in Belgium. A large number of people benefit directly from the system and a great many more are in a household with someone who does (for example, a spouse or a recently graduated child). Almost 1 million people – this equals 1 in 4 people in the work force – benefit directly from the UI system in one way or the other. The percentage of working-age households with an unemployment benefit in their household income package is even larger. These households are to be found in all layers of the income distribution. The system clearly has a vast constituency that stands to lose directly from less generous or stricter entitlements. Moreover, the potential gains would be uncertain – it is not certain at all that stricter entitlement rules would lead to lower social insurance contributions, given the deficits and rising costs in other branches of the social security system.

9   Conclusion

This chapter has tried to demonstrate that the gradual adaptation of the Belgian UI system, combined with expanded coverage and targeted benefit increases, initially went a long way in responding to the fundamental shift in the nature of the unemployment risk: the massive increase in its incidence, the shift from transitory to structural unemployment and the rise of secondary earner as opposed to sole breadwinner unemployment. The transformation of the UI system from a classic income insurance system pretty much in the Bismarckian mould to what effectively amounts to a basic minimum income protection system initially helped to contain the budgetary cost of the system while maintaining and in some respects improving its minimum income protection effectiveness. Yet, after the mid-1980s, the poverty alleviation effectiveness of the UI system nevertheless started to deteriorate, giving rise to claims that gradual adaptation of the UI system, especially in the direction of improving minimum income protection, had begun to run its course, both on an economic as well as a political level.

This chapter has taken issue with some of the arguments that have been put forward in support of these 'limits to incrementalism' claims. In essence, my critique is that the key arguments rely too heavily on a priori reasoning. I stress, however, that I do not claim that there are no limits to incrementalism nor is it my assertion that incrementalism within the social insurance/social assistance context is necessarily the preferred way forward. But the fact is that we do not know whether the limits to incrementalism have really been reached in the Belgian case. It would appear – but this is a hypothesis that requires further validation – that the poverty alleviation effectiveness of the Belgian UI system actually deteriorated from the mid-1980s on, and certainly during the 1990s, because the objective of improving benefit adequacy was sacrificed to other priorities, most notably budgetary cost control, and not because attempts to further improve minimum income protection adequacy flagrantly ran into any limits of economic or political feasibility. Kuipers' (2006) recent study of welfare state reforms in Belgium in the 1990s seems to add credence to this hypothesis.

PART 3

NEW POLICY RESPONSES ASSESSED

5   How Responsive Are Poverty Rates to Job Growth?

1   Introduction

The 1990s were marked by rising prominence of social policy doctrines which entailed a departure from incrementalism, particularly that which is understood as improved benefit adequacy within the social insurance/social assistance framework. At the centre of these doctrines is the idea that there is and must be a strong complementarity between labour participation and poverty reduction objectives. A noticeable exponent is the Netherlands, where a radical policy shift from passive benefit adequacy towards boosting labour market participation was initiated in the mid-1980s and where it has been vigorously pursued ever since. The Dutch government itself summed up its singular purpose in the catch phrase: 'work, work, work'. The idea that employment growth and poverty reduction are natural allies is also remarkably central to policy at the EU level as it is now taking shape within the framework of the Open Method of Coordination (OMC). On the employment front, the objectives are quite specific. There is the overall objective of increasing the employment ratio to 70 per cent by 2010 and, in addition, there are clear targets for specific subgroups of the population like women and older workers. On the poverty front, the ambitions remain less well-defined, but there is an effective commitment now to engage in serious efforts at the member country level to bring about significant reductions in relative income poverty, among other objectives. Though little is explicitly said in EU policy documents, aspirations in both domains are assumed to be complementary. Indeed, a very similar vocabulary is used to defend aspirations in both domains.

This chapter presents empirical evidence for a range of OECD countries which suggests that countries may well find it difficult to achieve significant progress on both objectives at the same time. It starts with a look at current policy discourse. Next we turn to the empirical evidence on the link between employment (growth) and poverty (reduction) in a range of OECD countries. Because broad cross-country comparisons provide little insight as to the exact role of policy, we focus in some detail on the recent experience in the Netherlands, a country that turned job growth into the central pillar of its social policy, making it a central reference point in current discussions about the benefits and pitfalls of activation policies.

2   The Renewed Primacy of Work in Social Policy

The recent decade has been marked by the advent of such doctrines as the 'Third Way' and the 'Active Welfare State', in which work and social inclusion are seen as natural allies.

The idea that, to put it simply, 'work is the best social policy' came to prominence during the 1990s. It was around that time that the idea gained ground that far too many healthy, able-bodied people were chronically 'trapped' in passive benefit dependency. The emphasis shifted towards bringing down levels of chronic benefit dependency and increasing economic self-reliance (Zeitlin and Trubeck 2003).

Up until then, the main concern in many European countries had been with providing adequate benefits to those who were seen as the victims of the deteriorating economic conditions and the collapse in worker demand. After all, the 1980s were characterised by mass layoffs and double digit unemployment rates. Many economists had come to believe that structural mass unemployment was here to stay.

The shift in attitude occurred on both sides of the Atlantic, though in some countries more conspicuously than in others. In the US, Bill Clinton conducted his successful 1992 presidential campaign largely on his famous promise 'to end welfare as we know it' (Blank and Ellwood 2001; Blank 2002). In what came to be known as the politics of triangulation, he acknowledged the conservative critique – powerfully spelled out during the 1980s by the likes of Charles Murray (1984) and Lawrence Mead (1986), but up till then ardently rejected by progressives – that chronic welfare dependency constituted an economic, social and moral problem of the first order. Clinton vowed to reduce welfare rolls but also, and this in his effort to triangulate between the traditional left and right, to enhance social protection for workers through an expansion of in-work benefits. His motto: to make work pay.

In Europe, something similar happened. Arguably, the most spectacular example is the Netherlands, where a radical policy shift from benefit adequacy towards stimulating labour market participation was initiated in the early 1990s and where it was vigorously pursued by the social democrat-liberal 'purple' coalition. Around the same time in the UK, Labour leader Tony Blair (who was looking more towards the US than Europe), made his own attempt at political triangulation, calling it the 'Third Way'. Blair started to emphasise the virtues of work and self-reliance, and the importance of individual responsibility, but he did so without adopting the traditionally hostile Conservative attitude against the welfare state and those living on benefits. He vowed to reform the welfare state so as to 'make work pay'. The Third Way debate in the UK spilled over into other countries. The Third Way was emulated by social democrats all across Europe, probably in part because Blair's discourse proved to be so electorally successful (Bonoli and Powell 2002; Hall 2002; Hemerijck 2002). In Belgium, for example, it inspired the 'The Active Welfare State' (Vandenbroucke 2001).

The idea that ultimately the best anti-poverty strategy is a work-based strategy circulated long before it became politically fashionable. Most notably the OECD has long argued for employment-centred anti-poverty policies. But the policy changes which the OECD used to promote – its position has shifted in recent years – were different from what the Third Way and the Active Welfare State are said to be about.

Basically, the case then was for labour market deregulation (lower minimum wages, less rigid wage setting) and less generous passive benefits, the idea being that what long-term benefit dependents with few marketable skills needed most was, above all, work experience and work discipline. It was recognised that deregulation and cuts in passive benefits could entail an expansion of low-paid jobs that would bring little immediate income progress and no relief from poverty – perhaps the opposite. But the claim was that work – any job – would provide the unemployed with a far better stepping-stone onto the ladder of economic mobility and self-reliance.

This is not what the Third Way or the Active Welfare State doctrines are about: labour market deregulation, less generous passive benefits and the belief that upward mobility will make any pain that might result short-lived. Almost by definition, the Third Way favours an approach different from a 'passive' benefits policy, on the one hand, and a free-market approach, on the other. Rather, the general idea is that a shift is needed from 'passive' support to 'active' support, i.e., training, in-work benefits and child care provisions.

This is being put into practice. In the US, the Earned Income Tax Credit (EITC) – a tax subsidy for households with low earnings – is now by far the most important system for direct income distribution for the working-age population (Blank and Ellwood 2001). At the same time, benefit availability for those not working has been drastically curtailed. In Europe, similar tax credits for the low-paid have been introduced or expanded. More resources have been directed to active labour market policies, training programmes, employment subsidies for the less-skilled, child care etc. Few countries in Europe have actually cut back on benefits, but benefits in many countries have eroded in real value (because of partial non-adjustments for inflation), and eligibility for benefits has been tightened. In many countries there has been a decline 'by stealth' of passive income protection.

The present preoccupation with increasing employment and reducing passive benefit dependence does not derive solely from a concern with eradicating poverty and social exclusion. Other considerations play a role arguably first and foremost among these budgetary imperatives. The large numbers of inactive persons are a big burden on public resources at the same time when needs in many other domains continue to expand – health care for example. And with populations ageing, such needs are structurally on the increase. Because tax increases are not popular and, moreover, widely deemed economically undesirable, there is the perceived need to reduce spending, especially since neither deficit spending nor higher levels of public debt are seen as valid alternatives. Moreover, within the euro area, agreements apply to the size of budgetary deficits and the size of public debt. In this context, working age individuals chronically living on benefits are now considered as legitimate targets for cost cutting, especially in countries where unemployment rates have reached frictional levels again and where employers complain of labour shortages.

3   Employment and Poverty: Some Basic Facts

Figure 5.1, which plots poverty rates against employment rates for the mid-1990s, serves to give a sense of the extent of cross-national variation in employment and poverty outcomes (see also table 1). One does not expect to find a simple cross-country correlation between a country's employment and poverty rate. Countries may have comparatively high or low poverty rates for reasons which have little or nothing to do with employment performance – for example the socio-demographic composition of their population, the extent of wage inequality or, of course, the effectiveness of their social protection system. And yet it is striking that the relative poverty rate for the working-age population in the US is almost twice as high as in Germany or France, and almost four times as high as in Belgium, although a far higher proportion of the working-age population has at least one job in the US. Likewise, poverty rates are comparatively high in Australia, Canada and the UK, all of which are countries with better employment records than most of the Continental European countries. More work is not always associated with less poverty, but neither is the reverse true – there is no inevitable 'trade-off' between work and poverty, as some have claimed. This is clearly demonstrated by the Nordic countries, which manage to combine employment rates that are among the highest in the OECD area with poverty rates that are among the lowest.

Figure 5.1   Employment rates and poverty

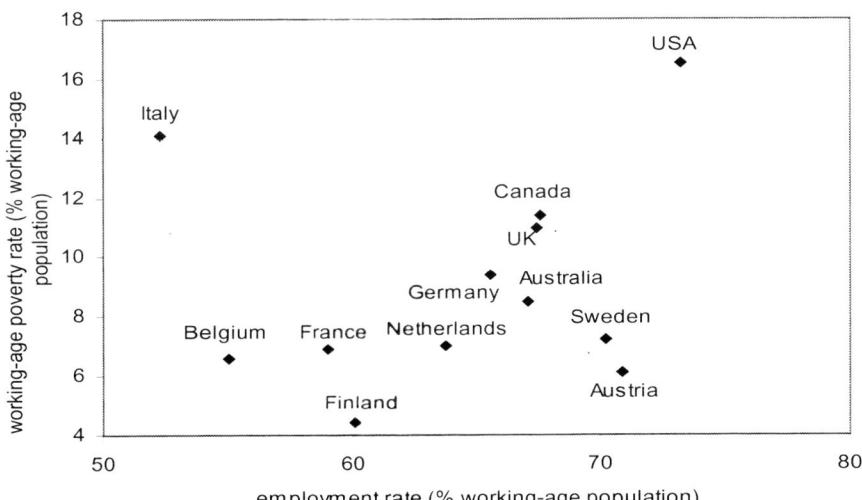

Sources: Employment rates: OECD (1998) Employment Outlook; poverty rates: Förster (2000); data for mid-1990s.

A snapshot of what we present here may well obscure higher degrees of economic mobility in high-poverty countries like the United States, Canada or the United Kingdom. Longitudinal research has revealed that there is extensive movement into and out of relative poverty but that those who escape poverty do not generally make large gains. But more importantly, studies (Duncan et al. 1995; OECD 2001) suggest that a rapid escape (after one year) is in fact more likely in countries with low poverty rates (like the Netherlands and Sweden) than in countries with high poverty rates (like Canada and the US). In other words, there appears to exist a marked *inverse* relationship between the incidence of poverty and escape rates. To some extent, this is due to the fact that the poverty threshold typically cuts higher up the income distribution ladder in high poverty countries. Hence, the higher the income increase required to escape poverty. A different approach, which examines escape from the bottom decile reveals essentially similar patterns of economic mobility across countries. It appears, at any rate, that high poverty countries do not enjoy significantly higher levels of economic mobility.

More relevant in the present context is the inter-temporal comparison. While we cannot assume that factors affecting poverty other than employment growth have remained unchanged, the picture we get if we set employment changes against poverty changes is rather more pertinent. The resulting graph is striking. Countries that have done well in terms of employment growth have not necessarily done well in terms of poverty – in fact, the reverse is the case. Figure 2 shows that the top 5 performers in terms of employment growth during the mid-1980s to mid-1990s period have actually seen rises in their relative poverty rates. Most striking is the example of the Netherlands where a dramatic rise in employment

Figure 5.2 Changes in employment and poverty rates, mid-1980s-mid-1990s (percentage points difference)

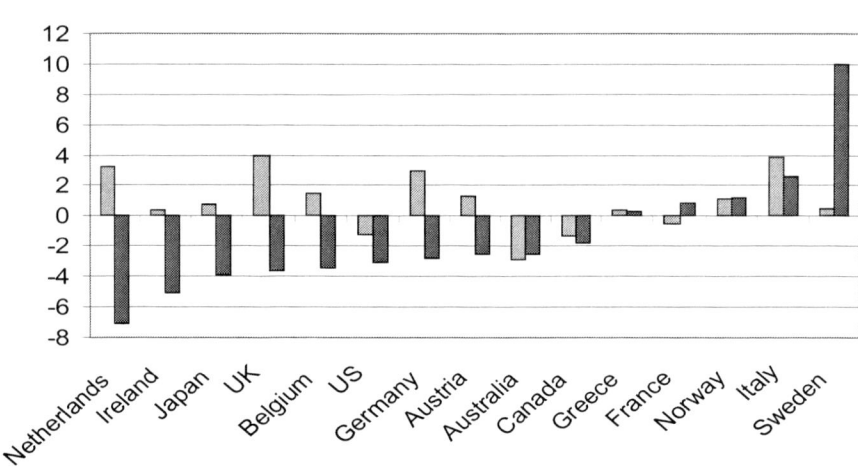

Notes: Relative poverty rates for working-age individuals.

Source: Poverty rates: Förster (2000); employment rates: OECD Employment Outlook (1998).

has gone accompanied with a substantial rise in relative poverty (see below). In only a few countries has employment growth been accompanied with reduced relative poverty, most notably in the US and Canada but in neither case has the drop been very impressive.

The household context is essential when analysing links between employment and poverty. Thus, in order to be useful further analysis needs to pursued at the household level. What we need to understand is how employment growth and policies aimed at boosting employment growth affect the labour market status not of individuals but of households.

4 Workless Households

Poverty exposure of work-less households

For arriving at an insight into the incidence and structure of poverty as it relates to employment at the household level we resort again to LIS data. Because poverty is measured on an annual income basis, employment status also has to be defined on that basis. 'Non-employed', consequently, are those individuals with zero annual labour earnings in the reference year, with consistency checks on the available labour force status variables. 'Employed' are said to be those with non-zero annual labour earnings. Jobless households, consequently, are households with no adults working during the focus period. The self-employed are excluded from the analysis. In addition, I add figures from an OECD study (Burniaux et al. 1998) for validation and comparison.

As tables 5.1 and 5.3 demonstrate, relative poverty rates for workless households are high in most OECD countries (in the 25 to 40 per cent range) and extraordinarily high in some countries (more than 50 per cent). Even in countries where poverty among workless households is comparatively low, the rates are around 15 per cent. The two tables, drawn from different data sources, provide a similar picture for most countries included in both series, be it that for some countries the estimates differ substantially, most notably for Australia and the United Kingdom. The reason may be that for table 5.1 a rather stricter definition of joblessness is used: all the adults in the household are required to have zero earnings during the reference period.

It is noteworthy, however that although poverty rates for workless households are extremely high, poverty is in most countries not principally concentrated among workless households; in most countries they make up less than half of the poor population of working age (tables 5.2 and 5.4).

Nevertheless, given the levels of poverty exposure of workless households, it seems imperative that they be the first to benefit from job growth.

Table 5.1 Poverty rates for various household types, working-age population, early 1990s (LIS data)

	All	Single-adult household		Two adult-household		
		In work	Not in work	Double earner	Single earner	No earner
Australia	14.5	10.1	65.6	1.1	9.0	47.5
Belgium	5.0	1.3	16.1	0.1	2.4	18.0
Canada	15.4	16.2	63.7	3.1	13.0	46.5
Denmark	6.1	8.6	20.1	0.4	2.0	7.9
Finland	7.5	12.1	30.3	1.0	1.8	8.9
France	8.4	3.8	32.5	0.2	7.8	25.6
Germany	10.4	10.5	44.2	1.5	7.0	32.4
Italy	13.3	3.2	27.1	1.2	16.3	23.5
Netherlands	8.3	12.1	27.8	0.7	3.5	17.1
Norway	7.5	10.0	28.3	0.1	4.6	11.2
Spain	12.5	8.8	28.7	4.0	10.7	27.3
Sweden	9.5	13.5	32.4	0.4	3.0	13.6
United Kingdom	17.5	7.0	57.7	1.0	12.7	52.3
United States	20.2	19.3	72.8	7.8	23.6	48.9

Source: LIS.

Table 5.2 The distribution of poor households with a working-age head across various household types, early 1990s (LIS data)

	All	Single-adult household		Two-adult household		
		In work	Not in work	Double earner	Single earner	No earner
Australia	100	17.2	47.1	3.0	11.9	20.8
Belgium	100	4.1	28.1	0.8	12.4	54.6
Canada	100	34.3	36.9	8.3	11.9	8.6
Denmark	100	53.4	37.8	2.6	3.0	3.2
Finland	100	58.8	30.0	6.1	2.1	3.0
France	100	8.8	43.6	1.0	24.6	21.9
Germany	100	27.2	38.2	5.1	16.2	13.3
Italy	100	1.5	8.8	2.4	56.1	31.2
Netherlands	100	29.0	40.9	2.6	12.3	15.2
Norway	100	60.6	31.8	0.7	5.4	1.5
Spain	100	6.9	16.4	5.7	46.1	25.0
Sweden	100	68.9	26.5	1.4	1.5	1.7
United Kingdom	100	7.8	49.2	2.1	13.6	27.2
United States	100	31.9	28.3	15.7	17.7	6.5

Source: LIS.

Table 5.3 Poverty rates by work attachment, working-age population (OECD data)

	No worker	One worker	Two workers
Australia	28.6	7.9	3.8
– change 1984-1994	-25.9	0.6	-0.5
Austria	19.8	8.8	0.7
– change 1983-1993	-5.8	5.9	-0.3
Belgium	18.0	7.9	0.6
– change 1983-1995	..	..	..
Canada	61.4	17.3	3.7
– change 1985-1995	-9.0	-0.7	-0.7
Denmark	16.0	8.6	0.6
– change 1983-1994	-12.8	-0.7	-0.4
Finland	21.0	8.4	1.7
– change 1986-1995	5.6	-2.6	-0.1
France	25.9	7.5	2.0
– change 1984-1994	2.2	2.0	-1.6
Germany	44.4	8.1	0.7
– change 1984-1994	14.8	4.2	-1.0
Greece	20.8	14.1	4.4
– change 1988-1994	-2.2	0.6	1.4
Italy	42.9	17.1	4.5
– change 1984-1993	3.6	4.1	2.8
Netherlands	27.0	7.6	1.0
– change 1984-1995	14.7	4.2	0.3
Norway	38.3	4.4	0.1
– change 1986-1995	-5.9	1.2	0.1
Sweden	25.8	12.7	0.8
– change 1983-1995	-22.9	0.7	-0.1
United Kingdom	36.9	15.2	2.6
– change 1985-1995	4.4	9.0	1.5
United States	74.5	26.9	6.0
– change 1985-1995	0.7	1.2	-1.6
Average, mid-1990s	35.7	13.0	3.4
– change mid-1980s-mid-90s	0.1	1.4	-0.3

Notes: Poverty rate: percentage of persons living in households with incomes below 50 per cent of median equivalent income; equivalence scale elasticity = 0.5
Two workers means two or more workers. Averages are not weighted and exclude Belgium and Finland.

Source: Burniaux et al. (1998).

Table 5.4 Poverty shares by work attachment, working-age population (OECD data)

	No worker	One worker	Two workers
Australia	46.2	28.9	24.9
– change 1984-1994	-10.9	5.3	5.6
Austria	38.2	56.0	5.7
– change 1983-1993	-22.1	25.7	-3.6
Belgium	35.7	60.8	3.5
– change 1983-1995	..	..	..
Canada	40.4	39.7	19.8
– change 1985-1995	6.9	-3.9	-3.0
Denmark	32.6	56.5	10.9
– change 1983-1994	-0.5	5.5	-5.0
Finland	32.9	39.8	27.2
– change 1986-1995	22.5	-18.8	-3.7
France	44.1	41.6	14.4
– change 1984-1994	5.7	6.1	-11.7
Germany	54.7	42.3	3.0
– change 1984-1994	0.9	9.3	-10.2
Greece	18.8	63.8	17.3
– change 1988-1994	-4.1	-3.9	8.0
Italy	30.5	55.1	14.4
– change 1984-1993	8.2	-14.3	6.2
Netherlands	54.4	38.5	7.1
– change 1984-1995	9.5	-9.0	-0.5
Norway	72.9	26.0	1.2
– change 1986-1995	2.9	-3.2	0.3
Sweden	28.8	64.8	6.4
– change 1983-1995	-2.4	3.4	-1.0
United Kingdom	44.9	41.8	13.3
– change 1985-1995	-16.3	11.9	4.4
United States	27.9	49.1	23.0
– change 1985-1995	-0.3	3.8	-3.5
Average, mid 1990s	38.2	46.1	15.7
– change mid 1980s-mid 90s	2.3	-0.2	-2.1

Notes: Poverty rate: percentage of persons living in households with incomes below 50 per cent of median equivalent income; equivalence scale elasticity = 0.5.
Two workers refers to two or more workers. Averages are not weighted and exclude Belgium and Finland.

Source: Burniaux et al. (1998).

The profile of jobless households

Although there is a positive correlation between non-employment rates for individuals and households, the relationship tends to be weak (OECD 1998b). A country's employment rate generally tells us little about a country's household joblessness rate. Countries with a low individual non-employment rate, or unemployment rate for that matter, do not always have a low proportion of households with no work. The UK is a striking example.

It is also true the other way around. For example, Italy and Spain have non-employment rates that are among the highest in the OECD area, but their household jobless rate is about the same as that of Germany or the Netherlands, and lower than in the UK. Household joblessness is significant all across the OECD area: in 1996 it varied from about 13 per cent to 22 per cent, with an average of around 18 per cent for the OECD area as a whole.

Table 5.5 shows the distribution of non-employed households by household type and the presence of children in the OECD as a whole. There is some cross-country variation but the OECD average distribution contained in table 5 is roughly representative for the distribution in most individual countries. About a third of jobless households are single-adult households. Single-parent households, a much-discussed category, constitute less than 8 per cent of the total jobless household population. This is because they make up only a small share of the total working age population. But their *risk* of non-employment (table 5.6) is quite high, on average 40 per cent in the OECD as a whole. Two-adult households with no children make up another one-third of the jobless household population. In part this is because two-adult households constitute a large share of the population as a whole. But an equally important factor is their relatively high risk of joblessness (around 26 per cent). Two-adult households with children and three-adult households constitute the final 20 per cent of the jobless household population. This is largely because of their dominance in the working age population as a whole; their risk of joblessness is relatively low.

Table 5.5   Non-employed working-age households by type (distribution in 1996, and percentage point changes between 1985-1996), OECD

	Single-adult, without children	Single-adult, with children	Two-adult, without children	Two-adult with children	Three or more adults without children	Three or more adults with children	All working age household
Levels	34.8	7.7	35.3	8.0	11.2	3.0	100.0
Changes	3.7	1.4	-3.2	-1.8	0.6	-0.6	-

Source: OECD (1998).

Table 5.6   Risk of non-employment of working-age households by type (as a percentage of households in each type in 1996, and percentage point changes between 1985-1996), OECD

	Single-adult, without children	Single-adult, with children	Two-adult, without children	Two-adult with children	Three or more adults without children	Three or more adults with children	All working age household
Levels	34.4	39.7	26.4	6.0	9.1	5.5	18.2
Changes	-1.8	-2.0	-1.1	-0.1	0.8	0.6	1.3

Source: OECD (1998).

Esping-Andersen (2002) points out that workless households are a diverse category. There is a hard core that exhibits signs of chronic exclusion. There also appears to be a 'softer element' that is more temporarily detached from the labour market. In an attempt to profile workless households in Europe (EU) Esping-Andersen (2002) finds that the following attributes are over-represented. (The author is not explicit about this, but I gather the attributes are individual-level characteristics of adults living in jobless households.) Approximately 45 per cent have less than a secondary education; 55 per cent are single, never-married people; 49 per cent are never-employed women; 50 per cent are unemployed men; 33 per cent are single adults with chronic disabilities or ill health; 65 per cent are those not looking for work. It is not clear how and to what extent these characteristics overlap.

The concentration of non-employment within the same households may be due to many factors. A correlation between the employment statuses of household members may reflect a tendency for individuals who share common characteristics to live together. Household members are usually looking for work in the same local labour market and a depressed labour market will have a common impact on them. In addition, household members often have similar levels of education attainment. Since people with fewer educational qualifications typically experience higher unemployment and non-employment rates, households with members who all have a low level of educational attainment are likely to be over-represented among work-less households.

The disincentive effects of tax and benefit systems probably also account for the polarisation between work-rich and work-less households. To get out of the dependency trap, both partners must sometimes find a job simultaneously, which may be particularly hard if they both have low educational levels. This problem is more severe in countries with extensive means-testing of welfare benefits based on family income.

Household formation, and hence the extent and composition of household joblessness, may also be affected by the generosity of public support. In southern Europe, for example, where youth unemployment rates are extremely high and benefits for jobless school leavers non-existent or inadequate, youngsters tend to stay at home for as long as they are not able to be economically self-sufficient. They rely on the household or the family for social protection. More generally, the low household jobless rates in some countries with high individual jobless rates (like Italy or Spain) are likely to be at least in part a reflection of the inadequacy of public support provisions.

Employment growth and its limited impact on work-less households

The apparent crux of the problem is that employment growth, where it did occur, did not result in marked drops in household joblessness. Job growth generally produced more double or multi-earner households rather than fewer no-earner households.

Paul Gregg and Jonathan Wadsworth (1996a) attracted a lot of attention with their finding that the much touted rise in UK employment rates during the 1980s and 1990s masked a polarisation between work-rich and workless households. The proportion of working-age individuals with work had risen in the UK, but so had the proportion of households with no one working. Job growth had mainly benefited households with one person already working.

Data for OECD countries for the period 1985-1996 shows something similar (OECD 1998b). While the proportion of non-employed working-age individuals declined in general, the proportion of jobless households increased in all but a few countries. Only in Ireland, the Netherlands and the United States – three of the most discussed 'employment miracles' of that period – was the rise in employment at the individual level been strong enough to lead to *some* reduction of in the incidence of non-employment at the household level (figure 5.3).

The point that employment growth does not tend to benefit workless households first and foremost is also apparent if we look again at the evolution of poverty rates and poverty shares (tables 5.1 through 5.4). In the striking case of the Netherlands, the poverty rate for no-earner households soared by almost 15 percentage points in the 1984-1995 period – a period of tremendous employment growth (see below). In the UK too, the poverty rate for no earner households increased, be it only marginally. Generally, employment growth failed to significantly reduce poverty among jobless households.

Figure 5.3   Changes in non-employment rates at the individual and the household level, mid-1980s-mid-1990s (percentage points difference)

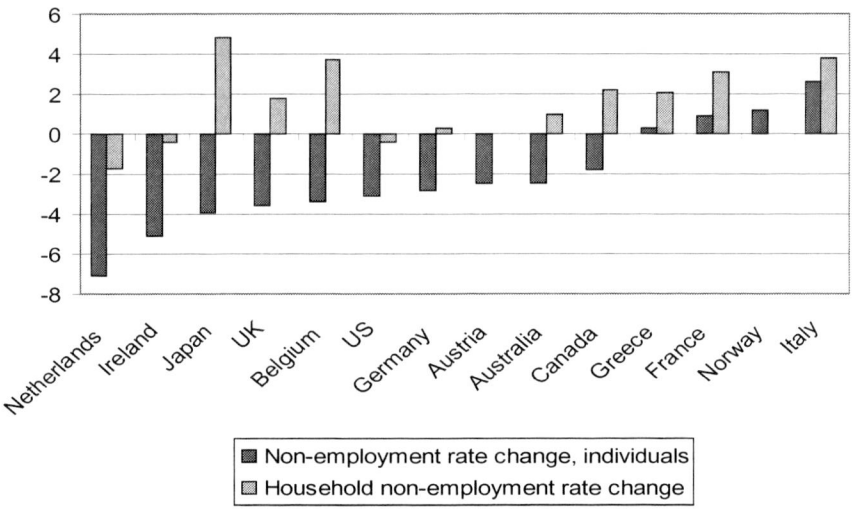

Source: OECD (1998), Employment Outlook.

180   HOW RESPONSIVE ARE POVERTY RATES TO JOB GROWTH?

Why is joblessness at the household level so persistent?

The OECD (1998b) decomposed the changes in the aggregate household non-employment rates into changes in the mix of household types and changes in non-employment rates within each. Their results show that over the period 1985-1996, increases in joblessness at the household level were largely due to a shift towards household types with a relatively high incidence of joblessness, i.e., single-adult households (OECD 1998b). But it is also the case that the risk of household joblessness has generally fallen less than the risk of individual joblessness. In the Netherlands, for example, the individual non-employment rate declined steeply between the mid-1980s and the mid-1990s. The household jobless rate fell only modestly, by comparison, as did the jobless rates for all household types, except single parents.

Workless households are a heterogeneous lot and so there is unlikely to be a single explanation why the joblessness at the household level is so persistent.

A substantial proportion of workless households are made up of one or two adults of a relatively advanced age (over 55) who have effectively retired from the labour market. (In Continental European countries, the typical situation is of a male partner who has retired early and who has a wife who has never or only briefly participated in the labour market.) These people are unlikely, and in some cases even unable, to return to the labour market, even if labour market conditions are excellent. One can even imagine that these people find it easier to obtain early retirement when economic conditions are good and public budgets are not under pressure.

A completely different sub-segment within the jobless household population is single parents. It is well documented that they often face formidable barriers on the labour market, both financially and practically (De Lathouwer and Marx 2004). A move from benefit dependency to work is often associated with immediate income loss, especially if the extra costs (child care, travel) associated with work are taken into account (OECD 1999a; Carone et al. 2004).

But for other sub-segments the explanations are less obvious. The levels and persistence of household joblessness among single adult households is for most countries less easily explained by the potential work disincentive effects of benefits. One potential reason, as Gregg and Wadsworth (2001) have illustrated for the UK, is the regional concentration of employment, or even the area concentration of employment. There clearly remains an important research agenda here.

> Would it necessarily make a difference if household joblessness was more responsive to employment growth?

It is quite likely that what workless households in poverty usually need is not just a job, but a job that pays significantly more than their benefits. From an anti-poverty perspective, the issue is not just 'making work pay' (i.e., tempting people to move out of dependency), but to make work pay enough to make sure that a move from dependency to work also implies a move from poverty to subsistence security. The living standard of working age households is often so far below the poverty threshold (especially in the case of single parents and households with children) that it is quite possible that a job that pays the minimum wage, or even more, would not be enough to lift them out of poverty.

Table 5.7 serves to succinctly illustrate this point for Belgium, a country that happens to have one of the highest minimum wages in the EU (in PPP terms and relative to average wage terms). As the table shows, a single minimum wage job would not have sufficed in every case to lift a nonworking household from poverty (especially if measured by the 60 per cent threshold favoured by the EU).

Again, this is an issue that requires more in-depth analysis. What we really need to gauge the potential poverty reduction effects of job growth is further analysis of the distribution of poverty gaps across various household types, and this combined with an analysis of the potential positive income effects of imputed or simulated wages, also taking into account the effects of taxation and work-related benefits. This, however, is beyond the scope of the present chapter.

Table 5.7 A job is not necessarily enough to escape poverty: illustrative table for Belgium, 1997, in Belgian francs

	Gross minimum wage	Net minimum wage	50 per cent poverty threshold	60 per cent poverty threshold
1 adult, no children	44,185	33,518	23,700	28,320
1 adult, 2 children	44,185	38,128	37,800	45,360
2 adults, no children	44,185	37,816	35,400	42,480
2 adults, 2 children	44,185	40,867	49,600	59,400

Source: Poverty thresholds derived from SEP.

5 Households with Work

Poverty in work is ubiquitous, but its structures differ

'Poverty in work' – poverty among households with at least one earner – is, contrary to widespread perception, by no means a uniquely American problem, or even a problem restricted to countries with a high incidence of low pay. As tables 5.2 and 5.4 demonstrate, single-earner households make up a substantial share of poor households in all OECD/EU countries. My estimates and the OECD estimates differ considerably for a number of countries, presumably in part because of differences in methodology. Also, my figures are at the household level, while the OECD figures are at the individual level; consequently, in the OECD tables, poverty in double or more adult households has greater 'weight'. However, there can be little doubt that households with at least one worker make up a large share of the poor working-age population in most European countries. There are, however, important cross-country differences in the structure of poverty at work.

In the Scandinavian countries, working-age poverty, comparatively low as it is, is to a surprisingly large extent concentrated among households with at least one worker. My figures suggest that the vast majority of these single-earner households are single adults. This is probably related to the fact that young adults in the Nordic countries gain economic independence at a relatively early age. They are at least expected to do so. Indeed, persons over the age of 18 are effectively assumed to be economically independent in the Swedish LIS survey, that is: they are counted as if they are in separate households. This also explains why poverty is generally found to be so heavily concentrated among young households in Sweden and, to a lesser extent, in other Nordic countries (see Cantillon, Marx and Van den Bosch 1996; Förster 2000).

In Southern European countries, where poverty rates are comparatively high, poverty at working age is also to a very large extent concentrated among single-earner households. But unlike Scandinavia, couples with only one working partner are more likely to be poor. In effect, working-age poverty, and it is a considerable phenomenon in Southern Europe, is overwhelmingly concentrated among traditional breadwinner-type households. This is also the case in other Continental European countries but the picture there is less clear-cut. In Continental Europe, working-age poverty is rather evenly spread across households with and without a worker, and across single-adult households and couples. But poverty among traditional breadwinner-type households is an important phenomenon nevertheless.

Single earnership and the female employment deficit in Europe

What all this shows is that what increasingly matters in advanced economies is the *combined* labour market position of household members. Single earnership has to some extent become a poverty risk in an era in which the average living standard, and hence the relative poverty threshold, is increasingly determined by the living standard of double earner households. Two working adults is the best protection against poverty that a household can have nowadays. The US is just about the only advanced economy where a significant proportion of double-earner couples live in poverty (table 5.1), and where they make up a really substantial proportion of working-age households in poverty (table 5.2). But in most countries, it does not matter much whether one or both partners in a two-adult household have a low wage or a part-time job.

It appears that many European households would do better with a second household income. This is certainly the case in the South, where female participation rates remain low. In Italy and Spain, well over one in two working-age couples still live on a single breadwinner wage. Female participation rates are higher in most other Continental European countries but remain far from capacity.

It has been suggested that unemployment rates, and, more broadly, non-employment rates for less-educated women are bound to remain high unless more flexible, relatively low-paid jobs are 'allowed' to emerge in the domestic services sector. Such jobs could then provide many single-earner households with the additional income they need to escape poverty. The idea here is that Continental European welfare states retain too strong a breadwinner bias. This, as Esping-Andersen (1996, 1999, 2002) has repeatedly argued, is to the detriment of the employment chances and hence (relative) living standards of less-skilled women. They, unlike their better-skilled counterparts, are negatively affected by the preservation of high minimum wages, job protection rules, etc. The high cost of mass benefit dependency has, moreover, led to excessively high costs for labour, hampering low-skilled job creation in the service sector.

The alleged result is that in modern-day societies the traditional breadwinner-bias in labour market institutions and social security arrangements perversely favours the highly skilled and is a disadvantage for the less-skilled, particularly less-skilled women. It is quite evident that unemployment and especially non-employment rates are particularly high for women with lower levels of education. Non-employment rates for women with tertiary education are around 25 per cent in Belgium, France, Germany, Italy and the Netherlands. By contrast, non-employment rates for women with less than upper-secondary educations tend to be far higher: around 55 per cent for France, 60 per cent for Germany, 65 per cent for the Netherlands and around 70 per cent for Italy (OECD 2002).

Double earnership is clearly more widespread in the Anglo-Saxon countries than it is in Continental Europe, perhaps in some measure because less-educated women find it easier there to acquire a job in the more flexible Anglo-Saxon labour markets, where low-paid jobs are more plentiful. At the same time, however, as wages are more dispersed in the Anglo-Saxon countries poverty rates for single-earner households, especially single-earner couples, tend to higher than in the Continental European countries, where low wage work is less prevalent, particularly among men of prime age. And as has been argued above, a high degree of wage dispersion (or a high incidence of low pay) is neither systematically nor proportionally related with higher employment rates for the less-skilled. It is striking that nonemployment rates for less-skilled women remain quite high in countries like the US and the UK, despite there being more low-paid jobs available.

Why more wage flexibility might give a boost to multi-earnership but lead to increased poverty

While more wage flexibility (e.g., lower minimum effective wages) could help boost multi-earnership and reduce single-earner poverty, the larger effect might well be increased poverty among households that would see their earnings deteriorate but fail to acquire a second household income either because there is no second adult or because the second adult fails to obtain a job even in a labour market where more (low-paid) jobs are available. In short, the potential poverty enhancing effects of more wage dispersion (more poverty among low earnings households) may well outweigh the poverty reduction effects (more multi-earner households).

There is one particularly interesting case in this context. The UK is one of the few OECD countries where earnings inequality has surged over the past two decades and where (relatively) low-paid work has become more prevalent. It is well documented that the United Kingdom saw major labour market deregulation during the 1980s and 1990s, culminating in the abolishment of the minimum wage in 1993. There is, however, considerable disagreement on the causal link between the various institutional reforms and the observed rise in inequality, which was quite significant (Gregg and Machin 1993; Machin 1996b). It is evident, for example, that much of the rise in earnings inequality predates the abolishment of the minimum wage. It is also the case that much of the vast increase in overall wage inequality is due to the exceptionally strong gains made by top earners and only to a lesser extent to widening inequalities in the low to median earnings segment.

What is important for us is that earnings inequality increased in the bottom half of the wage building and particularly that the incidence of low pay increased. This increase has gone accompanied, as we have seen, with a rise in individual employment levels but this did not lead to a decrease in the proportion of no-earner households (Gregg and Wadsworth 1996b). Relative poverty also increased in the 1985-1995 period. And what is most interesting: the strongest rise in poverty occurred among single-earner households (in fact, the rise for the UK is by far the largest of the 16 countries included in table 5.3). In addition, there was a remarkably strong poverty shift towards single-earner households. By 1995, single-earner households made up an almost equally large share of the poor working age population as no earner households. This is all the more striking since the share of single-earner households in the total working age population declined: they after all were the ones who benefited most from employment growth though not, apparently, single-earner households most in need of a job.

6 The Case of the Netherlands

Broad cross-country comparisons of employment and poverty rates tell us only so much. They provide a broad idea of how employment and poverty correlate, but they offer little insight into the mechanisms underlying the relationship. And most crucially, they reveal rather little about the role of policy. It is for this reason that we now want to focus on one particularly interesting case study, the Netherlands, a country where social policy reform has been guided by a singular preoccupation with promoting job growth.

The 'Dutch miracle', in the words of Visser and Hemerijck (1997) is often singled out as the country that has shown the way forward in employment and social policy (Kenworthy 2004), particularly by Third Way and Active Welfare State enthusiasts (Hemerijck and Visser 1999; Becker 1999, White 2001), but also by organisations like the OECD. They praise the Netherlands for achieving a meteoric rise in employment while maintaining a big welfare state, extensive social protection and low levels of poverty and inequality.

The transformation of the Dutch welfare state has been remarkable but the received wisdom in much of the international literature is generally rather too generous, specifically with respect to the poverty outcomes. Massive employment growth has in fact gone accompanied with a comparatively modest reduction in absolute poverty and comparatively strong rise in relative poverty among the working-age population.

The employment 'miracle'

Some 15 years ago, the Netherlands was widely known as, in the words of Therborn, one of 'the most spectacular employment failures in the advanced capitalist world' (cited in Visser and Hemerijck 1997). In the mid-1980s, the OECD broad unemployment rate, which includes the registered unemployed, beneficiaries of disability benefits, people on early retirement or social assistance, workers in state-sponsored training schemes and public labour pool, had soared to 27 per cent of the labour force.

In the period since, the Netherlands has succeeded in bringing down its unemployment rate from almost 14 per cent in the mid-1980s to an extraordinarily low level of just over 2 per cent in 2000. Employment growth has been massive: the employment rate has risen from well under 60 per cent in the mid-1980s to well over 70 per cent currently. The male employment rate has risen by some 5 percentage points, while in the EU as a whole it has declined. The female employment rate has risen by more than 15 percentage points in less than two decades, be it from a comparatively low level of around 40 per cent. In terms of annual job growth over the past two decades, the Netherlands leaves virtually every other European country well behind. It is the only European country that rivals the US 'jobs machine'.

The figures on the employment front are impressive. Critics are right however when they point out that the Netherlands had a lot of catching up to do. The female employment rate in particular was comparatively low up until the mid-1980s, particularly for a Northern European country. Even now the female employment rate is not particularly high compared to say Germany or Belgium. Critics also point out that many of the new jobs are part-time jobs. But one can easily argue that this makes the Netherlands even more remarkable. The Netherlands is today a country where paid work, care and leisure are far more evenly spread across the working-age population than two decades ago (Visser 2002). More men work part-time in the Netherlands than anywhere else – something that governments everywhere try to promote in vain.

A more valid point is that exceptionally strong job creation has not had the expected impact on re-employment of long-term benefit recipients. It is certainly true that the Netherlands has achieved a steeper decline in its I/A ratio than any of its neighbours in Europe. This ratio, which figures prominently in Dutch public debate and in the literature, relates the number on benefits (expressed in full-time equivalents) to the number or people working (again, in full-time equivalents) The evolution of the I/A ratio is shown in table 1.1. But the I/A ratio has declined because first and foremost the number of people working has increased dramatically, boosting the denominator, not because the number of people on benefits has substantially declined. On the contrary, benefit dependency continued to rise even until the mid-1990s. In the period 1985-1995, the employment rate increased by 5.5 percentage points, a steeper increase than almost anywhere in Europe. But the dependency rate increased in the same period by 2 percentage points (de Beer 2001). It must be added, however, that the further increase in benefit dependency was in major part due to further extensions in social security entitlement rights, for example the introduction of the Law on Social Assistance in 1985. The rise does mask some degree of success in curbing fresh inflows into certain benefit programmes, for example the famed Dutch disability scheme.

But what is particularly interesting and relevant is the fact that massive job growth resulted only to a very limited extent in people moving out of benefit dependency, particularly long-term benefit dependency. In the period 1985-1995 more than a million new jobs were created, theoretically enough to annihilate benefit dependency to 1960s levels. In fact, virtually all of these new jobs were taken by newcomers on the labour market, recent school graduates and women (re-)entering the labour market.

Policies

The drastic policy shift towards job creation was prompted by the dire state of the Dutch economy was in the early 1980s (Visser and Hemerijck 1997; Becker 1999; de Beer et al. 2002). Economic growth at the time was virtually zero, benefit dependency rampant and fiscal deficits were rising fast. It could almost be described as a panic reaction to steer clear of what looked at the time like an impending economic disaster. It was only later that the active welfare state doctrine developed. It was not until the late 1980s, when the sense of urgency regarding the economy was fading, that the Dutch government started to tout the social policy virtues of its obsession with job creation. A report published in 1990 by the Netherlands Scientific Council for Government Policy, an influential advisory board, laid down the doctrine. It advocated a policy of maximising the rate of labour market participation as the single most important policy goal of any sustainable welfare state. Dutch ministers started to proclaim that 'a job is the best social policy'. The strategy had two major components.

First, the macro-economic component: sustained general wage moderation. Wage moderation started with the so-called Wassenaar accord in late 1982, a now-historical agreement between trade unions and employers which marked a turning point in industrial relations. There is widespread agreement in the Netherlands that sustained wage moderation has been by far the single most important contributing factor in Holland's extraordinary employment performance (Kleinknecht and Naastepad 2001; OECD 2002). According to Visser and Hemerijck (1997), the Central Planning Bureau estimated that for the second half of the 1980s, a period during which employment growth was particularly strong, two-thirds of job growth could be attributed to wage moderation and one-third to the expansion of the world economy. Wage moderation was by and large maintained throughout the 1990s.

Secondly, from the mid-1980s on, minimum wage and benefit policies became far more strongly geared towards stimulating labour participation and job creation. Minimum wages and benefits were 'allowed' to erode in relative and even real value through non-adjustments for inflation. To illustrate this: the minimum wage, expressed as a percentage of the average monthly wage, fell from almost 70 per cent in the early 1980s to well below 55 per cent in the late 1990s. This quite strong decline in the value of the minimum wage is also reflective of what has happened with minimum benefits because of the legal linkage between minimum wages and minimum benefits in the Netherlands. The idea, of course, was that lower (relative) minimum wages would boost job creation for the low-skilled and that lower (relative) welfare benefits would make low-skilled, low-paid work more attractive than benefit dependency. The goal was to get people off benefits and into work.

During the 1990s, the government even started to push employers and unions to effectively use the lowest wage scales laid down in collective agreements – the perceived problem was that low-paid (prospective) workers typically received higher wages than the official minimum wage. It did so by threatening to refuse to make sector agreements generally binding unless the lowest wage scales remained near the minimum wage and were more often applied. In addition, a series of special programmes geared towards the integration or reintegration of unemployed low-skilled workers were deployed and the public employment service sector was reformed.

The poverty consequences

Income policy after the mid-1980s and especially during the 1990s became totally and explicitly geared towards labour market participation partially in the hope that an effective employment policy would also turn out to be a good anti-poverty policy. So, what has happened on the poverty front?

Poverty in the Netherlands is conventionally measured using a constant poverty line. This poverty line equals the living standard of a single person household on social welfare benefits in 1979, the year in which welfare benefits reached their highest level in real terms. The poverty thresholds for other households are obtained with an equivalence scale devised by the Dutch Statistical Office.

A study by De Beer (2001) shows that absolute poverty in 1997 increased slightly from 13 per cent in 1977 to 15 per cent in 1997. However, this trend was not linear. Absolute poverty increased quite strongly in the period 1981 to 1985 (to around 22 per cent), and dropped again thereafter, until the early 1990s when the decline stalled. The period from the early 1990s to 1997 was essentially a period of stable absolute poverty.

Of particular interest to us is the period 1985 to 1997, when Dutch employment soared. Absolute poverty in this period dropped about 6 percentage points, following a rise of similar magnitude during the early 1980s. De Beer shows that employment growth was a marginal factor in this decline. The reason, he argues, is that employment growth did not result in a rise in the number of households with at least one labour market income. The proportion of single-earner households dropped dramatically in this period, but the proportion of jobless households declined only marginally.

It is illustrative in this context to compare it to Belgium, a country that experienced far weaker aggregate employment growth, but where minimum wages and minimum benefits also eroded less than in the Netherlands (Cantillon et al. 2004). In order to make a more or less standardised comparison with De Beer's figures I set the initial poverty threshold (i.e., the threshold for 1985) for Belgium at the level which produces an overall poverty rate equal to that of the Netherlands at the time. In this way, the poverty threshold is cut off at a similar point in the income distribution. This is important if we want to make a 'fair' comparison because the effort required to achieve a certain percentage point reduction in the poverty headcount rate depends on the initial poverty level. After all, large numbers are found in the middle of the income distribution than in the tails. A country with a high initial level of poverty will find it much easier to achieve a say 5 percentage point reduction in the headcount rate than a country with a low initial level (see also De Lathouwer and Marx 2002).

Table 5.8 shows that Belgium achieved a larger reduction in absolute poverty than the Netherlands despite the fact that the share of non-active households increased in Belgium, while declining in the Netherlands. Most striking is the markedly stronger decline in poverty among households with a non-employed head in Belgium, a finding that appears reflective of differential real minimum wage and real benefit trends (table 5.9).

Table 5.8 Absolute poverty incidence: standardised comparison between Belgium and the Netherlands, 1985-1997. Percentage point difference (initial levels for 1985)

	Belgium	Netherlands
Poverty incidence		
– total population	-8.4% (21.6)	-6.2% (21.6)
– active households	-6.6% (8.6)	-4.6% (11.1)
– non-active household	-12.9% (39.1)	-7.3% (36.4)
– head below age 65	-4.0% (36.0)	-0% (42)
– head over age 65	-18.6% (40.7)	-11% (31.4)
Share		
– active households	-3.1% (56.7)	+2.2% (58.5)
– non-active household	+3.1% (43.3)	-2.2% (41.5)
– head below age 65	+0.3% (18.3)	-3.5% (20.2)
– head over age 65	+2.8% (25.0)	+1.3% (21.3)

Source: Own calculations for Belgium on SEP, Dutch figures from de Beer (2001).

Table 5.9 Key trends in Belgium and the Netherlands (1985 = 100)

	Belgium	Netherlands
Employment rate	+ 7%	+ 18%
Real gross minimum wage level	+ 2%	- 10%
Real social assistance level for working-age couple	+ 11%	+ 3%

Source: Employment rate: OECD, Employment Outlook; real minimum wage and real social assistance: Cantillon et al. (2004).

Household joblessness has, as we have seen, remained high in the Netherlands and so has working-age benefit dependency. These households, which rely entirely on benefits, have suffered the consequences of the nominal freeze policy pursued by successive Dutch governments over the past two decades. The real value of social assistance benefits declined by 15 per cent in the period 1977 to 1997, with the decline being particularly strong in the first part of this period, a high inflation period. Hence, households on benefits experienced a strong decline of their living standards until roughly the mid-1980s. After that, they were confronted with virtually stagnant living standards.

One would suspect that the position of non-active households relative to the general standard of living would have deteriorated substantially. Unfortunately, time series analyses on relative poverty are seldom presented in Dutch publications, which tend to stick to the rather idiosyncratic official absolute poverty measure. Figures published by the OECD, however do confirm the suspicion that relative poverty in the Netherlands increased quite substantially in the period under investigation (figure 5.2). According to the OECD figures, the incidence of relative poverty, which stood at a comparatively low 6.3 per cent in the mid-1970s, rose by 0.6 percentage points between the mid-1970s and the mid-1980s, and by 3.2 percentage points between the mid-1980s and mid-1990s. The recorded rise after the mid-1980s was quite significant; among OECD countries as a whole relative poverty rose by an average of only 0.3 percentage points (Burniaux et al. 1998; Förster 2001).

Even more telling is the evolution of the poverty rates split up by the labour market status of the household (table 5.3). According to the same OECD source, households with a working age head but with not a single adult in work faced in 1995 a poverty risk of 27 per cent. Ten years earlier, their relative poverty risk was around 12 per cent. Working age households with a single-earner, too, have become more exposed to poverty: their poverty risk doubled to 8 per cent in the 1984-1995 period. Double-earner households are almost never poor (1 per cent was in 1995) and their poverty risk has remained constant.

Why employment growth resulted not in less relative poverty, but more

Sustained aggregate wage moderation, general non-adjustments of replacement benefits and minimum wages for inflation and targeted cuts in benefits and minimum wages were the main ingredients of Dutch employment policy. As we have seen, employment rates of the most needy have increased only modestly relative to the employment rates of households that were comparatively well-off already, i.e., non-poor single-earner households. So what essentially has happened is that many of those at the bottom have felt the immediate income consequences of the wage and benefit growth restraint policies: stagnant or even declining real living standards. At the same time, aggregate employment growth did result in a huge increase in double earnership, which in turn pushed up average living standards and, consequently, relative poverty thresholds. Because those who got jobs ended up not with the people stuck at the bottom of the income distribution but primarily with those already in the middle – relative poverty increased. Households who have joined the ranks of double-income households have been the main – and in effect only – winners of the Dutch employment miracle.

The obvious question now is: why have the new jobs not gone to the households that most needed an earned income, i.e., no-earner households and poor single-earner households? The explanation is not simply that the Dutch employment miracle only produced jobs for the better-skilled. Various figures suggest that the less-skilled also benefited from job growth (De Grip and Dekker 1993; De Grip and Van Loo 2000). Notwithstanding this, the supply of less- or unskilled workers has remained far bigger than the demand. There are simply far more unemployed or non-employed people with low educational levels than there are jobs that require only basic skills.

De Beer (2001) demonstrates that, on the basis of panel data analysis, the poor, non-employed have not seen an improvement in their employment chances. Despite the vast expansion of employment in the Netherlands, the chance that a poor non-employed person will find a job remained stable throughout the late 1980s and the entire 1990s at around one in six. After correcting for business-cycle effects and controlling for a vector of personal characteristics, educational attainment emerges as the single most important determinant of employment probability (De Beer 2001: 284). The employment prospects of the less-skilled have, according to this study, even worsened quite substantially. The reason that the chances of a poor non-employed person getting a job has remained stable appears largely due to the fact that the share of the low-skilled has declined substantially.

The skill-biased nature of job growth would appear to be one of the limits of an employment-based social policy. But there are alternative and probably complementary explanations. One is that the largely simultaneous decline of benefits and minimum wages did little to alter the relative pay-off to (minimum-wage) work vs. benefit dependency, i.e., to eradicate unemployment traps. This, combined with a rise in the population share of particular segments prone to get stuck in unemployment traps provides another explanation for the persistence of household joblessness.

Concretely, the rise in the share of single-parent households, essentially a socio-demographic trend, probably also accounts for the persistence of household-level non-employment. Single-parent households, in the Netherlands as elsewhere, remain particularly prone to becoming trapped in welfare dependency. This is not only a matter of financial incentives; single adults with children often find it extremely difficult to combine their role as sole breadwinner and sole care provider, especially when their earnings potential is low and when they have to pay for child care. This is not to imply, however, that the boosting of work participation among segments like single parents would necessarily make much difference for poverty rates. Welfare entrapment and non-employment are not the fundamental reason why poverty among sole parents is high. The fundamental problem is that they are in an inherently disadvantaged economic position in the double earner dominated era, whether they are working or not. As we have seen, even jobs that pay considerably above the minimum wage can be insufficient to lift single-earner households with children above the poverty line.

In the specific case of the Netherlands, there is indeed evidence that transitions from full-time social assistance dependency did not always result in an escape from poverty. An analysis by Hoff (2003) on a sample of labour market re-entrants during the 2001-2002 suggests that about half of the full-time benefit recipients who actually made the transition to work – selective as this segment is – escaped poverty, as defined by the official Dutch poverty line. This estimate should be considered indicative since no information on household income was available in the data set that was used, only on individual income. Furthermore, the data set did not allow to gauge the length of the period during which re-entrants were able to hold on to a job. Still, the finding reinforces the point that the policy challenge goes beyond getting (poor) people jobs.

7 Conclusion

The 1990s saw the rise of doctrines that promoted work as the prime vehicle for achieving social policy objectives, particularly less poverty and social exclusion. Within the context of the EU employment and social inclusion processes, governments have proclaimed their intention of achieving progress on the employment and poverty fronts simultaneously.

The idea that increased work participation and poverty reduction are somehow natural allies sits uneasily with the facts. This chapter has presented empirical evidence pertaining to employment and poverty trends during the 1980s and 1990s for a range of OECD countries. The analysis has shown that few countries managed to achieve significant progress on both fronts simultaneously during this period. The main reason appears to be that job growth did not primarily benefit the neediest households. New jobs tended to end up with households that already had earned income. Strong job growth, where it occurred over this period, effectively reinforced the gap between work-rich and work-poor/work-less households. This was notably the case in the Netherlands, a country that experienced extraordinary job growth during the 1980s and 1990s.

The conclusion, however, is not that the policy challenge simply exists in making sure that the most disadvantaged benefit more strongly from job growth. It is not obvious that this in itself would suffice to bring about more substantial drops in poverty. For many of the poor non-employed, a job alone, even a job paying substantially above the minimum wage, would probably not suffice to lift them from poverty. Single-earner households with low earnings-capacities are inherently disadvantaged in present-day society, where the average living standard and hence the relative poverty threshold is largely determined by the double-earner household living standard. This certainly applies to low earnings-capacity households with children. But the extent of this problem remains to be charted. Micro-simulation models that allow the estimation of incomes in and out of work could help ascertain the poverty effects of targeted employment measures, combined or not with additional in-work benefits and child support benefits. Clearly, there is an important research agenda here that remains to be pursued.

6 Alternatives to Passive Income Support: The Verdict of Empirical Evaluation Studies

1 Introduction

As noted in the previous chapter, the past decade has been marked by increased efforts to re-integrate those who have slipped into passive, long-term benefit dependency back into the labour market. The approach is two-pronged: 'to make work possible' and 'to make work pay', that is to say, to stimulate labour demand and to stimulate labour supply.

This chapter looks at the empirical evaluation literature. In the first section, we look at measures aimed at boosting labour demand, specifically through employment subsidies and reductions in employers' social security contributions for the recruitment of long-term unemployed persons and other vulnerable groups in the labour market. In the second section, we focus on the effects of measures to stimulate labour supply, specifically of long-term benefit dependents. The particular focus is on benefits and tax credits for low-paid workers or households with a modest earned income.

2 Employers' subsidies

In Europe and elsewhere, employment subsidies and cuts in employers' social security contributions are being used to improve the labour market prospects of the unemployed and other vulnerable groups in the labour market. According to OECD (2003) figures, such programmes account for a significant share (on average 24 per cent of expenditures on active labour market programmes among the OECD countries. Some countries, Belgium and Ireland for example, devote half or more of their active labour market spending to such programmes; meanwhile, the UK and the US spend well under 10 per cent. An average of 0.18 per cent of GDP is spent on such programmes in the OECD as a whole, with Belgium (0.69 per cent) and Ireland (0.53 per cent) again being notable exceptions. Spending on targeted employment subsidies is also significantly above the OECD average in countries like the Netherlands (0.38 per cent), France (0.34 per cent) and Spain (0.33 per cent). At the other end of the scale, the US spends only 0.01 per cent of its GDP on employment subsidies, the UK 0.03 per cent.

Policymakers here and elsewhere in Europe often justify this strategy by referring to theoretical analyses which suggest that such measures could have strong positive effects on the employment chances of vulnerable groups – the long-term unemployed and people with low skills. Snower (1994, 1997) and Phelps (1997, 1997b), for example, are noted advocates. Snower, for example, has claimed that well-targeted employment subsidies could reduce long-term unemployment by about one-third and that the subsidy scheme would pay for itself in the longer run. Others economists (Richardson 1998) have asserted that the indirect positive effects of employment subsidies and the like could turn out to be even more considerable in the long term. The claim here is that the long-term unemployed constitute a labour reserve only in theory and that they, consequently, exert very little downward pressure on wages. Employment subsidies for the long term unemployed could result, so the argument goes, in these outsiders, or at least some of them, being incorporated into the effective labour reserve, resulting in a dampening effect on wage demands and hence a further positive effect on employment.

Policymakers, at least in countries like Belgium, France and the Netherlands, also seem to place great trust in simulations such as those conducted by Bossier et al. (1995, 1998) and others (Jongen 1998; Malinvaud 1998; Sneessens and Shadman 2000). These generally show that selective reductions in employers' social security contributions have a substantial impact on employment. However, the outcomes of such simulations are sensitive to the theoretical and parametric assumptions (see for example Hui and Trivedi 1986; Jongen 1999; Granier and Nyssen 1995; Nickell and Bell 1997). Most crucially, the demand for low-skilled labour is assumed to be fairly sensitive to its cost. Most simulation models tend to use demand elasticities for low-skilled labour that are broadly supported by the empirical literature (Hamermesh 1993), i.e., in the order of -0.4 to -0.5. However, surveys of enterprises suggest that employers tend to be very reluctant when it comes to hiring less-skilled people with specific characteristics, e.g., people who have been unemployed for a long period of time. De Beer (1996), for example, reports some employers as saying that they would be unwilling to hire long-term unemployed people at almost any cost. Moreover, it is legitimate to ask whether empirical estimations of the elasticity of demand provide an adequate instrument for simulating the response of employers to subsidies. Not all employers may be aware that such subsidies exist and there are usually administrative and other costs involved in applying (Katz 1998). It may also be the case that the temporary nature of a subsidy and the costs involved in subsequent redundancies have a dissuasive effect. Such costs may be substantial in many cases, not only the direct administrative cost, but employers may also want to avoid strained relations with trade unions and their work forces.

So it is interesting to see what we can learn from practical experience with employment subsidies and related measures like reductions in social security contributions. We bring together the findings of empirical assessment studies in relation to the following two questions:
a. What is known about the employment effects of subsidising jobs?
b. What is known about the degree of mobility from subsidised to regular employment?

The take-up of subsidies by employers

The empirical evaluation material available suggests that the response to employment subsidies and cuts in employers' social security contributions varies quite considerably (OECD 1993; Fay 1997; Katz 1998; Martin 1998). There appears to be a connection in this respect between the scope, the generosity and the duration of such initiatives. Relatively generous measures with a relative broad scope involving a substantial subsidy or reduction generally generate a greater response. Ignorance is often a reason for non-take-up, which would appear to be related to the fact that these schemes are often of an experimental, local or temporary nature. Also, employers indicate that the (perceived) bureaucratic fuss and the expenses involved often dissuade them from applying, especially in the case of schemes with restricted eligibility. Voucher schemes, whereby employees carry the right to a subsidy with them as it were, appear to be more effective if one intends to target very specific groups (Sianesi 2001).

A survey of Belgian industrial companies employing many low-skilled workers conducted in the early 1990s found that a considerable proportion of companies – often between 50 and 60 per cent – were not aware of (temporary) cuts in social security costs for the employment of certain target groups, such as youngsters or long-term unemployed persons. Small companies in particular appeared to be inadequately informed (Lamberts 1993). The percentage of companies that actually took advantage of the measures was even lower, as many companies that were aware of the existence of certain reductions deemed them to be (largely) inapplicable. Again, this was especially the case among smaller companies. Lamberts (1993) attributes the relatively limited familiarity with and applicability of measures to the complexity and variability of legislation. This might explain why small companies in particular were less likely to take advantage of a measure, despite the fact that they involved quite considerable, albeit temporary, cuts in social security payments. A similar survey conducted by Ameels et al. (1994) offers further indications that the perceived complexity and administrative cost is seen by employers as a reason not to make use of certain measures.

More recent research in the Netherlands focused on a measure known as SPAK (*Specifieke Afdrachtskorting Lage Lonen*). SPAK, introduced in 1996, encompasses a reduction in fiscal and social security payments by employers for workers whose wages do not exceed 115 per cent of the statutory minimum wage. The reduction is highest at the level of the minimum wage and cuts employers' contributions by around 60 per cent or 13 per cent of gross pay. SPAK targeted low-paid workers, including those already working. A survey conducted by Van Nes et al. (1998) suggests that 72 per cent of all eligible enterprises made use of SPAK at the time of the survey. Public services are reported to make the most extensive use of the measure, while the lowest percentages were recorded in business services, wholesale trade, the hotel and catering industry, the metal industry, the building industry, and the transportation and communication sectors. Yet, some of the latter industries are often considered to be industries with problems regarding the cost of less-skilled labour. Large companies are more inclined to make use of SPAK than smaller firms (Van Nes et al. 1998). The question arises then why enterprises do not take full advantage of the possibilities offered by SPAK. According to the survey, some 12 per cent of companies feel that the projected savings on labour costs would not compensate for the additional administrative cost. About two-thirds of the companies who would otherwise qualify for SPAK did not register because they were unaware that the scheme existed. Ignorance appears to be a factor mostly among small and medium-sized companies (Van Nes et al. 1998).

Table 6.1   Brief survey of the measures discussed

Measure	Target Group	Description
Vermeend-Moor Act (NL)	long-term unemployed	• reduced social contributions for a period of 4 years • one-off recruitment bonus
RAP (NL)	long-term unemployed	• reduced social security contributions for a period of 4 years • recruitment bonus (increases with period of unemployment)
Workstart (UK)	long-term unemployed	• temporary wage subsidy
Jobstart (Australia)	long-term and quasi long-term unemployed	• temporary wage subsidy
Employment Incentive (Ireland)	long-term unemployed	• temporary wage subsidy
Jongerenbanenplan (Belgium)	unemployed youngsters	• temporary, regressive reduction in social contributions
VLW (NL)	long-term unemployed	• reduced social security contributions for a period of 4 years
SPAK (NL)	low-paid	• permanent reduction in social contributions

Deadweight losses

Still, measures like SPAK are used to employ large numbers of workers. A similar scheme in Belgium (i.e., a small but structural reduction in social security contributions for relatively low-paid workers) applies to around 2 million workers. Even strongly targeted measures – temporary reductions or waivers generally generate a substantial response in terms of the sheer number of people who benefit.

Policymakers like to quote these kinds of figures as evidence of what they see as the strong impact of such measures on employment, ignoring the fact that there tends to be substantial deadweight losses, i.e., that many subsidised individuals would also have found employment had the employment subsidy not existed. This is clearly not just an efficiency issue; it is also a fairness issue.

Most subsidies or reductions are aimed at specific target groups that are considered to be in need of special attention, for example the long-term unemployed (usually defined as those seeking work for over 6 months or more). But even a specific segment like the long-term unemployed is surprisingly heterogeneous, comprising high as well as low-skilled persons, youngsters and older people, people with work experience and people with no work experience, etc. There is, in other words, room for companies to recruit selectively. Indeed, there is every indication that this is occurring to a very significant extent. For example, the proportion of unskilled persons in a job with a so-called KRA-subsidy (a Dutch subsidy for engaging long-term unemployed workers) amounted to barely 11 per cent, while they constituted half of the target group. Moreover, one of every six of these jobs were occupied by high-skilled workers (De Beer 1996: 256). Likewise for Belgium, there is evidence that the least-skilled are seriously underrepresented in subsidised jobs, although they constitute the prime target group (Bollens et al. 1996).

Many subsidies are of the same type as those granted under the Vermeend-Moor Act or RAP (*Reguliere Arbeidsplaatsvariant*) in the Netherlands. Both schemes offered employers a substantial 4-year reduction in social security contributions for every additional recruitment of a long-term unemployed individual. In addition, employers could claim a one-off recruitment bonus. An assessment by Koning et al. (1995) estimated the deadweight loss for RAP at just over 42 per cent (see table 3). De Koning (1993) previously arrived at a comparable estimate for the Vermeend-Moor Act. Roughly four of every ten long-term unemployed people recruited with a subsidy would have also found a job without any governmental financial incentive. This is a relatively favourable result, as most evaluation studies estimate the deadweight loss to be considerably higher.

The British Workstart scheme of the early 1990s granted a temporary but substantial subsidy to employers offering a full-time job to a person who had been out of work for at least 2 years. An evaluation of a pilot scheme arrived at a 53 per cent complete deadweight loss and a 27 per cent partial deadweight loss. The latter refers to jobs that would have been offered to the target group regardless of the subsidy, but not on a full-time basis (Atkinson and Meager 1994).

These results are more in line with findings regarding similar measures in other countries. The deadweight loss for the Employment Incentive scheme in Ireland and the Jobstart scheme in Australia was, for example, estimated to be around 70 per cent (OECD 1993, on the basis of Breen and Halpin 1989 and Department of Employment, Education and Training 1989). Van der Linden (1997) estimated the deadweight loss of a series of temporary social security reductions for the employment of youngsters, the unemployed and other weak groups that were introduced in Belgium in the early 1990s at 53 per cent.[1] (Only this overall estimate is reported, although the study covered a range of very similar but not identical measures.)

A more recent Dutch study (Van Polanen Petel et al. 1999) estimates the deadweight loss of a scheme known as *Vermindering Langdurig Werklozen* (VLW) – a reduction in employers' social security contributions of up to around 2,140 euros per year for a period of 4 years for the recruitment of long-term unemployed people – at between 27 and 60 per cent (the broad margin is due to the statistical confidence interval applied). This study also explicitly gauged employers' motivation for recruiting the long-term unemployed. Some 40 per cent of respondents indicated that they did so to evaluate whether the individual involved was able to function within the organisation. About one-third mentioned a 'social motive'.

More recently, an evaluation was made of the more general SPAK measure, which involves a permanent reduction in employers' contributions for workers earning up to 115 per cent of the statutory minimum wage. It does not exclusively target the unemployed, but low-wage earners in general, including those already employed. One would expect the deadweight loss associated with this more general measure to be quite substantial and this is indeed what Van Polanen Petel et al. (1999) find; they estimate it at 93 per cent.

Virtually all of the above evaluation studies are based on interviews with employers. It is quite conceivable that these studies underestimate the deadweight loss as a result of selection distortion and opportunistic responses. An approach whereby the direct employment effects are estimated on the basis of interviews of interested parties clearly has a number of limitations. For one thing, the response rate is generally rather low. The aforementioned assessment study of SPAK, for example, yielded

---

[1] Van der Linden evaluates the following measures: a reduction in employers' contributions for a period of 8 months for the recruitment of youngsters or long-term unemployed individuals, a digressive reduction in employers' contributions for the recruitment of youngsters after a training period, a temporary subsidy for the unemployed within the framework of certain projects, the schemes in Wallonia known as "Primes plus" and "Prime d'employ" and incentives for the recruitment of the disabled.

a response rate of roughly 10 per cent. Secondly, and probably more importantly, the estimates of deadweight loss are based on statements by the employers themselves. In most of the studies cited, employers were asked directly whether the subsidised unemployed or low-paid worker(s) concerned would have been hired without the subsidies. The limitations of this methodology seem to be illustrated by the results of a study on a small-scale British project for long-term unemployed people in certain Scottish regions (involving a 50 to 100 per cent subsidy over a period of 26 weeks). This study concluded that the deadweight loss amounted to no more than between 15 and 20 per cent. This atypical finding may well be related to the fact that, in order to qualify, employers were required to state formally that they would not have offered the job without the subsidy (Fay 1996).

Table 6.2 Summary of some important findings

Name (country)	Deadweight	Substitution	Displacement	Sum (deadweight + substitution)	Reference
Vermeerd-Moor Act (Netherlands)		80-85%	28%	> 80%	De Koning et al. (1995)
RAP (Netherlands)	42%	47%	36%	> 89%	De Koning et al. (1995)
Workstart (UK)	55%	25%	33%	> 80%	Atkinson and Meager (1994)
Jobstart	67-79%	–	–	> 67%	OECD (1993); Byrne (1994)
Employment Incentive (Ireland)	70%	21%	4%	95%	OECD (1993); NERA (1995)
Voordeelbanenplan (Belgium)	53%	36%	–	> 89%	Van der Linden (1995)
VLW (Netherlands)	27-60%	37-63%	–	57-87%	NEI (1999)
SPAK (Netherlands)	93%	-	–	93%	NEI (1999)

Substitution cost

Another often-voiced criticism is that subsidised jobs come at the expense of non-subsidised jobs. Targeted groups need to be clearly demarcated and this inevitably leads to distortions at the margins. As a consequence, non-subsidised employees may be excluded or not recruited for the benefit of cheaper, subsidised workers. In some instances this may actually be desirable. Therefore, the question of who benefits at whose expense is quite relevant. It may, for example, be a policy objective to have older workers replaced by young unemployed persons. Or it may be deemed desirable that a subsidy makes the labour market more accessible to low-skilled workers rather than high-skilled employees whose long-term employment prospects are at any rate more favourable. But it is generally not the intention to create an advantage for specific segments of the labour market (e.g., unemployed young people) at the detriment of other vulnerable groups (e.g., the long-term unemployed). It is, for that matter, prohibited under the terms of most schemes to dismiss workers with the purpose of replacing them with subsidised employees.

The few available studies which have looked at substitution effects invariably provide general estimations. They rarely indicate which specific groups are prized out of the market by subsidised workers. Estimates range fairly widely, from around 20-25 per cent for the Irish Employment Incentive and the British Workstart schemes to around 50 per cent for the Dutch RAP and VLW schemes. Van der Linden (1997) estimates the substitution costs of a series of Belgian measures (cf. above) at 36 per cent. Such estimates suggest that substitution effects can be quite substantial but, again, the limitations of getting at reliable estimates of substitution effects on the basis of employers' surveys are quite apparent.

A time-series analysis of the so-called *Jongerenbanenplan*, a Belgian scheme the aim of which was to increase employment among longer-term unemployed youngsters also brought to light important substitution effects. Introduced in 1993, the measure involved a regressive reduction in employers' social security contributions for up to three years (100 per cent in the first year, 75 per cent in the second and 50 per cent in third) for each recruitment of someone under the age of 26 who had been unemployed for at least 6 months. The measure was implemented at the beginning of a period of economic recovery so that the overall response exceeded the initial expectations by quite a margin. Unemployment dropped significantly among long and short-term unemployed youngsters alike. However, Koevoets (2000) found that this measure still had a negative impact on the relative employment chances of short-term unemployed youngsters who saw their relative chances of employment reduced quite considerably after the implementation of the scheme.

Displacement cost

The least amount of empirical data is available regarding the displacement effects of job subsidies. These are, after all, the hardest to measure. It concerns job losses through the distortion of competition, i.e., job losses caused by the fact that enterprises that do not receive subsidies lose market share. This negative impact on employment is not easy to estimate, as it is difficult to attribute an increase or decrease in market share to one single factor. Determining the relation between loss of market share and employment at a company is usually not easy. It is almost impossible to arrive at reliable estimates by means of evaluation studies on the basis of interviews with employers. Nevertheless, it is likely that displacement effects do come into play, as all empirical evaluation studies suggest that many subsidised workers would have found employment regardless of the subsidy (cf. above). This means that the measures constitute a de facto subsidy to the companies in question, and it is quite conceivable that this is beneficial to the competitive position of the enterprise. Some 28 per cent of companies receiving a subsidy under the Dutch Vermeend-Vermoor Act indicated that the subsidy had enabled them to improve their competitive position. A similar advantage was realised by 36 per cent of companies obtaining subsidies under the Dutch RAP scheme (De Koning et al. 1995) and 33 per cent of enterprises claiming subsidies under the Workstart programme in the UK. It seems likely that, to some extent, this gain was realised at the expense, to some extent at least, of (employment at) competing enterprises. But as already indicated, it is hard to assess how substantial these negative employment effects at companies that make no or less use of subsidised labour actually are.

Net employment effects: estimates on the basis of time series

A number of studies have tried to assess the overall employment impact through time series analysis. The approach taken in these studies is to ascertain whether the introduction of a particular measure coincided with additional job growth (or slower job destruction) that could not be attributed to any other measurable factor. The significance of these estimations therefore depends on the thoroughness with which one tests for other potential explanatory factors, such as cyclical movements of the economy.[2] This type of evaluation was carried out for a number of US

---

[2] Interestingly, measures aimed at stimulating job growth are often implemented at a time when the economy is already recovering. This has been the case

programmes, such as the Targeted Job Tax Credit (TJTC), which was in force between 1979 and 1994. It encompassed substantial tax deductions (amounting to 50 per cent of wages in the first year and 25 per cent in the second) for companies recruiting additional staff from disadvantaged categories, including youngsters from deprived areas, welfare recipients, etc. By the mid-1980s, the number of beneficiaries of the programme had reached 650,000. A time-series analysis specifically examined the impact of the scheme on the employment of youngsters (18- to 24-year-olds). Katz (1998) estimates the net employment effect of TJTC at around 7 per cent among youngsters occupying a vulnerable position in the labour market, a figure which he finds to be consistent with a demand elasticity of -0.5.

For France, Kramarz and Philippon (2001) have looked at the employment effects of cuts in employers' social security contributions on minimum wages. The French government introduced its policy of reduced contributions on minimum wages and wages just above the statutory minimum in 1993. Employers' contributions were cut from roughly 40 per cent at the beginning of the 90s to around 22 per cent in 1996. The gross minimum wage, on the other hand, increased over that same period. Kramarz and Philippon (2001) look at the net employment effect of the changes in labour costs between 1990 and 1997. They compare the transition from work to non-work and vice versa of people earning approximately the minimum wage who did not enjoy selective cuts in employers' social security contributions. They find that an increase in labour costs at the minimum-wage level clearly had a negative impact on employment. (They estimated the elasticity at -1.5.) At the same time, however, they observe that reductions in the cost of minimum-wage labour did not really coincide with any net job growth, a finding which they link with anecdotal evidence that employers were not convinced that the reductions were permanent. In other words, they find an asymmetrical effect: A rise in the cost of minimum-wage labour resulted in job losses, while a reduction in the cost resulted in a substitution of low-paid workers for slightly better-paid workers.

---

in the US (Katz, 1998), as well as other countries. This underlines how vitally important it is to correct for other policies and circumstantial factors when evaluating a measure (Van Trier, 1998).

Table 6.3   Employment effects: Findings from time-series/DDD analysis

Type of measure	Findings	Source
Targeted Jobs Tax Credit (US) – target group: youths, public assistance and SSI recipients, veterans, certain ex-convicts – tax credit for employer amounting to 50% of first and 25% of second year earnings	– Net employment effect of 7.7% or 3 percentage points	Katz (1996)
SPAK (Netherlands) – permanent reduction in employers' social security contributions for low-paid workers (up to 115% minimum wage)	– Zero net employment effect	Muhlau and Salverda (2000)
France – permanent reduction in employers' social security contributions (from 36.5% in 1993 to 21.8 per cent in 1996) for minimum wage workers	– Small but statistically insignificant effect	Kramarz and Philippon (2000)

There is also research available that pertains to the impact of a permanent reduction in employers' social security contributions on low wages. Previous evaluation research (Polanen Petel et al. 1999) estimated that the net employment effect of the Dutch SPAK scheme was 7 per cent at the most. Muhlau and Salverda (2000), on the basis of time-series analysis, assert that the introduction of SPAK did not cause any measurable additional employment growth, including in such sectors as the hotel and catering industry or retailing. They carried out a time-series analysis of job growth per sector, controlling for a series of factors that may influence variations in employment. Interestingly, the authors find that already expanding companies were more inclined to make use of the subsidy than companies with a relatively stable staff level in years prior to the introduction of the subsidy. It is therefore unlikely that the employment-stimulating effects are underestimated as a result of self-selection of enterprises that are not performing well.

Evidence from experimental research

There is also some evidence available from experiment-based research. Experimental studies are few but quite revealing. A particularly interesting study was conducted in the US in the 1980s (Burtless 1985). In a controlled experiment, a group of welfare recipients were given a voucher entitling an employer to a substantial tax credit on recruitment of the person in question. A second group was given a voucher that entitled the employed to a direct cash subsidy. The individuals making up a third, control group were not given a voucher, even though they qualified in principle. The individuals were assigned to one or the other group randomly, so that the groups were comparable in terms of composition. All three groups got two weeks of job search training. Efforts were made to ensure that the three groups were not treated differently by administrators or trainers.

Table 6.4	Findings from experimental research: Dayton voucher experiment		
Group	Sample size	Number placed in jobs	Percentage placed in jobs
Tax credit voucher	247	32	13.0
Direct rebate voucher	299	38	12.7
Control	262	54	20.6
Total	808	124	15.3

Source: Burtless (1985).

Astonishingly, the non-subsidised group was actually significantly more successful in finding work than the subsidised groups. Also, only in one-quarter of the cases did the employer who hired the vouchered worker request payment. Indeed, there was evidence that a substantial number of voucher holders declined to use the voucher because there were afraid of being labelled problem cases. This fear was apparently not entirely ungrounded. Anecdotal evidence did suggest that employers used the voucher to screen out applicants known to be public assistance recipients. However, it is important to keep account of the fact that the experiment concerned a rather specific segment of job seekers: social assistance recipients who suffered from a rather unfavourable image among employers. A second, comparable, study came to a similar conclusion (Hollenbeck and Wilke 1991, cited by Katz 1998).

Transition to the regular labour market

We move now to the second question: What is known about the degree of mobility from subsidised to regular employment?

An Australian study examined the effects of Jobstart, a subsidy to employers for the recruitment of the unemployed. Participants were screened six months after termination of their subsidised employment. The findings revealed that their prospects of employment had improved considerably (Byrne 1994). It should be noted, however, that the study failed to correct for selection distortions. This is a serious shortcoming since beneficiaries tend to have a considerably more favourable profile than those entitled, at least in terms of their observable characteristics. This might explain why people who have completed a period of subsidised employment perform better than those who are merely entitled to the subsidy. A different study examined the effect of another Australian subsidising scheme, known as the Special Youth Employment Training Programme. After controls for selection distortion on observable variables, this study too found a positive effect on the job prospects of participants two years after the period of subsidised employment had ended (Richardson 1998). This positive result could be due to the fact that the scheme linked the subsidy to training requirements.

In a study for Belgium, Bollens et al. (1996) studied the employment prospects of people 24, 30 and 36 months after leaving a job that entitled the employer to reduced social security contributions. They found that the employment prospects were comparable to those of previously non-subsidised unemployed people. However, this is another study which did not involve a correction for possible selection bias. In a methodologically more advanced study, Cockx et al. (1998) examined the effects of employment subsidies on individuals' job tenure. This study did correct for selection distortion and found that pure employment subsidies had a positive yet statistically insignificant effect of on beneficiaries' ability to keep a job. In contrast, a significantly positive effect, however, was measured for subsidised training programmes.

Eichler and Lechner (2002) evaluate the effect of subsidised jobs (one-year time limit) for the longer-term unemployed (over 6 months), with priority being given to unskilled youngsters, older workers, disabled workers and the extremely long-term unemployed. They find that participants have a higher probability of being employed than non-participants with the same observable characteristics. By contrast, Bardaji (2001), in an evaluation of a similar programme in France (albeit limited to the non-market sector), finds that very few people find work after their spell of subsidised employment has ended. It would appear that the experience gained in a subsidised job is not very highly valued. This is another study which did not correct for selection bias.

Table 6.5 Summary of findings on mobility from subsidised to regular work

Type of measure	Findings	Source
Jobstart (Australia) – employer subsidy for recruitment of unemployed persons	– improvement of employment chances 6 months after subsidised job – no correction for selection bias	Byrne (1994)
Special Youth Employment Training Scheme (Australia) – employment subsidy coupled with training	– positive effect on employment chances two years after – correction for selection bias	Richardson (1998)
Voordeelbanenplan (Belgium) – targeted, temporary reduction in social security contributions	– employment prospects 24, 30 and 36 months after leaving subsidised employment comparable to non-subsidised unemployed – no correction for selection bias	Bollens et al. (1996)
Voordeelbanenplan (Belgium) – targeted, temporary reduction in social security contributions	– positive yet statistically insignificant effect on employment chances – correction for selection bias	Cockx et al. (1998)
PEP (Germany) – subsidised jobs (1 yr. max.) for long-term unemployed	– participants have higher probability of being in work than non-participants with similar observable characteristics	Eichler and Lechner (2002)
France – subsidised jobs for long-term unemployed in non-market sectors	– few participants move to regular work after their spell of subsidised employment has ended	Bardaji (2001) (from OECD, 2003)
Slovakia – subsidised jobs for the unemployed, maximum duration expanded first from 6 to 9 months, then to 12	– short term subsidised jobs have positive effect on job finding rate, opposite effect as maximum duration got expanded ('lock-in')	Van Ours (2002)

Gauging from the available evidence, subsidised jobs do not seem to have a significant positive effect on the employment chances of beneficiaries in the regular labour market.

One possible explanation is that beneficiaries get locked into their subsidised jobs. Van Ours (2002) reports on an analysis of data from what he calls a 'natural experiment' in Slovakia's labour market in the mid-1990s. He observes the transitions to the regular labour market by participants in a subsidised job scheme the duration of which was expanded first from

6 to 9 months and then from 9 to 12 months. His finding is that short-term subsidised jobs have a positive effect on the regular job finding rate, but that the effect became exactly the opposite as the maximum duration got expanded.

A second explanatory factor that has been mentioned in the literature is stigmatisation. It is argued that subsidised work has a stigmatising effect on the beneficiary, thus compromising their prospects of finding regular employment. The reasoning behind this argument is that individuals in subsidised jobs are easily perceived as lacking in ability and being unable to find a regular job. At least an unemployed person applying for a job can claim that his or her unemployment was, to a certain extent, 'voluntary', in the sense that they might have been looking for a 'suitable job'. By contrast, a person with a history of subsidised work indicates that he or she is willing to work, but implicitly concedes to be unable to find a regular job.

A third explanation for the apparently poor transition rate from subsidised to regular labour is that the type of job experience acquired in subsidised employment does not suffice to escape from the so-called 'productivity trap'. This suggests that the weak position in the labour market of certain groups, such as the long-term unemployed, is not merely a matter of a lack of job experience and contact with the labour market. Katz (1998) concludes that, on the basis of an evaluation of a number of US projects, employment subsidies only work in combination with training and counselling. This conclusion is corroborated by results obtained by Richardson (1998) and Cockx et al. (1998). Martin and Grubb (2001) argue that such schemes also produce better outcomes when programme participants are allowed to do more regular work. In other words, they claim that private sector subsidies are more effective than public sector subsidies or public sector employment. The idea here is that the type of work experience gained in the private sector is more relevant and transferable to a regular work situation than public sector jobs.

The tentative verdict on demand-oriented subsidies

General conclusions are difficult to draw because of the rather significant differences between the measures discussed here across a very wide range of dimensions: the economic and institutional context in which they are embedded, the design features of the measures (is it a direct cash subsidy or a social security charge reduction, the size and length of the measure, the definition and delineation of the target group), the administrative procedures. Also, there are significant differences in evaluation methodology. It is also important to note that many results come from studies that employ methodologies (employer interviews) that must be questioned as to their validity.

But, on the whole, two striking findings emerge from the evaluation literature. First, the measured net employment effects tend to be consistently lower than what theoretical models and simulations predict, even under relatively conservative assumptions. Deadweight losses in particular tend to be consistently higher than is generally assumed. Estimates for targeted programmes range in the order of 50 to 70 per cent. Studies pertaining to more general measures arrive at estimates as high as 85 to 90 per cent. Furthermore, there is evidence that enhanced recruitment among the target groups tends to be to the detriment of employment among categories that are (narrowly) ineligible (e.g., the relatively short-term unemployed). Evaluation studies for targeted measures report substitution effects in the order of 20 to 35 per cent. Little is known about job losses resulting from competition distortion, mainly because these job losses are difficult to measure. It is also suggested in some studies that this effect may be considerable. But the cumulative effect of deadweight loss and substitution alone is large enough to conclude that the net employment impact of selective wage subsidies to the unemployed and comparable groups in the labour market tends to be rather small, often at approximately 10 per cent. The net employment effect of more general measures, such as cuts in employers' social security contributions on low wages is probably even smaller. The cost-effectiveness of labour cost reductions and job subsidies therefore appears to be relatively small: a substantial drop in revenue for the treasury or the social security system on the one hand, and relatively few new jobs on the other.

The biggest problem is that most subsidised workers *who are actually recruited* would also have found a job without the subsidy. Even within fairly strictly defined target groups there is evidence of selective recruitment – the most promising workers are 'skimmed off'. This is probably the main reason why the measured dead weight losses are consistently higher than what tends to be assumed in theoretical analyses such as those by Snower (1994). This could perhaps be resolved by defining the target groups even more sharply, so that subsidies remain restricted to the very long-term, unskilled unemployed. However, the question then arises whether a subsidy, especially a temporary one, will provide a sufficiently strong incentive for employers to recruit apparently unsuitable job applicants. Moreover, there is a danger that extremely selective subsidies will have an even stronger stigmatising effect.

The second striking conclusion that emerges from our survey is that there is little evidence that targeted subsidies have a beneficial effect on the later careers of beneficiaries. There are indications that very selective, targeted schemes can have a reverse effect if they stigmatise beneficiaries, that is to say, if they label individuals coming from subsidised jobs as 'problem cases'. However, there are also indications that subsidies that are coupled with training and job counselling can have a significant positive impact on the longer-term employment prospects for vulnerable groups.

Policymakers apparently face the following dilemma. A rather general measure, such as a subsidy for all the long-term unemployed, is probably the least stigmatising, but its net employment effect is likely to be rather modest. Limited additional employment among the target group would be realised at the cost of a substantial income transfer to companies. The budgetary cost for each additional job, moreover, would be rather high.

This could be resolved by defining the target groups even more sharply, so that subsidies are restricted to the very long-term, unskilled unemployed. However, the question then arises whether a subsidy, especially a temporary one, will provide a sufficiently strong incentive for employers to recruit apparently unsuitable job applicants. Moreover, there is a danger that extremely selective subsidies will have an even stronger stigmatising effect, i.e., that individuals in subsidised jobs will, more than ever before, be labelled 'problem cases' once they try to (re-)enter the regular labour market.

3 Subsidising the Low-Paid

Why subsidise low-paid workers?

Let us turn to subsidies which seek to influence labour supply. Subsidies to low-paid workers or families on a low earned income aim a) to make work more attractive than passive benefit dependency and b) to improve the living standard of individuals or households on low earned income.

Subsidies to low-paid workers have become especially important in the Anglo-Saxon world. In the US, the Earned Income Tax Credit (EITC) – a negative income tax for families on a low earned income – has effectively become the main pillar of social security for working age people. In many Continental European countries this form of subsidising has gained ground in the shape of targeted reductions in employees' social security contributions and personal taxes.

Is the subsidising of individuals or households on a low earned income a good idea? Those in favour argue that it allows one to achieve two goals at once, i.e., integration into the labour market and reduction of poverty. After all, the main critique of 'passive' benefits is that they represent a disincentive for labour market participation and are thus conducive to exclusion. On the other hand, sceptics point out that there is the risk that the poverty trap will shift from subsidised passivity (i.e., unemployment) to subsidised low-paid work. Some critics question whether there is really a need for combating poverty among the employed. Finally, it is suggested that the subsidising of low wages will actually stimulate wage erosion. The reasoning behind this particular argument is that employers will tend to offer even lower wages if low-paid workers are subsidised by the government. Workers, for their part, may be inclined to accept lower wages, or slower wage development at least, realising that the government will compensate the difference in income to a certain extent.

List-wise, these are the principal questions and issues:
a. To what extent do supplementary income benefits actually increase effective labour supply and do the additional employment and resulting benefits outweigh the budgetary cost?
b. What is the potential redistributive impact of subsidies on employees and to what extent do they help combat poverty?
c. Is there any empirical evidence that wage supplements merely cause a shift in the dependency trap, i.e., what is the degree of upward mobility from subsidised low-paid labour and is it greater than that from passive benefit dependency?

Is there empirical evidence that the subsidising of low-paid work actually aggravates the problem it seeks to alleviate, i.e., that it causes erosion of wages at the bottom end of the labour market?

The empirical evidence available today remains fairly limited and pertains mostly to the United States, Canada and the UK. Particularly interesting, quantity as well as quality-wise, are the studies relating to the American EITC. Hence, most of our focus will be on the recent US experience. The US is still looked upon by many in Europe as the country where economic objectives override social concerns to such an extent that we can safely disqualify the US 'model' as a reference point for the European debate. And yet, the United States seems to be one of the few countries where employment growth has effectively been accompanied with some drop in poverty, at least among certain population segments. It also seems to me that the United States is also one of the few OECD countries that has genuinely experienced a paradigmatic shift in its approach to social policy. The introduction of time limits on 'passive' social assistance represents a radical departure from past policy. And the shift towards in-work benefits has nowhere been as large or radical as in the United States. This shift has not been successful in every respect, but it has delivered at least some striking results.

The Earned Income Tax Credit (EITC)

History and context

Stimulating economic self-reliance has always been a pivotal objective in American social policy. For a long time, the centrality of self-reliance in American social policy was evident in the virtual absence of income protection provisions for wide sections of the population. Before the expansion of the EITC, a negative income tax that provides substantial income supplements to the low-paid, it was basically the case that if you were of working-age, childless and healthy, you were expected to be able get by on your own. Direct income support in the form of cash transfers was generally restricted to non-employed households, most often single parents, with dependent children. The main social assistance programme was called Aid to Families with Dependent Children (AFDC). Americans referred to this programme as 'welfare'. Despite its limited size and its almost negligible budgetary importance by European standards, this program was for many years the subject of virulent criticism.

One of the principal critiques was that AFDC undermined self-reliance. This critique was widely shared in American society, which places an enormous value on virtues such as individual effort, hard work and personal responsibility, and AFDC was, especially during the 1980s, when welfare caseloads were rising, a favourite target of commentators and politicians from the right. But this was not only because AFDC was perceived as corrupting the work ethic. There was also a widespread belief that the welfare system encouraged dependency, the break-up of families and the proliferation of single-parent households. The majority of AFDC recipients were black single mothers. The racist undertones in many of the critiques of the time were often far from subtle.

During the American presidential campaign of 1992, then candidate Clinton offered a new vision of social policy. Two key objectives were 'to make work pay' and 'work-oriented welfare reform'. Clinton wanted to enforce work and personal responsibility. He insisted that people who were able to work ought to work. He, quite uncharacteristically for a Democrat politician at that time, called for time limits on welfare. At the same time, he advocated a role for government in rewarding work, providing training and even community service jobs. To achieve the objective 'to make work pay' he proposed, among other things, an expansion of the EITC, a programme that had existed since 1975. Clinton did not call for a scaling back of government support for the needy, but for a redirection of government effort and expenditure. He sought to move away from long-term cash payments to the non-active toward greater support for workers, especially low-paid workers.

At the start of his first term in office, Clinton proposed and was able to pass a dramatic expansion of the EITC. According to Blank and Ellwood (2001), levels were chosen to ensure that the combination of minimum wages, EITC and food stamps available to a family of four would be sufficient to move that family out of poverty, as measured by the official American poverty line.

The Earned Income Tax Credit (EITC)

The EITC was first introduced in the US in 1975 as an exemption from employees' social security payments for poor working households with children. The system was subsequently expanded in 1986, 1990 and 1993. The 1993 reform in particular turned the scheme into the country's pre-eminent anti-poverty programme for families at active age. Eligibility for the EITC hinges on three conditions. First, the household must have an earned income. Other sources of income are deducted from the work income. Second, the earned income must not exceed a given amount. A household with two children, for example, may not earn more than US\$30,000 annually. Third, there must be a dependent child in the family who is either under the age of 19 or under the age of 24 if a full-time student. Households with a disabled child are also eligible.

Benefits are tied to the level of earnings and the number of children. For each dollar earned up to a maximum, the parent gets a refundable tax credit. For a parent with two or more children, the credit is 40 per cent of earnings up to a maximum credit of roughly US\$3,800. This is roughly triple the maximum for such families in 1992. For a minimum wage worker, this amounted to a 40 per cent pay raise. As a family's earned income rises above US\$13,000, the credit is gradually reduced at a rate of 21 cents per additional dollar earned, and the credit is fully phased out for families with incomes over US\$30,000. The effect of the EITC on the living standard of low-earning households was reinforced by an increase in the minimum wage in 1997 from US$4.25 per hour – the level at which it had stood since 1992 – to US$5.15.

The EITC is not only granted to households under the poverty line. In fact, only about half of EITC expenses go to poor families (Scholz 1996). This is due to the fact that the scheme is not intended to combat poverty, but to encourage people on a low earned income to work longer hours.

The EITC generally comes in the shape of a one-off payment at the end of the year. Few people choose to receive periodical advance payments. People do not receive EITC automatically; they need to claim the credit. It appears that a large proportion of those eligible for EITC make use of the scheme. Scholz (1996) estimates that the take up rate is between 75 and 90 per cent. This is considerably higher than registration rates for other provisions and benefits for the poor. One explanation for this observation is that there appears to be no stigma attached to claiming EITC. Nor is it perceived as a welfare provision. There are however indications that non-take up is higher among the unskilled. Moreover, the number of people applying is far greater than the number actually entitled. The self-employed in particular sometimes try to claim EITC inappropriately.

Accompanying policy reforms

The expansion of EITC went accompanied with a number of other reforms in the social policy domain. The State Children's Health Insurance Program, established under the Balanced Budget Act of 1997, provides federal matching funds for state-designed programmes to provide health insurance to low-income children. Children are generally eligible if their family's income is below 133 per cent of the poverty line, with many states adopting even higher limits. This reform aimed to ensure that people do not lose health insurance for their children when they move from welfare dependency to low-paid work. In addition, child care funding was expanded. The Taxpayer Relief Act of 1997 included a $500 per child non-refundable tax credit offering support to working families.

As Blank and Ellwood (2001) show, the combined effect of policy changes have dramatically affected work incentives. The payoff for working has increased quite substantially since 1988. They calculate that a full-year, full-time minimum-wage single parent who would otherwise be on welfare in 1988 would have a net gain of only $2,325, and she would likely lose her Medicaid benefits, which might easily be worth more than that gain. In 1999, that gain was over $7,000, the children would keep Medicaid health insurance and even the women would be eligible to keep it for a time. A higher minimum wage and slightly lower welfare benefits contributed to this gain, but it is mainly the result of a sizeable rise in the EITC and greater child support.

This calculation probably understates the real change in work incentives. The abolition of the 30-year-old AFDC programme, which was replaced in 1996 by the less generous Temporary Assistance to Needy Families (TANF) put far greater pressure on welfare applicants and recipients to look for work and to accept low-paying jobs. The option not to work and collect benefits is now much more unavailable than it was 10 years earlier. One of the main features of TANF is a lifetime limit of five years on TANF-funded aid.

The effects on passive benefit dependency

How have the dramatic policy changes that took place during the 1990s affected outcomes in the United States? Generally speaking, the outcomes have been almost equally dramatic. The number of Americans, especially lone parents, on welfare (AFDC later TANF) has plummeted and the proportion of less-skilled, previously non-employed people in work has increased, though not by the same magnitude as the drop in welfare dependency.

The principal purpose of the welfare reforms during the 1990s was to reduce passive benefit dependency. During the 1970s and 1980s, the number of households on welfare (AFDC) remained persistently high, at just under 4 million recipients, even during periods when the American economy was booming. The number of families receiving AFDC even rose sharply during the economic slowdown of 1990-1991, and continued to rise through the early 1990s, to a high of just under 5 million. After the mid-1990s, caseloads started to decline and welfare dependency plummeted during the late 1990s. By 2000, just over 2 million households were on welfare. The enormous decline during the late 1990s stood in marked contrast to the persistence of welfare dependency during the preceding decades.

The 1990s were, of course, a period of stellar economic performance in the US. A number of studies have attempted to separate the effects of the economy from the effects of policy. As one would expect, most studies find a significant effect of both policy and the economy. The prolonged economic expansion of the 1990s produced exceptionally low unemployment rates, especially towards the late 1990s. The late 1990s were also a period of rising real wages, even for low-skilled workers, who had generally experienced real wage decline in the preceding 25 years. Some studies (Ziliak 2002) have implausibly argued that policy effects were not significantly related to the welfare caseload decline. It is difficult to see how economic growth alone can account for a more than 50 per cent drop in dependency levels in the late 1990s, given that the very strong economy of the late 1980s pushed down unemployment yet did not produce noticeable effects on welfare dependency levels. Most studies (Schoeni and Blank 2000; Blank 2001) conclude that the marked drop is the product of the combined effect of economic growth and policy reform. But it is generally acknowledged that the effects of welfare reform, the expansion of EITC, the expansion of child care and health coverage, and the economy are interactive and difficult to disentangle.

The effects on labour supply and employment
Quite a lot of research has been done in recent years on the labour supply and employment effects of the American EITC scheme. Since these effects seem to be quite large, there may be important lessons to be learnt for other countries that are introducing or expanding similar schemes. But I think it is crucial to re-emphasise the fact that the expansion of EITC in the US happened in a very specific context.

Firstly, the labour supply effects have occurred in exceptionally favourable economic circumstances characterised by, among other things, very strong job growth and low unemployment. Secondly, the expansion of the EITC went hand in hand with a noticeable toughening up of passive unemployment benefit policy, particularly the introduction of strict time limits on passive benefit dependency. Thirdly, the introduction of the EITC went hand in hand with concerted efforts to provide training, day care and access to healthcare (more in particular, an extension of healthcare to the working poor). Fourthly, the statutory minimum wage was substantially increased.

One of the main reasons for introducing the EITC was to encourage single mothers to participate in the labour market. This appears to have worked. The employment rate among single mothers has risen about 10 percentage points in less than 10 years (from 73 to 83 per cent). The rise was largely realised after 1993, when the EITC was gradually increased. The percentage of single mothers on welfare has dropped from 19 per cent in 1992 to 8 per cent in 1997. To an extent, this strong decline in welfare dependency and the simultaneous increase in labour market participation on the part of single mothers is due to the unprecedented economic expansion experienced in the US since the beginning of the 1990s. But the likely impact of policy factors is evident from the fact that employment rates for other vulnerable groups, such as lone women without children, rose significantly less strongly.

Econometric analyses conclude unanimously that the EITC in combination with other policy measures, particularly the consecutive increases of the minimum wage, must have contributed to the significant increase in labour market participation by lone mothers (Eissa and Liebman 1996; Meyer and Rosenbaum 1999; Blank, Card and Robins 1999). There are also indications that the impact on the labour supply would be even more apparent if expressed in terms of hours worked, as the EITC makes it more lucrative for mothers with a low-paying part-time job to work longer hours.

Other studies have focused on the impact of the EITC on the labour supply from other groups. Eissa and Hoynes (1998), for example, have looked into its effect on married couples. They found that there was a small positive effect on the labour supply of married men, but a significant negative impact on that of married women. Consequently, the net effect was deemed to be a decline in the supply of labour of married couples.

In other words, the empirical results draw quite a mixed picture. On the one hand, it is clear that the EITC makes work much more lucrative for those who are unemployed. They are encouraged to work a minimum number of hours, as the scheme explicitly set out to achieve. On the other hand, it is inherent in a scheme such as the EITC that those who already hold a job but whose income is below-average are encouraged to work less. The problem in the US is that quite a large proportion of families have work incomes that lie in the phase-out zone, i.e., the interval in which the subsidy received declines as earnings get more substantial. These people may therefore be inclined to reduce their working hours in order to receive higher supplements.

The labour supply effects of EITC and associated policy reforms have been rather impressive, especially as far as single parents are concerned. In a sense, it would have been really surprising if there had been no such an effect. After all, the reforms added up to a huge increase in the financial rewards to work, especially for lone parents. In a way, the really puzzling question is why a significant proportion of lone parents has remained unemployed. For as one may have noticed, the drop in the welfare case load during the 1990s was considerably bigger than the rise in employment among former welfare recipients. A study found that a substantial minority (around 30 per cent) of those who left the welfare roles remained unemployed for a substantial period of time (Loprest 1999).

Loprest (1999) looked at the reasons, as perceived and reported by the non-employed who left the welfare roles themselves. It should be stressed that this study reports on the period 1997-1998, when the mandatory 5-year time limit on welfare dependence introduced in 1996 was not yet being fully felt. There is, however, some evidence to suggest that welfare leavers were already being treated less leniently and that many exited from the welfare system under duress. More than one in four of the non-employed leaving welfare reported health problems, a disability or an illness. Fifteen per cent reported that they could not find work and another 12 per cent reported lack of child care or transport facilities. A large number also reported involvement in non-work activities, such as child care or caring for other family members.

The effects on income and poverty
The most widely used poverty measure in the US is the official poverty line, which is an absolute, monetary resources based poverty line that has been essentially unchanged in real terms for 35 years. Poverty measures are sensitive to which income components are and are not included in the measure of household resources. The picture changes somewhat depending on the treatment of taxes and social security contributions, housing and in-kind benefits, food stamps, child care and transportation costs etc.

But by no measure has there been a really dramatic improvement in the area of poverty, i.e., an improvement that is in any way comparable to the phenomenal decline in welfare dependency or the almost equally impressive rise in employment among single mothers and some other categories. Poverty in the United States has remained high. Dickens and Ellwood (2001) show that absolute poverty (EITC, food stamps, and housing aid added) among non-elderly households declined from just under 15 per cent to around 11 per cent in the late 1990s. This decline is almost similar in magnitude to the decline that occurred during the late 1980s, also a period of strong economic growth but with less dramatic policy change. Dickens and Ellwood (2001) also show that relative poverty among the non-elderly in the United States has remained remarkably stable at around 30 per cent throughout the entire 1980s and 1990s.

Poverty rates for some disadvantaged groups declined by several percentage points during the (late) 1990s, particularly those for female-headed households. The EITC was specifically designed to lift full-time working families above the official poverty line. The combined effect of higher statutory minimum wages (+9 per cent) and the EITC (+38 per cent) between 1993 and 1997 was such that the ratio between the net earned income and the poverty line for full-time working single parents rose from 0.93 to 1.06 (CEA 1998). This is at least the case in theory. Most recipients choose for a single payment at the end of the fiscal year, even though they could opt for advance payments in the course of the year. Critics argue that the EITC does not help poor families to make ends meet at times when they are most in need of the money. Research suggests that the money is often not spent on current expenses, but that it is invested in training, in buying or fixing a car, in durable consumer goods. About one-quarter of the recipients save the money for later use (Smeeding et al. 1998).

The Census Bureau estimates that, in 1997, the EITC helped 4.3 million Americans escape poverty, which is twice as many as in 1993, the year in which the scheme was expanded. There was a notable decline in poverty among children, especially children living in lone-parent households. This decline was due to a combination of greater labour market participation on the part of single mothers and an increase in their income. In addition, female-headed households with children at the bottom end of the income distribution, those most affected by the policy changes, gained in terms of their average income.

However, Blank and Ellwood (2001) cite evidence suggesting that the poorest single mother families (those roughly in the bottom quintile within this category) have lost ground in income terms and have slipped into severe poverty. Clearly, welfare recipients who have been sanctioned or time-limited off welfare and who have been unable to replace their welfare income with earned income have become much worse off. As I have noted, studies of those leaving welfare indicate that a substantial proportion (around 30 per cent in the mid-1990s) remained unemployed or non-employed for some time after leaving welfare (Brauner and Loprest 1999; Loprest 2001).

So it appears that the results on the poverty front are quite mixed. The policy reforms have made one segment of the previously poor substantially better off - those who found low-paid work and now enjoy EITC and other in-work benefits. But another segment has clearly become worse off - those who have lost their welfare entitlement and failed to find a job. The problem with the shift from passive income support to in-work support is that it is to the detriment of those who for one reason or another fail to find employment. Even in the US, where there are plenty of low-paying jobs (or ought to be plentiful, given that by various measures its labour market is among the most flexible in the world) and where the (relative) financial incentive to take up low-paid work is now bigger than anywhere else, low-skilled unemployment remains a real problem.

The Canadian Self-Sufficiency Project

The Canadian Self-Sufficiency Project (SSP) offered an experimental earnings supplement to single parents who had slipped into long-term benefit dependency. Although a limited scale programme that was deployed in only two Canadian provinces, the SSP deserves mention because of its experimental set-up, which ensured the existence of a perfectly comparable control group.

The project provided generous wage supplements, which in some cases exceeded the beneficiary's earned income. The purpose of the scheme was to elevate the income of single parents with a full-time job to the average earned income of full-time working women in the two Canadian provinces where the experiment was being conducted. Crucially, one only qualified for the supplement if one held a full-time job (30 hours per week). The supplement was restricted to a period of 36 months. Non-earned income and income from any other household members did not affect the amount received. So in contrast to the EITC, entitlement depended on the recipient's personal income, not the household income.

Under the project, two groups were created: a group that actually received the supplement and a control group. In order that the two groups would be perfectly comparable in terms of composition, assignment to one group or the other happened on an entirely random basis. Initial results after 18 months showed that 30 per cent of those who were offered the supplement were working, compared to 16 per cent of those in the control group. It also appeared that the newly fully employed made a transition from non-participation rather than from part-time work (Card and Robbins; Lin et al. 1998).

An evaluation was also made of the employment effects of a variant of the SSP, known as SSP-plus. This variant not only offered a bonus as an incentive to work, but also involved active assistance to long-term unemployed welfare recipients. This assistance consisted mainly in job-interview training. Of the experimental group receiving a wage supplement and assistance, some 33 per cent were working after a period of 18 months, which is 17 percentage points more than in the control group and 3 more than in the group receiving an earnings supplement only (Card and Robbins 1996).

The difference in the poverty rates between the test group and the control group was reported to be on the order of 11 per cent (21 versus 32 per cent), while the difference in terms of the poverty gap was in the order of

17 per cent. It appears that SSP-households used predominantly the additional funds to pay off debts, purchase durable consumer goods or save (Lin et al. 1998).

The UK's Family Credit / Working Families Tax Credit / Employment Tax Credit

Introduced in 1988, the UK's Family Credit (FC) was a social security allowance for working families with dependent children. In order to qualify, at least one adult in the family had to work a minimum of 16 hours per week. In 1995, the basic allowance stood at £45.10 per week per adult. For each child, an additional amount was granted of between £11.40 and £32.80 depending on the age of the child. The amount a family actually received depended on the differential between the earned income and a reference income. If the reference income was exceeded, the amount received was cut at a rate of 70 per cent.

The number of families receiving FC rose from around 300,000 in 1988-1989 to some 500,000 in 1994-1995. The take-up rate was estimated to be around 70 per cent (Evans 1996). In 1994, some 44 per cent of families receiving FC were single-parent households, 39 per cent were couples with a male breadwinner, and 17 per cent consisted of families with a female breadwinner.

The Working Families Tax Credit (WFTC) was an extension of the FC and offered a tax credit to families with children where at least one adult works a minimum of 16 hours per week. If household income after tax and National Insurance contributions exceeded GBP 90 per week, the tax credit was reduced by 55 pence for each pound above this mark. Recently, the WFTC was generalised for all working families and individuals, including those with no children.

Labour supply effects were estimated using sophisticated supply models. Simulations of the Working Families Tax Credit (WFTC) suggested a positive effect on the labour supply from lone mothers and women with a non-working partner. At the same time, a negative effect was predicted on the labour supply from married women. Moreover, a negative effect was predicted on the number of hours worked by this particular group, mostly among women with a low-paid partner. Still according to these simulations, the overall effect on the labour supply was modestly positive (Duncan and Giles 1998; Duncan and MacCrae 1999). In other words, the simulations suggested an impact is similar to that of the American EITC scheme: an unequivocal positive impact on employment among those who were not in the labour market and a slight negative impact on the labour supply from working partners in double-income households with a low-paid breadwinner.

It is worth pointing out that households in the phase-out zone of the British WFTC were de facto confronted with a marginal tax rate of 55 per cent, as for each additionally earned pound above the income that entitled them to maximum benefit the family received 55 pence less. The phase-out zone of the American EITC is considerably flatter: depending on the number of children, it varies between roughly 21 and 8 per cent. Consequently, the phase-out zone of EITC stretches out to families on an about-average earned income.

The empirical evaluation research suggests that the WFTC credit increased the proportion of lone parents who work but seems to have had little overall effect on the proportion of adults in couples with children who work. Overall, the WFTC seems to have increased the employment rate, because the number of previously work-less families who found employment probably outweighed the number of previously double-earner households who decided to reduce their labour participation or hours (Brewer and Browne 2006).

The tentative verdict on supply-oriented measures

The available empirical evidence suggests that offering financial rewards to people preferring low-paid jobs to benefits can have a considerable positive effect on employment among groups that are traditionally hard to activate, such as long-term benefit recipients. It would appear, however, that the subsidy that is made available must make low-paid labour significantly more remunerative than benefits.

Consequently, such subsidies can contribute towards improving the level of welfare of households with a low earned income. Obviously, the condition is that one subsidises households rather than low-paid individuals. After all, the overwhelming majority of low-paid individuals belong to dual-income households and therefore enjoy a relatively high standard of living. Reductions in employers' social security contributions for low-paid workers and the like therefore contribute minimally to improving the level of welfare of poor households.

However, subsidising households with a low-earned income seems to have at least one important drawback. The selective nature of such subsidies implies that households with an earned income in the phase-out zone, i.e., the zone where the subsidy becomes smaller with each additionally earned income unit, are confronted with high marginal tax rates. The high marginal tax rates that seem inevitable in the phase-out zone may be a serious impediment to upward mobility. Selective subsidising of low-paid work may actually dissuade individuals with a below-average earning capacity to realise their earning capacity fully. If selective wage supplements stand in the way of upward mobility, this not only represents a problem from an economic and social perspective, but it also undermines one of the most important reasons for implementing welfare-to-work programmes in the first place. The goal, after all, is to reduce long-term benefit dependency and encourage economic independence. If former benefit recipients get stuck in low-paying subsidised work despite having the potential to move on to more remunerative employment, there may be repercussions in terms of the political legitimacy of such schemes.

In the case of the British WFTC, for example, low-earning households in the phase-out zone faced a marginal tax rate of 55 per cent, implying that they effectively faced the highest marginal tax rates in the UK. In principle, this could have been remedied by broadening the phase-out zone, for example by extending it to households with an average earned income. The phase-out zone of the American EITC, for example, is far flatter: depending on the number of children, it varies between roughly 21 and 8 per cent. It effectively stretches out to families on an about-average earned income. But the flatter the phase-out zone, the more expensive the scheme, especially, one would think, in European countries where wage structures are more compressed. Moreover, there is a risk of a negative effect on the supply of labour from households who already have a below-average or average earned income. Analyses of the system of EITC in the US have shown this is a realistic concern. But even if the overall effect on the labour supply, expressed in terms of working hours, is negative, policymakers would still find it desirable to put more people to work, even if this entails that some will work fewer hours.

Little is known about the mobility of EITC recipients, but, as we have seen, there are empirical indications that the EITC has a slightly negative effect on the labour supply from families in the phase-out zone, and especially on the labour supply from partners. No empirical data is available for either the old or the new British schemes, but simulations also suggest that there is a substantial negative impact on the labour supply from working families on an earned income in the phase-out zone. These findings indicate that there may indeed be a negative impact on the income mobility of families with a low earning potential. EITC-type schemes may also hamper mobility through the way they affect skill formation. A recent study by Heckman et al. (2002) suggests that EITC recipients may have cut down on their training efforts.

Finally, there is the matter that subsidising of low wages could lead to opportunistic behaviour on the part of employers. After all, if they realise that their low-paid workers are receiving a government subsidy, they may be inclined to pay even lower wages, hoping that workers will accept lower pay or slow wage developments knowing that the government will fully or partially make up for the financial loss anyway. Little is known empirically about the impact on wages. The introduction of the EITC in the US, the most adequately assessed wage subsidy scheme yet, went hand in hand with a gradual increase in the minimum wage. For that matter, the expansion of the EITC played a part in the decision to raise the minimum wage. The minimum wage represents a lower limit for any downward pressure that may develop on wages of EITC-recipients. But many people qualifying for EITC actually earn more per hour than the minimum wage, so that downward pressure could still manifest itself. However, no or very little research results into this aspect is currently available. Some argue that the effect on wage developments is probably limited, as employers are often not aware that their employees receive EITC or are entitled to it. The workers themselves are often unaware of how much EITC they will receive at the end of the year, as the amount is calculated on the basis of the earned income over an entire fiscal year. Still, a substantial minimum wage may well be a prerequisite for in-work benefit programmes to be efficient and sustainable in the longer run.

EITC a model for Europe?

The evaluation literature on the EITC is encouraging as far as the potential of such schemes is concerned. However, it is crucial to point out that findings for the United States cannot be generalised in a simple way. The socio-demographic composition of the US work force is different from most European countries. There are more single-adult (parent) households, but also more multi-earner households. The US also has an earnings structure that is totally different from virtually every European country – earnings are far more compressed in Europe. Significant low-pay subsidies are likely to be more expensive for that reason. Also, one would think that *ceteris paribus* more European households have earned incomes that fall within the phase-out zone where work incentive effects – particularly on secondary earners – tend to be negative. And there are likely to be important and complex interactions with the other parts of the tax/benefit system. All this makes it impossible to make general statements about the likely net effects of a policy of in-work benefits. As an assessment of the new tax credits introduced in the UK makes clear, apparent details in the specific design of the tax credit and in the institutional environment in which they are embedded can be important (Brewer, Clark and Myck 2001).

The impact of in-work benefits is probably highly contingent on the generosity of the benefits and on their ability to raise earned income above certain threshold. But many of the benefits/tax credits that have recently been introduced in Europe provide only small financial gains (for an overview see OECD 2001). In Belgium, for example, low-paid individuals have become entitled to a small tax credit. The amount is so small that it is difficult to imagine there being a significant work incentive effect. The dominant effect appears to be that it raises net income of people already in (full-time) work. Analysis suggests, moreover, that middle- to high-income households benefit the most from this measure (Cantillon, Kerstens and Verbist 2000) An *ex ante* analysis of the French scheme, which is similar to the Belgian one (i.e., low and aimed at individuals), comes to an equally pessimistic conclusion as far as the likely employment effects are concerned (Cahuc 2002).

4   Conclusion

One general conclusion clearly emerges from the empirical evaluation literature: financial incentives, if substantial and well designed, trigger favourable behavioural responses. Employers react to subsidies to hire certain types of workers and benefit recipients react to financial incentives to find employment. At the risk of over-simplifying, measures that seek to influence supply-side behaviour seem to have more of a net impact than measures that seek to influence labour demand. Much depends of course on the magnitude, length and design of the subsidy for either the employer or the potential employee, but on balance the evidence seems more encouraging as far as supply-aimed subsidies are concerned. There is rather more evidence that long-term benefit recipients have been drawn into the labour market through employee rather than employer subsidies. Moreover, such subsidies have (almost by definition) more of a direct effect on the income position of poor households. But little remains know about the longer-term effects of targeted subsidies, be it whether these are employer or employee aimed. There are good reasons to suspect that these might well be substantially less positive from the short term benefits, especially in the case of employee subsidies, which seem to trigger the strongest behavioural response. After all, if the behavioural effects are strong in the desired direction, then these are also likely to be strong in more undesirable ways. In other words, the impact on such aspects as mobility, wage bargaining behaviour, skill formation etc., on which less is empirically known at present, may in fact turn out to be rather significant too.

It would appear that, as always, the problem remains of striking a balance right between universalism and selectivity. In dealing with poverty, the eternal dilemma remains that well-targeted measures are in theory the most-cost effective but that these tend to come with serious disincentive effects which in turn tend to undercut their longer-term effectiveness and political sustainability. Particularly when one takes the potential implications of the dynamic perspective seriously, it is likely that to be effective, targeted policies need to fit within a broad-based anti-poverty strategy that builds to a large extent on universalistic programmes, such as universal child benefits, that can have an immediate impact on poverty without adversely affecting work incentives one way or the other.

Overall Conclusion

It has become a central tenet of the current welfare state literature that we now live in an economic environment that is fundamentally different from the one which prevailed when the core institutions of modern income protection came to maturity. French sociologist Pierre Rosanvallon has suggested that advanced welfare states are confronted with as much as a 'New Social Question'. Many others have made or have come close to making similar claims. The following quote from Esping-Andersen et al. (2002, p. 2) is reflective of much of current thinking:

> We are in the midst of economic upheaval, the emergence of a very different kind of integrated global economic order from that which reigned in our grandfathers' time. Technological transformation and the dominance of service employment provoke major changes in the social risk structure, creating a wholly new set of societal winners and losers. The standard production worker and the low-skilled could by and large count on a decently paid and secure job in the welfare capitalism era. This is unlikely to be the case in the twenty-first century. The basic requisites needed for a good and secure life are growing and changing at the same time. Those with insufficient skills or cultural and social resources may easily slide into a life course marked by low pay, unemployment, and precarious jobs. Our contemporary preoccupation with social exclusion appears very much as an echo of the 'social question' that permeated debates in the 1930s.

The core claim here is that people who lack adequate schooling or the intellectual, creative or social talents that new technologies and work practices seem to require will find it increasingly hard to acquire an adequate income in the labour market, even if they do everything they reasonably can to achieve their full earnings potential.

If this is true, the consequences for social policy are bound to be profound, especially for minimum income protection policy. Income protection systems in advanced welfare states are after all to a greater or lesser degree grounded on the institutional and doctrinal premise that people of working age have no need for social income and that they cannot legitimately claim social income, unless they are incapacitated or otherwise involuntarily unemployed. The assumption, by and large, is that redistribution is only required and, indeed, appropriate, to alleviate risk-induced and, as a general rule, temporary need. It seems that it is exactly this crucial assumption that is becoming increasingly untenable.

This can be said to be the generic problem. In addition to that, and more specifically, the demand shift against the less-skilled appears to be generating specific problems and pathologies across the various welfare state regimes.

Poverty in work, though obviously not a new phenomenon, is widely thought to have become a more salient problem in the Anglo-Saxon welfare states. The challenge facing the Anglo-Saxon cluster is said to be deteriorating (relative) wages for the less-skilled, increasing poverty in work, which is coupled to ever-more unequal access to social insurance and deficient skill-formation because of inadequate public investment in education, especially for the disadvantaged.

In the Bismarckian Continental European welfare states, where regulatory practices, wage structures and social protection provisions have supposedly not adapted sufficiently to post-industrial realities, the problem is said to be inadequate employment growth, mass chronic benefit dependency and entrapment at working age.

The position of the Nordic countries in this context is said to be of a rather different nature. The Scandinavian regime has traditionally been less reliant on the assumption that working age people can and should be economically self-reliant. The state there has long taken active responsibility in ensuring full employment (for men and women alike), catering specifically to the needs of the less-skilled. The main difficulty confronting the Scandinavian model, it is argued, is their continued ability to finance the set of public policies that sustain high employment in the context of egalitarian wages. In an increasingly competitive and non-egalitarian internal context, the Nordic countries are said to face a hard choice between liberalising private services, which would presumably entail more wage inequality, or a continued adherence to wage equality which, under conditions of tightening budgetary constraints, might imply more unemployment.

The challenges that the demand shift against the less-skilled is said to be posing for advanced welfare states, in the context of present-day economic and political constraints, has been captured in what Iversen and Wren dubbed the 'Service Economy Trilemma'. This trilemma suggests that welfare states today increasingly confront a choice between full employment, wage equality and fiscal sustainability.

Coming back to the specific focus of this volume – minimum income protection – the claim is not just that the traditional systems are dealing inadequately with the new social risks that economic change has given rise to, but that there is no hope in gradual reform, particularly of the kind that remains true to the paradigmatic principles of the conventional models of social protection. We have seen the rise of social policy doctrines such as 'The Third Way' or 'The Activating Welfare State' that entail a radical shift from 'passive' use of resources (adequate replacement benefits for the non-employed) to a more 'active' use, in the form of employment subsidies for the long-term unemployed or wage supplements for the low-paid. Others have called for an even more profound paradigmatic shift, for example in the direction of an unconditional basic income.

This book began by tackling the notion that certain sections of the active age population are finding it increasingly difficult to be economically self-sufficient in the advanced economies.

The proportion of working-aged people dependent on benefits to stay out of poverty has increased substantially. Patterns and magnitudes differ across countries, but the OECD-wide pattern clearly is one of rising dependency on direct income redistribution to stay out of poverty. Socio-demographic change, particularly the increase in single-parent and single-adult households, is one major factor but cannot provide the whole explanation. It is also evident that economic self-reliance dropped most strongly among the least skilled.

While such evidence is consistent with claims that people with fewer educational qualifications are finding it increasingly hard to acquire an adequate income in advanced economies, the interpretation of dependency trends is beset by difficulties. Observed trends are the result of complex causal mechanisms including feedback mechanisms (both of an economic as of a political nature) that prove very difficult to disentangle from 'exogenous' labour market shifts.

In the subsequent chapter, we turned to the extensive empirical labour economics literature to gain more insights into the magnitude and nature of the labour demand shifts that are often thought to be behind the increases in dependency. The evidence leaves little doubt about the reality of the demand shift against the less-skilled. Deindustrialisation and technological change seem to be major driving factors. But a more striking finding is the labour market position of the less-skilled – as measured by their employment rate and their relative earnings – has not deteriorated everywhere to the same extent. The degree of cross-country variation in this respect is in fact quite striking.

In some countries, most conspicuously the US, the less-skilled have experienced a very marked, even dramatic deterioration of their labour market position. In most European countries the picture is less dramatic and rather more mixed. Earnings differentials have generally remained stable. Stability on the earnings inequality side has in some countries come at the cost of (relative) drops in employment and rises in unemployment but this has not happened everywhere, certainly not to the same extent.

Why is this? Some studies suggest that the falling demand for less-skilled workers has not been accompanied with increases in economic inequality or economic redundancy in countries where the rate of upskilling has kept pace with these demand shifts. Other studies have linked the mostly episodic changes in inequality, where these have occurred, to country-specific institutional and policy changes.

What the evidence in effect suggests is that it appears unduly fatalistic to predicate social policy reform on the assumption that the economic marginalisation of the less-educated is an inescapable feature of post-industrial society. By the same token, the idea that countries are increasingly and inevitably faced with a choice between more wage inequality or more structural labour market exclusion does not seem to be borne out by the weight of the empirical evidence as it presents itself today either. Countries can demonstrably still achieve high levels of labour market integration within the context of relatively egalitarian wage settings even in absence of large-scale direct or indirect government employment.

The problem here is perhaps not so much that certain trade-offs are intrinsically impossible to overcome today, but that there remain considerable practical barriers to actually doing so. Providing people with the right initial skills as well as with continuing upskilling is one such crucial challenge. This, clearly, is easier said than done. Changing the skills profile of the work force is never done overnight. Some countries are demonstrably more successful in providing the less-talented segments of their populations with skills, knowledge and credentials that are worth something in the labour market. But much less remains known as to why this is the case. And even if one were able to quickly identify all the factors that distinguish a good educational system from a less adequate system, it is unlikely that the required organisational and cultural changes could be made quickly.

All this implies an important continued role for remedial redistribution and this brings us to the notion that the traditional pillars of minimum income protection are not doing an adequate job in this respect and are, moreover, inherently incapable of doing so.

I have argued in this book that at least some social security systems have proved more adaptive in the face of economic and social change than is often recognised. I have looked in some detail at the Belgian case because it is a fascinating case of a social security system that did not remain 'frozen' in the face of changing circumstances. Belgium's system evolved from a social insurance system fairly much in the classic Bismarckian mould into what effectively amounts to a minimum income protection system. Improving the poverty alleviation effectiveness of the system was a prime and explicit policy objective in that process of gradual transformation. The reforms did have a substantial impact on the poverty alleviation effectiveness of the system. What the Belgian case shows is that the scope for gradual adaptation may be considerably larger than often assumed. At the same time, however, the Belgian case also hints at both the economic as well as political limits to gradual reform. Specifically, gradual reform clearly failed at the objectives of reintegrating benefit recipients in the labour market and improving their prospects of upward income mobility and economic self-sufficiency.

And yet a satisfactory policy response to the problem of low-skilled labour market exclusion should clearly entail more than adequate minimum income protection. Over the past decade or so we have witnessed the rise of social policy doctrines that seek to achieve a synthesis between the objectives of providing adequate minimum income protection and promoting self-sufficiency. These doctrines all put labour market reintegration and job creation at the very centre of policy effort.

I have argued in this book that rather than a natural complementarity there appears to be more of a tension between the objectives of boosting labour market participation and reducing poverty (relative income poverty that is). I have documented instances where strong rises in labour participation went accompanied with rises rather than drops in relative poverty. This happened not so much because more employment growth came at the cost of more low-paid (service) employment and more 'poverty in work'. (The link between low-paid work and poverty is weak at any rate.) Instead, strong job growth, where it occurred, did not benefit first and foremost those most in need of a job: the unemployed and the non-employed living in poverty. Instead, it reinforced rather than reduced the gap between work-rich and work-poor/work-less households. The Dutch case provides a telling illustration in this respect.

A further point made in this book is that even special measures aimed at drawing into the labour market those who have slipped into passive, long-term benefit dependence have not always managed to generate the impact that was hoped for. Many countries have put very significant resources into measures like employment subsidies and reductions in employers' social security contributions to give an added boost to the employment prospects of segments with a high risk of chronic labour market exclusion.

My reading of the empirical evaluation literature as presented in this volume is that the measured net employment effects are consistently much lower than what theoretical models and simulations tend to predict, even under relatively pessimistic assumptions. The available evidence certainly raises many doubts as to the effectiveness, particularly the cost-effectiveness, of demand-side-oriented measures if it comes to reintegrating those with the weakest chances on the labour market. At the same time, the empirical evaluation literature is rather more encouraging when it comes to the effects of measures that address the supply side. It appears that well-designed financial rewards for accepting low-paid work can have a considerable positive effect on the labour market participation and living standards of long-term benefit recipients. However, concerns about chronic entrapment in low-paid work also appear to be legitimate. In addition, little remains known about how such subsidies enter into wage setting processes and how they affect wage structures and skills in the longer run, especially at the lower end of the spectrum.

I would, in conclusion, argue that the focus today is perhaps rather too much on new policy paradigms and instruments, many of which remain after all of unproven effectiveness, and that there is an undue disregard for the continued role of the traditional pillars of income protection. If we are to take the objective of reducing poverty seriously, the traditional pillars of social protection arguably need to be brought back into the picture again. I strongly suspect that these are bound to remain an important, if not crucial component of any truly effective poverty reduction strategy. Adequate 'passive' benefits have after all a direct and immediate impact on the living standards of vast sections of the poor population since their effectiveness does not depend on the extent to which assumed behavioural effects occur, or at least much less so. Moreover, the experience in a number of countries shows that passive benefit adequacy can go together with a well-functioning labour market and high levels of labour market integration, including of the least skilled. What is required, it seems, is that benefit adequacy is accompanied by strictly enforced training, job search and work requirements as well as stimuli to accept a job if it is actually offered.

Similarly, I believe that new policy instruments such as in-work benefits for the low-paid need to be seen as complements rather than substitutes for traditional institutions. After all, in-work benefits may well induce further wage erosion in the absence of externally enforced wage floors, i.e., minimum wages and collective bargaining. Moreover, in order to be effective as an anti-poverty device, low-pay supplements need to be strongly targeted, which almost inevitably implies a high cost in terms of disincentive effects. This again places the focus on the continuing importance of traditional instruments such as (universal) child benefits that can have an immediate impact on poverty – both among those depending on earnings and those on replacement benefits – without adversely affecting work incentives. A strong case can be made that in order to be effective, policies aimed at the working poor will have to fit within a broad-based anti-poverty strategy in which the classic instruments of income support play a crucial role. This is particularly true when one takes the implications of possible longer term behavioural effects seriously. These questions of complementarity between traditional and new instruments deserve to be at the centre of the current debate.

List of Tables and Figures

List of Tables

Table 1.1   Benefit dependency: benefit recipients at working age as a percentage of the working-age population (15-64 years), 1980-1999 (in FTE)   30

Table 1.2   Poverty rates before taxes and transfers: per cent of poor[2] individuals in each group, and changes in percentage points   34

Table 1.3   Structure of poverty before taxes and transfers: per cent of all poor individuals belonging to each group, and changes in percentage points   36

Table 1.4   Educational profile Flemish population of working age, 1976-1997 (change in percentage points)   40

Table 1.5   Living standard by formal level of qualification, 1976-1997. Level in 1997 (1997 euros) and 1976-1997 percentage point difference   41

Table 1.6   Poverty rate by formal level of qualification, 1976-1997. Level in 1997 and 1976-1997 percentage point difference   41

Table 1.7   Living standard by educational quartile, 1976-1997. Level in 1997 (1997 euros) and 1976-1997 percentage point difference   42

Table 1.8   Poverty rate by educational quartile, 1976-1997. Level in 1997 and 1976-1997 percentage point difference   42

Table 1.9   Indicators of employment, income and welfare state dependence, men aged 45-65 years, levels for 1997 and 1976-1997 trend, percentage point difference, except for living standard (percentage change)   45

Table 1.10   Indicators of employment, income and welfare state dependence, women aged 25-45 years, levels for 1997 and 1976-1997 trend, percentage point change, except for living standard (percentage change)   46

Table 1.11   Joint labour income, couples with head aged between 25 and 45, by level of educational attainment head, Flanders 1976-1997   47

Table 1.12   Pre-transfer poverty rate by formal level of qualification, 1976-1997. Level in 1997 and 1976-1997 percentage point difference   48

Table 1.13   Pre-transfer poverty rate by educational quartile, 1976-1997. Level in 1997 and 1976-1997 percentage point difference   49

Table 2.1   Skill composition by economic sector, OECD average 1998   64

Table 2.2   Employment, wage and labour-market inequality trends, men 1970s-1990s   73

Table 3.1   The extent of poverty, low pay, and poverty among the low-paid, based on LIS data, late 1980s/early 1990s   100

Table 3.2   The overlap between poverty and low pay, based on ECHP data, 1993   102

Table 3.3   The probability of being low-paid for employees in poor households, based on ECHP data, 1993   103

Table 3.4   Location of employees in the household income distribution, based on ECHP data, 1993   104

Table 3.5   Location of low-paid employees in household income distribution, based on ECHP data, 1993   105

Table 3.6   Poverty rates for low-paid individuals by age and sex, based on LIS data, late 1980s   106

Table 3.7   The distribution of low-paid workers by number of earners in the household, based on LIS data, late 1980s   107

Table 3.8   Poverty rates and the impact of social transfers and taxes for low-paid household heads, couples with dependent children   108

Table 3.9   Poverty for low-paid full-time full-year workers versus all low-paid, the Netherlands, the UK and the US, 1993   110

Table 3.10   Poverty rates for households of low-paid employees in the absence of their earnings, Ireland 1994   111

Table 3.11   Percentage of employees experiencing low pay who are in poor households over different periods, Germany, the Netherlands, the UK and the US   112

Table 4.1	The robust labour market position of the male breadwinner: Labour market position of prime-age men in a European perspective, 1997 128
Table 4.2	Evolution of the number of people entitled to unemployment insurance benefits for full-time unemployment, Belgium 1970-2000 130
Table 4.3	Distribution across benefit categories in unemployment insurance, Belgium, 2000 132
Table 4.4	Poverty incidence by labour market status, Belgium 1985-1997 139
Table 4.5	Poverty exposure of unemployed persons by household type, 1997 140
Table 4.6	Profile of households receiving unemployment benefits (UEB), Belgium, 1997 140
Table 4.7	Adult minimum wage relative to a range of average earnings measures, mid-1990s-1997 155
Table 5.1	Poverty rates for various household types, working-age population (LIS data) 174
Table 5.2	The distribution of poor households with a working-age head across various household types (LIS data) 174
Table 5.3	Poverty rates by work attachment, working-age population (OECD data) 175
Table 5.4	Poverty shares by work attachment, working-age population (OECD data) 176
Table 5.5	Non-employed working-age households by type (distribution in 1996, and percentage point changes between 1985-1996), OECD 178
Table 5.6	Risk of non-employment of working-age households by type (as a percentage of households in each type in 1996, and percentage point changes between 1985-1996), OECD 178
Table 5.7	A job is not necessarily enough to escape poverty: illustrative table for Belgium, 1997, in BEF 182
Table 5.8	Absolute poverty incidence: standardised comparison between Belgium and the Netherlands, 1985-1997. Percentage point difference (initial levels for 1985) 191
Table 5.9	Key trends in Belgium and the Netherlands (1985 = 100) 191

Table 6.1 Brief survey of the measures discussed 205
Table 6.2 Summary of some important findings 208
Table 6.3 Employment effects: Findings from time-series/DDD analysis 212
Table 6.4 Findings from experimental research: Dayton Voucher Experiment 213
Table 6.5 Summary of findings on mobility from subsidised to regular work 215

List of Figures

Figure 1.1 Living standard trend by level of educational attainment, 1942-1951 cohort (25-34 years old in 1976) in Flanders 1976-1997 44
Figure 1.2 Determinants of living standard rise among working-age population (25-65 years), Flanders 1976-1997 50
Figure 1.3 Determinants of living standard rise among working-age population (25-65 years), Flanders 1976-1997 50

Figure 2.1 Changes in male employment and earnings inequality (1970s, 1980s, 1990s), OECD countries 74

Figure 3.1 Incidence of low pay and poverty 99

Figure 4.1 Minimum UI benefit levels, in 2001 prices 133
Figure 4.2 Relative poverty rates for the working-age population, OECD, mid-1990s 137
Figure 4.3 Relative poverty (50% mean equivalent household income) among the unemployed, 1994 138
Figure 4.4 Poverty rates for households receiving UI benefits, 1985-1997 141
Figure 4.5 Households receiving UI benefits, share in total population, 1985-1997 142
Figure 4.6 Adequacy of minimum UI benefits, expressed as percentage of relative poverty threshold for relevant category 143
Figure 4.7 Minimum UI benefit levels relative to national income per head 144
Figure 4.8 Average living standard, wages and UI benefits: real terms trend between 1985 and 1997 144

Figure 4.9   How the minimum wage and UI benefits have drifted from the average standard of living   145
Figure 4.10   Real minimum wages 1970-1995; 1975 = 100   152
Figure 4.11   Distribution of unemployment insurance benefits across household income deciles, 1997   159

Figure 5.1   Employment rates and poverty   171
Figure 5.2   Changes in employment and poverty rates, mid-1980s–mid-1990s (percentage points difference)   172
Figure 5.3   Changes in non-employment rates at the individual and the household level, mid-1980s–mid-1990s (percentage points difference)   180

References

Acemoglu, D. (1998), 'Why Do New Technologies Complement Skills? Directed Technical Change and Wage Inequality', *Quarterly Journal of Economics*, 113, 1055-1090.

Acemoglu, D. (1999a), 'Changes in Unemployment and Wage Inequality: An Alternative Theory and Some Evidence', *American Economic Review*, 89, 1259-1278.

Acemoglu, D. (1999b), *Patterns of Skill Premia*. Working Paper 7018. Cambridge: National Bureau of Economic Research.

Acemoglu, D. (2002), 'Technical Change, Inequality and the Labour Market', *Journal of Economic Literature*.

Acemoglu, D. and J.-S. Pischke (2001), 'Changes in the Wage Structure, Family Income, and Children's Education', *European Economic Review*, 45, 890-904.

Alderson, A.S. and F. Nielsen (2002), 'Globalization and the Great U-Turn: Income Inequality Trends in 16 OECD Countries', *American Journal of Sociology*, 107, 1244-1299.

Allen, S. (1996), *Technology and the wage structure*, Working Paper 5534. Cambridge: National Bureau of Economic Research.

Alvarez, P.B. (2001), *The Politics of Income Inequality in the OECD: The Role of Second Order Effects*. Luxembourg Income Study Working Paper 284.

Ameels, J.C., M. Lopez-Movella and B. Van der Linden (1994), *Rapport d'une enquête auprès des firmes à la définition des politiques favorisant l'embauche des groupes concernés par l'objectif 3, Recherche pur l'établissement du plan 1994-1999 de la Belgique*. Louvain-la-Neuve: IRES.

Amiel, Y., F.A. Cowell and A. Polovin (2001), 'Risk Perceptions, Income Transformations and Inequality', *European Economic Review*, 45, 964-976.

Andries, M. (1996), 'The Politics of Targeting: the Belgian Case', *Journal of European Social Policy*, 6 (3) 209-233.

Arrow, K., S. Bowles and S. Durlauf (2000), *Meritocracy and Economic Inequality*. Princeton: Princeton University Press.

Arryn, P. (1995), *De werkvloer als leerschool: Doelmatigheid van werkervaringsprojecten*. RIAT.

Ashenfelter, O. and C. Rouse (1999), *Schooling, Intelligence and Income in America: Cracks in the Bell Curve*, Working Paper 6902. Cambridge: National Bureau of Economic Research.

Ashenfelter, O. and C. Rouse (2000), 'Intelligence and Income in America', in: K. Arrow et al. (eds.), *Meritocracy and Economic Inequality*. Princeton: Princeton University Press.

Ashton, D., B. Davies, A. Felstead and F. Green (1999), *Work Skills in Britain*. Oxford: Centre for Skills, Knowledge and Organisational Performance.

Atkinson, A. (1973), 'Low Pay and the Cycle of Poverty', in: F. Field (ed.), *Low Pay*. London: Arrow.

Atkinson, A. (1987), 'On the Measurement of Poverty', *Econometrica*, 55 (4) 749-64.

Atkinson, A. (1993), 'Work Incentives', in: A.B. Atkinson and G.V. Mogensen (eds.), *Welfare and Work Incentives: A North European Perspective*. Oxford: Clarendon Press.

Atkinson, A. (1995), *Incomes and the Welfare State*. Cambridge: Cambridge University Press.

Atkinson, A. (1997a), 'Bringing Income Distribution in from the Cold', *Economic Journal*, 107, 297-321.

Atkinson, A. (1997b), *Measurement of Trends in Poverty and the Income Distribution*. Cambridge: University of Cambridge: Cambridge.

Atkinson, A. (1999a), *Increased Income Inequality in OECD Countries and the Redistributive Impact of the Government Budget*. Paper presented at UNU/WIDER conference on Income Inequality and Poverty Reduction, July, Helsinki.

Atkinson, A. (1999b), *Is Rising Inequality Inevitable? A Critique of the Transatlantic Consensus*, Wider Annual Lecture 3.

Atkinson, A. (1999c), 'The Distribution of Income in the UK and OECD Countries in the Twentieth Century', *Oxford Review of Economic Policy*, 15 (4) 56-75.

Atkinson, A. (2000), 'The Changing Distribution of Income: Evidence and Explanations', *German Economic Review*, 1.

Atkinson, A., F. Bourguignon and C. Morrison (1992), *Empirical Studies of Earnings Mobility*. Philadelphia: Hardwood Academic Publishers.

Atkinson, A. and A. Brandolini (2001), 'Promise and Pitfalls in the Use of "Secondary", Data-Sets: Income Inequality in OECD Countries', *Journal of Economic Literature*, 34, 771-799.

Atkinson, A., B. Cantillon, E. Marlier and B. Nolan (2001), *Social Indicators: The EU and Social Inclusion*. Oxford: Oxford University Press.

Atkinson, J. and N. Meager (1994), *Evaluation of Workstart Pilots*. Institute for Employment Studies Report 279.

Atkinson A. and J. Micklewright (1991), 'Unemployment Compensation and Labour Market Transitions', *Journal of Economic Literature*, 24, 1679-1727.

Atkinson, A., L. Rainwater and T. Smeeding (1995), *Income Distribution in OECD Countries*. Paris: OECD.

Austen, S. (2000), *Fairness and Skills Differentials: an International Comparison*, CLMR Discussion paper 00/3.

Autor, D. and L. Katz. (1999), 'Changes in the Wage Structure and Earnings Inequality', in: O. Ashenfelter and D. Card (eds.), *Handbook of Labour Economics*. Amsterdam: North-Holland.

Autor, D., A. Krueger and L. Katz (1998), 'Computing Inequality: Have Computers Changed the Labour Market?', *Quarterly Journal of Economics*, 113 (4) 1169-1214.

Autor, D., F. Levy and R. Murnane (2000), *Upstairs, Downstairs: Computer-Skill Complementarity and Computer-Labour Substitution on Two Floors of a Large Bank*, Working Paper 7890. Cambridge: National Bureau of Economic Research.

Baldwin, P. (1990), *The Politics of Social Solidarity: Class Bases of the European Welfare State 1875-1975*. Cambridge: Cambridge University Press.

Baldwin, R. (1995), *The effect of trade and foreign direct investment on employment and relative wages*. Working Paper 5037. Cambridge: National Bureau of Economic Research.

Barr, N. (1998), *The Economics of the Welfare State*. Oxford: Oxford University Press.

Barr, N. (2001), *The Welfare State as Piggy Bank: Information, Risk, Uncertainty, and the Role of the State*. Oxford: Oxford University Press.

Barrett, A., T. Callen and B. Nolan (1997), *Earnings Distribution and Returns to Education in Ireland, 1987-94*, ESRI Working Paper 85.

Bartel, A. and F. Lichtenberg (1997), 'The Comparative Advantage of Educated Workers in Implementing New Technology', *Review of Economics and Statistics*, 69, 1-11.

Baumol, W., S. Batey Blackman and E. Wolff (1989), *Productivity and American Leadership*. Cambridge, MA: MIT Press.

Bazen, S. (1988), *On the Overlap Between Low Pay and Poverty*, Discussion Paper 120, Programme on Taxation, Incentives and the Distribution of Income. London: London School of Economics.

Bazen, S. and N. Skourias (1997), 'Is There a Negative Effect of Minimum Wages in France?', *European Economic Review*, 41, 723-732.

Beaudry, P. and D. Green (1998), *What is driving U.S. and Canadian wages: Exogenous technical change or endogenous choice of technique?*, Working Paper 6853. Cambridge: National Bureau of Economic Research.

Beaudry, P. and D. Green (2000), *The Changing Structure of Wages in the US and*

Germany: What Explains the Differences?, Working Paper 7697. Cambridge: National Bureau of Economic Research.

Becker, I. (1998), *Zur personellen Einkommensverteilung in Deutschland*, EVS- Projekt, Arbeitspapier Nr. 13, Frankfurt am Main: Universität Frankfurt am Main.

Becker, U. (1999), *The 'Dutch Miracle': Employment Growth in a Retrenched but still Generous System*, SPRC Discussion Paper no 99.

Bell, B., R. Blundell and J. Van Reenen (1999), 'Getting the Unemployed Back to Work: The Role of Targeted Wage Subsidies', Institute of Fiscal Studies Working Paper no W99/12.

Bell, B. and M. Pitt (1995), *Trade Union Decline and the Distribution of Wage in the UK: Evidence from Kernal Density Estimation*, Discussion Paper 107. Oxford: Nuffield College.

Belleville, A. (2001), 'L'utilisation des aides à l'emploi par les entreprises: permanence ou logique conjonturelle?', *Premières Synthèses*, no. 25.1, DARES, Ministère de l'Emploi et de la Solidarité, France.

Berlin, G.L. (2000), *Encouraging Work, Reducing Poverty: The Impact of Work Incentive Programs*, Manpower Demonstration Research Corporation.

Berman, E., J. Bound and S. Machin (1998), 'Implications of Skill-Biased Technical Change: International Evidence', *Quarterly Journal of Economics*, 113 (4) 1215-44.

Berman, E., J. Bound and Z. Griliches (1994), 'Changes in the Demand for Skilled Labour Within US Manufacturing: Evidence from the Annual Survey of Manufacture', *Quarterly Journal of Economics*, 109: 367-397.

Berman, E. and S. Machin (2000), *SBTC Happens! Evidence on the Factor Bias of Technological Change in Developing and Developed Countries*, mimeo.

Bertola, G., F.D. Blau and L.M. Kahn (2002), *Labour Market Institutions and Demographic Employment Patterns*, Working Paper 9043. Cambridge: National Bureau of Economic Research.

Bertola, G. and A. Ichino (1995), 'Wage Inequality and Unemployment: U.S. vs. Europe', *NBER Macroeconomics Annual 1995*. Cambridge, MA: MIT Press.

Beveridge, W. (1945), *Full Employment in a Free Society*. London: Allen and Unwin.

Bhagwati, J. (1964), 'The Pure Theory of International Trade: a Survey', *Economic Journal*, 74, 1-84.

Bhagwati, J. and V. Dehejia (1994), 'Freer trade and wages of the unskilled: Is Marx striking again?', in: J. Bhagwati and M. Kosters (eds.), *Trade and Wages: Leveling Wages Down?*, pp. 37-75. Washington, DC: American Enterprise Institute.

Bingley, P. and I. Walker (1997), 'The Labour Supply, Unemployment and Participation of lone-mothers in in-work transfer programmes', *The Economic Journal*, Sept.

Bishop, J. and R. Haveman (1979), 'Selective Employment Subsidies: Can Okun's Law be Repealed?', *American Economic Review, Papers and Proceedings*, 69, 124-130.

Bishop, J. and M. Montgomery (1994), 'Does the Targeted Jobs Tax Credit Create Jobs at Subsidized Firms?', *Industrial Relations*, 32 (3) 289-306.

Bjorklund, A. and R. Freeman (1997), 'Generating Equality and Eliminating Poverty – The Swedish Way', in: R. Freeman, B. Swedenborg and R. Topel (eds.), *The Welfare State in Transition Reforming the Swedish Model*. Chicago: SNS-NBER Conference Volume. Chicago: University of Chicago Press.

Blanchard, O. and J. Wolfers (2000), 'The Role of Shocks and Institutions in the Rise of European Unemployment: The Aggregate Evidence', *The Economic Journal*, 110, Cl-33.

Blanchflower, D. and A. Bryson (2003), *What Effect Do Unions Have on Wages and Would 'What Do Unions Do' Be Surprised?*, Working Paper 9973. Cambridge: National Bureau of Economic Research.

Blank, R. (1995), 'Changes in Inequality and Unemployment over the 1980s: A comparative cross-national perspective', *Journal of population economics*, 8, 1-21.

Blank, R. (1997a), *Is There a Trade-Off Between Unemployment and Inequality? No Easy Answers: Labour Market Problems in the United States versus Europe*. Public Policy Brief no. 33. City Levy Economics Institute.

Blank, R. (1997b), *It Takes a Nation: A New Agenda for Fighting Poverty*, Princeton: Princeton University Press.

Blank, R. (2002), *Evaluating Welfare Reform in the United States*, Working Paper 8983. Cambridge: National Bureau of Economic Research.

Blank, R., R. Card and P. Robins (1999), *Financial Incentives for Increasing Work and Incomes among Low-Income Families*, Working Paper 6998. Cambridge: National Bureau of Economic Research.

Blank, R. and D. Ellwood (2001), *The Clinton Legacy for America's Poor*, Working Paper 8437. Cambridge: National Bureau of Economic Research.

Blau, F. and L. Kahn (1996), 'International Differences in Male Wage Inequality: Institutions versus Market Forces', *Journal of Political Economy*, 104, 791-837.

Blau, F. and L. Kahn (2001), *Do Cognitive Test Scores Explain Higher US Wage Inequality?*, Working Paper 8210. Cambridge: National Bureau of Economic Research.

Blondal, S. and M. Pearson (1995), 'Unemployment and Other Non-Employment Benefits', *Oxford Review of Economic Policy*, p. 136-169.

Blum, A. and F. Guerin-Pace (2000), 'Weaknesses and Defects of IALS', in: S. Carey (ed.), *Measuring Adult Literacy: The International Adult Literacy Survey in the European Context*. London: Office for National Statistics.

Blundell, R. (2000), 'Work Incentives and "In-Work", Benefit Reform: A Review', *Oxford Review of Economic Policy*, 16 (1) 27-44.

Blundell, R. and T. MaCurdy (1999), 'Labour Supply: A Review of Alternative Approaches', in: O. Ashenfelter and D. Card (eds.) *Handbook of Labour Economics, vol. 3*. Amsterdam: North-Holland. (Also published as Institute of Fiscal Studies Working Paper no. W98/18.)

Boeri, T., A. Borsch-Supan and G. Tabellini (2000), 'Would you like to shrink the welfare state?', *Economic Policy*, 32, 9-50.

Bollens J., C. Claeys and I. Nicaise (1996), *Koopjes op de arbeidsmarkt. De micro-economische effectiviteit van RSZ-verminderingen bij tewerkstelling van risicogroepen in België*. Leuven: Hoger Instituut voor de Arbeid.

Bonoli, G. and M. Powell (2002), 'Third Ways in Europe', *Social Policy and Society*, 1(1), 59-66.

Borjas, G., R. Freeman and L. Katz (1997), 'How Much Do Immigration and Trade Affect Labor Market Outcomes?', *Brookings Papers on Economic Activity*, 1, 1-67.

Borjas, G. and V.A. Ramey (1995), 'Foreign Competition, Market Power, and Wage Inequality', *Quarterly Journal of Economics*, 110, 1075-1110.

Borland, J. (1999), 'Earnings Inequality in Australia: Changes, Causes and Consequences', *Economic Record*, 75, 177-202.

Bossier, F., Th. Brechet, M. Englert, L. Masure, M. Saintrain, C. Streel and F. Van Horebeek (1995), *Simulaties betreffende een vermindering van de werkgeversbijdragen voor sociale zekerheid en vormen van alternatieve financiering*. Planning Paper 75. Brussels: Federaal Planbureau.

Bossier, F., K. Hendrickx and C. Streel (1998), *Macro-economische impact van bijkomende patronale bijdragevermindering in het Belgische Actieplan voor Werkgelegenheid*, Working Paper 7-98. Brussels: Federaal Planbureau.

Bound, J. and G. Johnson (1992), 'Changes in the Structure of Wages in the 1980s: An Evaluation of Alternative Explanations', *American Economic Review*, 82, 371-392.

Bouwen, M. et al. (1978), *Bijzonder tijdelijk kader en tewerkstelling van werklozen*. Leuven: HIVA.

Bowles, S. and H. Gintis (2000), *The Inheritance of Economic Status: Education, Class and Genetics*. Department of Economics, University of Massachusetts.

Bowles, S., H. Gintis and M. Osborne (2002), 'The Determinants of Earnings: A Behavioral Approach', *Journal of Economic Perspectives*, 16 (3).

Breen, R. and B. Halpin (1989), *Subsidizing Jobs: An Evaluation of the Employment Incentive Scheme*. Dublin: The Economic and Social Research Institute.

Bresnahan, T. (1999), 'Computerisation and Wage Dispersion: An Analytical Reinterpretation', *Economic Journal*, 109, F390-F415.

Brewer, M and J. Browne (2006), 'The Effect of Working Families Tax Credit on Labour Market Participation', IFS Briefing Note no. 69, London: Institute for Fiscal Studies

Bryson, A. and A. Marsh (1996), *Leaving Family Credit*. London: HMSO.

Buhman, B., L. Rainwater, G. Schmaus and T. Smeeding (1988) 'Equivalence Scales, Well-being, Inequality and Poverty: Sensitivity Estimates Across Ten Countries Using the Luxembourg Income Study Database', *Review of Income and Wealth*, 33 (2) 115-42.

Burkhauser, R. and T. Finnegan (1989), 'The Minimum Wage and the Poor: The End of a Relationship?', *Journal of Policy Analysis and Management*, 8 (1) 53-71.

Burniaux, J-M., T-T. Dan, D. Fore, M. Förster, M. Mira d'Ercole and H. Oxley (1998), *Income Distribution and Poverty in Selected OECD Countries*. Working Paper 189. Paris: OECD.

Burtless, G. (1985), 'Are Targeted Wage Subsidies Harmful? Evidence from a Wage Voucher Experiment', *Industrial and Labour Relations Review*, 39, 105-114.

Burtless, G. (1995a), 'International Trade and the Rise in Earnings Inequality', *Journal of Economic Literature*, 33, 800-16.

Burtless, G. (1995b), 'The Case for Randomized Field Trials in Economic and Policy Research', *Journal of Economic Perspectives*, 9 (2) 63-84.

Byrne, A. (1993), *An Evaluation of JOBSTART*, Department of Employment, Education and Training, EMB Report 7/93.

Cahuc, P. (2002), A quoi sert la prime pour l'emploi?, *Revue Française d'Economie*, 16 (3) 3-61.

Callan, T. and B. Nolan (1991), 'Concepts of Poverty and the Poverty Line', *Journal of Economic Surveys*, 5 (3) 243-261.

Calmfors, L. (1994), 'Active Labour Market Policy and Unemployment – A Framework for the Analysis of Crucial Design Features', *OECD Economic Studies*. Paris: OECD.

Cantillon, B. (1993), 'De beperkingen van de sociale zekerheid', *Belgisch Tijdschrift voor Sociale Zekerheid*, 35 (1) 3-43.

Cantillon, B., L. De Lathouwer, I. Marx, R. Van Dam and K. Van den Bosch (1999), 'Sociale indicatoren 1976-1997', *Belgisch Tijdschrift voor Sociale Zekerheid*, 41 (4) 747-800.

Cantillon, B., V. De Maesschalck, V. and R. Van Dam (2001), *Welvaartsvastheid en adequaatheid van de sociale minima 1970-2001*, Berichten / UFSIA, Antwerp: Centrum voor Sociaal Beleid.

Cantillon, B., B. Kerstens and G. Verbist (2000), *De verdelingseffecten van het ontwerp van fiscale hervorming (plan Reynders)*, Berichten / UFSIA, Antwerp: Centrum voor Sociaal Beleid.

Cantillon, B., I. Marx and V. De Maesschalk (2003), *De bodem van de welvaartstaat*, Berichten / UA, Antwerp: Centrum voor Sociaal Beleid.

Cantillon, B., I. Marx and K. Van den Bosch (1997), 'The Challenge of Poverty and Social Exclusion', in: OECD (ed.), *Family, Market and Community: Equity and Efficiency in Social Policy*. Paris: OECD.

Cantillon, B., I. Marx and K. Van den Bosch (2003), 'The Puzzle of Egalitarianism: About the Relationships between Employment, Wage Inequality, Social Expenditure and Poverty', *European Journal of Social Security*, 5 (2) 108-127.

Cantillon, S. and B. Nolan (1998), 'Are Married Women More Deprived than their Husbands', *Journal of Social Policy*, 27 (2) 151-71.

Cantillon, B., J. Peeters and E. De Ridder (1987), *Atlas van de Sociale Zekerheid in België*. Leuven: Acco.

Cantillon, B., N. Van Mechelen, I. Marx and K. Van den Bosch (2004), 'De evolutie van de minimumbescherming in 15 Europese welvaartsstaten in de jaren negentig', *Belgisch Tijdschrift voor Sociale Zekerheid*, 3, 509-548.

Cappelli, P. (2000), *Computers, Work Organization, and Wage Outcomes*, Working Paper 7987. Cambridge: National Bureau of Economic Research.

Card, D. (1992), 'The Effects of Unions on the Distribution of Wages: Redistribution or Relabelling?', Working Paper 4195. Cambridge: National Bureau of Economic Research.

Card, D. (1998), *Falling Union Membership and Rising Wage Inequality: What's the Connection?*, Working Paper 6520. Cambridge: National Bureau of Economic Research.

Card, D. and J. DiNardo (2002), *Skill Biased Technological Change and Rising Wage: Inequality: Some Problems and Puzzles*, Working Paper 8769. Cambridge: National Bureau of Economic Research.

Card, D., F. Kramarz and T. Lemieux (1999), 'Changes in the Relative Structure of Wages and Employment: A Comparison of the US, Canada and France', *Canadian Journal of Economics*, 32 (4) 843-77.

Card, D. and A. Krueger (1995), *Myth and Measurement: The New Economics of the Minimum Wage*. Princeton: Princeton University Press.

Card, D., T. Lemieux and W.C. Riddell (2003), *Unionisation and Wage Inequality: A Comparative Study of the US, the UK and Canada*, Working Paper 9473. Cambridge: National Bureau of Economic Research.

Card, D. and P. Robbins (1996), *Do Financial Incentives Encourage Welfare Recipients to Work? Evidence from a Randomised Evaluation of the Self-Sufficiency Project*, Working Paper 5701. Cambridge: National Bureau of Economic Research.

Carling, K. and K Richardson (2001), *The Relative Efficiency of Labour Market Programmes: Swedish Experience from the 1990s*. IFAU Working Paper 2.

Caroli, E. and J. Van Reenen (1999), *Skills and Organizational Change: Evidence from British and French establishments in the 1980s and 1990s*, Institute for Fiscal Studies Working Paper.

Carone, G., H. Immervoll, D. Paturot and A. Salomäki (2004), *Indicators of Unemployment and Low-wage Traps*, Working Paper 18. Paris: OECD.

Casey, B. and G. Bruche (1985), 'Active Labour Market Policy: An International Overview', *Industrial Relations*, 24, 37-61.

Cassiers, I., P. De Villé and P. Solar (1996), 'Economic Growth in Post-War Belgium', in: N. Crafts and G. Tonioli (eds.), *Economic Growth in Europe since 1945*. Cambridge: Cambridge University Press.

Centre d'Etudes des Revenus et des Coûtes (1991), *Les Bas Salaires dans les Pays de la Communauté Economique Européenne*. Paris: CERC.

Clegg, D. (2006), 'Unemployment Reforms in Bismarckian Welfare States: the Case of Belgium, France, Germany and the Netherlands, Paper presented at the Conference A Long Goodbye to Bismarck', Harvard University, June 2006.

Cockx, B., B. Van der Linden en A. Karaa (1998), 'Active Labour Market Policies and Job Tenure', *Oxford Economic Papers*, 50, 685-708.

Cornia, G.A. (1999), *Liberalisation, Globalisation and Income Distribution*, WIDER Working Paper 157. Helsinki: UNU/WIDER.

Coulter, F., F. Cowell and S.P. Jenkins (1992), 'Equivalence Scale Relativities and the Extent of Inequality and Poverty', *Economic Journal*, 102, 1067-1082.

Council of Economic Advisers (1998), *Good News for Low Income Families: Expansions in the Earned Income Tax Credit and the Minimum Wage*. Washington, DC: Council of Economic Advisers.

Crepon, B. and R. Desplatz (2001), 'Une nouvelle évaluation des effets des allégements de charges sociales sur des bas salaires', *Economie et statistique*, 348, 8.

Crouch, C. (1997), 'Skills-Based Full Employment: the Latest Philosopher's Stone', *British Journal of Industrial Relations*, 35, 367-391.

CSERC (1996), *L'allégement des charges sociales sur les bas salaires*. Paris: La Documentation Française.

Dahlberg, M. and A. Forslund (1999), *Direct displacement effects of labour market programmes: the case of Sweden*, IFAU Working Paper. Uppsala: University of Uppsala.

Daly, M. (2000), 'A fine balance: Women's La*bour* Market participation in international comparison', in: F.W. Scharpf (ed.), *Welfare and Work in the open economy, Responses to common challenges*, vol. II, pp. 467-510. Oxford: Oxford University Press.

Davis, D.R. (1998), 'Technology, Unemployment and Relative Wages in a Global Economy', *European Economic Review*, 42, 1613-1633.

De Beer, P. (1996), *Het onderste kwart*. Rijswijk: Sociaal en Cultureel Planbureau.

De Beer, P. (1999), 'De paradox van banengroei en armoede', *ESB*, pp. 950-952.

De Beer, P. (2001), *Over werken in de postindustriële samenleving*. Den Haag: SCP, 424 p. (proefschrift).

De Beer, P., L. De Lathouwer and K. Vos (2002), 'Twintig jaar na Wassenaar. Succesformule of overleefd model?', *Tijdschrift voor Arbeidsvraagstukken*, 18 (4) 279-282.

De Grip, A. and R. Dekker (1993), 'Winnaars en verliezers op de arbeidsmarkt in de jaren '80', *Tijdschrift voor Arbeidsvraagstukken*, 9 (3) 220-229.

De Grip, A. and J. Van Loo (2000), 'Winnaars en verliezers op de arbeidsmarkt 1990-1995', *Tijdschrift voor Arbeidsvraagstukken*, 16 (1) 6-17.

De Koning, J. (1993), 'Measuring the Placement Effects of Two Wage-Subsidy Schemes for the Long-Term Unemployed', *Empirical Economics*, 18 (3) 447-468.

De Koning, J., J. Gravesteijn-Lighthelm, J. t' Hoen, A. Verkaik (1995), *Met subsidie aan het werk: samenvattend rapport evaluatie KRA*, Centraal Bureau Arbeidsvoorziening.

De Lathouwer, L. (1997), 'Twintig jaar beleidsontwikkelingen in de Belgische Werkloosheidsverzekering', *Belgisch tijdschrift voor sociale zekerheid*, 39 (3-4) 817-879.

De Lathouwer, L. and K. Bogaerts (2000), *Een studie naar het schorsingsbeleid in de Belgische werkloosheidsverzekering en de herintrede op de arbeidsmarkt*. Antwerp: Centrum voor Sociaal Beleid.

De Lathouwer, L. and K. Bogaerts (2001), *Financiële incentieven en laagbetaald werk. De impact van de hervormingen in de sociale zekerheid en de fiscaliteit op de werkloosheidsval in België*, Berichten / UFSIA, Antwerp: Centrum voor Sociaal Beleid.

De Lathouwer, L. and I. Marx (2002), 'Werkgelegenheid en armoede: de prestaties van België en Nederland in vergelijkend perspectief', *Tijdschrift voor Arbeidsvraagstukken*, 18 (4) 335-350.

De Lathouwer, L. and I. Marx (2004), 'Low Wage Employment and Social Protection', in: I. Marx and W. Salverda (eds.), *Low Wage Employment in Europe: Perspectives for improvement*. Leuven: Acco.

De Swaan, A. (1988), *In Care of the State*. Cambridge: Polity Press.

De Witte, H. (1992), *Tussen optimisten en teruggetrokkenen. Een empirisch onderzoek naar het psychosociale profiel van langdurige werklozen en deelnemers aan Weer-Werkactie in Vlaanderen*, Leuven: HIVA.

Deleeck, H. (2001), *De architectuur van de welvaartsstaat opnieuw* bekeken. Leuven: Acco.

Department of Employment (1998), *New Earnings Survey*, HMSO: London. Department of Employment (1999), *New Earnings Survey*. HMSO: London.

Desjonqueres, T., S. Machin and J. Van Reenen (1999), 'Another Nail in the Coffin? Or Can the Trade Based Explanation of Changing Skill Structures be Resurrected?', *Scandinavian Journal of Economics*, 101 (4) 533-54.

Devroye, D. and R. Freeman (2002), *Does Inequality in Skills Explain Inequality in Earnings in Advanced Economies?*, Working Paper 8140. Cambridge: National Bureau of Economic Research.

Dewatripont, M., A. Sapir and K. Sekkat (1999), *Trade and Jobs in Europe*. Oxford: Oxford University Press.

Dickens, R. (1996), *The Evolution of Individual Male Earnings in Great Britain: 1975-1994*, Discussion Paper 306. London School of Economics.

Dickens, R. and D. Ellwood (2001), *Whither Poverty in Great Britain and the United States? The Determinants of Changing Poverty and Whether Work Will Work*, NBER Working Paper, W8253.

Dickert-Conlin, S. and D. Holz-Eakin (1999), *Helping the Working Poor: Employer vs. Employee-Based Subsidies*, Public Finance Policy Brief 14. Syracuse: Syracuse University.

DiNardo, J., N. Fortin and T. Lemieux (1996), 'Labour Market Institutions and the Distribution of Wages, 1973-1992: A Semi-parametric Approach', *Econometrica*, 64, 1001-1044.

DiNardo, J. and T. Lemieux (1997), 'Diverging Male Wage Inequality in the United States and Canada, 1981-1988: Do Institutions explain the Difference?', *Industrial and Labor Relations Review*, 50, 629-651.

DiNardo, J. and J. Pischke (1997), 'The Returns to Computer Use Revisited: Have Pencils Changed the Wage Structure Too?', *Quarterly Journal of Economics*, 112, 291-303.

DiPrete, T. A., Goux, D., Maurin, E. and Tåblin, M. (n.d.), 'Institutional Determinants of Employment Chances. The Structure of Unemployment in France and Sweden', *European Sociological Review*, 17 (3) 233-254.

Dixit, A.K. and V. Norman (1980), *Theory of International Trade*. Cambridge: Cambridge University Press.

Dixon, S. (1996), 'The Distribution of Earnings in New Zealand, 1984-94', *Labour Market Bulletin*, 1, 45-100.

Dolado, J., F. Felgueroso and J. Jimeno (2000), *The Role of the Minimum Wage in the Welfare State: An Appraisal*. IZA Discussion Paper 152.

Dolado, J., F. Kramarz, S. Machin, A. Manning, D. Margolis and K. Teulings (1996), 'The Economic Impact of Minimum Wages in Europe', *Economic Policy*, 319-372.

Doms, M., T. Dunne and K. Troske (1997), 'Workers, Wages and Technology', *Quarterly Journal of Economics*, 112, 253-290.

Doudeijns, M., M. Einerhand and A. Van de Meerendonk (2000), *Financial Incentives to Take up Low-Paid Work: an International Comparison of the Role of Tax and Benefit Systems.* OECD Working Paper. Paris: OECD.

Duncan, A. and C. Giles (1996), 'Labour Supply Incentives and Recent Family Credit Reforms', *Economic Journal,* 106, 142-155.

Duncan, G., R. Gustafsson, R. Hauser, G. Schmaus, S. Jenkins, H. Messinger, R. Muffels, B. Nolan, J.C. Ray and W. Voges (1995), 'Poverty and Social Assistance in the United States, Canada and Europe', in: K. McFate, R. Lawson and W.J. Wilson (eds.), *Poverty, Inequality and the Future of Social Protection,* New York: Russell Sage Foundation.

Duncan, A. and J. MacCrea (1998), *The Labour Market Impact of the Working Families Tax Credit in the UK.* Institute of Fiscal Studies Working Paper.

Duncan, A. and J. MacCrea (1999), *Household labour Supply, Childcare Costs and In-Work Benefits: modelling the impact of the Working Families Tax Credit in the UK.* Institute of Fiscal Studies Working Paper.

Dunnewijk, B. and E. Vogels (2000), 'Loonkostensubsidie werkt!', *Economisch-Statistische Berichten* 19/5/2000.

Edin, P.-A. and B. Holmlund (1995), 'The Swedish Wage Structure: The Rise and Fall of Solidarity Wage Policy?' in: R.B. Freeman and L. Katz (eds.), *Differences and Changes in Wage Structures,* pp. 307-344. Chicago: University of Chicago Press for NBER.

Edin, P.-A. and R. Topel (1997), 'Wage Policy and Restructuring: The Swedish Labor Market Since 1960', in: R.B Freeman, R. Topel and B. Swedenborg (eds.), *The Welfare State in Transition: Reforming the Swedish Model,* pp. 155-201. Chicago: University of Chicago Press.

Eichengreen, B. and T. Iversen (1999), Institutions and Economic Performance: Evidence from the Labour Market, *Oxford Review of Economic Policy,* 15 (4) 121-138.

Eichler, M. and M. Lechner (2002), 'An Evaluation of Public Employment Programmes in the East German State of Sachsen-Anhalt', *Labour Economics,* 9 (2) 143-186.

Eissa, N. and H.W. Hoynes (1998), *The Earned Income Tax Credit and the Labour Supply of Married Couples,* Working Paper 6856. Cambridge: National Bureau of Economic Research.

Eissa, N. and J. Liebman (1996), 'Labour Supply Response to the Earned Income Tax Credit', *Quarterly Journal of Economics,* 112 (2) 605-637.

Eriksson, C. and A. Ichino (1995), 'Wage Differentials in Italy: Market Forces, Institutions and Inflation', in: R. Freeman and L. Katz (eds.) *Differences and Changes in Wage Structures,* pp. 265-306. Chicago: University of Chicago Press for NBER.

Esping-Andersen, G. (1996), 'Welfare States without Work: the Impasse of Labour Shedding and Familialism in Continental European Social Policy', in:

G. Esping-Andersen (ed.), *Welfare States in Transition: National Adaptations in Global Economies*. London: Sage.

Esping-Andersen, G. (1999), *Social Foundations of Post-industrial Economies*. Oxford: Oxford University Press.

Esping-Andersen, G. with D. Gallie, A. Hemerijck and J. Myles (2002), *Why We Need a New Welfare State*. Oxford: Oxford University Press.

European Commission (1997), *Employment in Europe*, Brussels.

European Commission (n.d.), *European Social Statistics, Social Protection: Expenditures and Receipts 1980-1999*.

Eurostat (1998), *Low Income and Low Pay in a Household Context (EU-12)*. Luxembourg: Office for Official Publications of the European Communities.

Eurostat (2001), *European Social Statistics: Income, Poverty and Social Exclusion*. Luxembourg: Eurostat.

Evans, M. (1996), *Giving Credit Where It's Due? The Success of Family Credit Reassessed*, Working Paper 121, London School of Economics Welfare State Programme.

Fay, R.G. (1996), *Enhancing the Effectiveness of Active Labour Market Policies: Evidence from Programme Evaluations in OECD Countries*. Paris: OECD.

Federaal Ministerie van Sociale Zaken, Volksgezondheid en Leefmilieu (n.d.), 'Sterkte-zwakte analyse van de sociale bescherming voor werknemers in België', *Belgisch Tijdschrift voor Sociale Zekerheid*, 44 (2) 265-362.

Feenstra, R. and G. Hanson (1999), 'The impact of outsourcing and high-technology capital on wages: Estimates for the United States 1979-1990', *Quarterly Journal of Economics*, 114, 907-940.

Ferrera, M. and A. Hemerijck (2003), 'Recalibrating Europe's Welfare Regimes', in: J. Zeitlin and D.M. Trubeck (eds.), *Governing Work and Welfare in the New Economy. European and American Experiments*, Oxford: Oxford University Press.

Ferrera, M., A. Hemerijck and M. Rhodes (2000), *The Future of Social Europe: Recasting Work and Welfare in the New Economy*. Oeiras: Celta Editora.

Finn, D. (1997), *Working Nation: Welfare Reform and the Australia Job Compact for the Long-Term Unemployed*. London: Unemployment Unit.

Fischer, C., M. Hout, M. Jankowski, S. Lucas, A. Swidler and K. Vos (1996), *Inequality by Design: Cracking the Bell Curve Myth*. Princeton: Princeton University Press.

Fitoussi, J.-P. and P. Rosanvallon (1996), *Le Nouvel Age des Inégalités*. Paris: Seuil.

Forslund, A. and A.B. Krueger (1994), *An Evaluation of the Swedish Active Labour Market Policy: New and Received Wisdom*, Working Paper 4802. Cambridge: National Bureau of Economic Research.

Förster, M. (1994), *Family Poverty and the Labour Market*, LIS Working Paper 114. Luxembourg: Luxembourg Income Study/CEPS.

Förster, M. (2000), *Trends and Driving Factors in Income Distribution in the OECD Area*. Paris: OECD.

Fortin, N., and T. Lemieux (1997), 'Institutional Changes and Rising Wage Inequality: Is There a Linkage?', *Journal of Economic Perspectives*, 11 (2) 75-96.

Foster, J.E. and A.F. Shorrocks (1988), 'Poverty Orderings', *Econometrica*, 56, 173-177.

Fougère, D., F. Kramarz and T. Magnac (1999), *Youth Employment Policies in France*, CEPR Discussion Paper 2394. London: CEPR/LSE.

Freeman, R. (1991), *How Much Has De-unionisation Contributed to the Rise in Male Earnings Inequality?*, Working Paper 3286. Cambridge: National Bureau of Economic Research.

Freeman, R. (1995), 'The Limits of Wage Flexibility to Curing Unemployment', *Oxford Review of Economic Policy*, 11 (1) 63-72.

Freeman, R. (1996), 'The Minimum Wage as a Redistributive Tool', *Economic Journal*, 106, 639-649 and 842-849.

Freeman, R. (1998), 'War of the Models: Which Labour Market Institutions for the 21st Century', *Labour Economics*, 5, 1-24.

Freeman, R. (2001), *The Rising Tide Lifts...?*, Working Paper 8155. Cambridge: National Bureau of Economic Research.

Freeman, R. and L. Katz (1994), 'Rising Wage Inequality: The United States versus other Advanced Countries', in: R. Freeman (ed.), *Working under Different Rules*, pp.29-62. New York: Russell Sage Foundation.

Freeman, R. and L. Katz (1995), 'Introduction and Summary', in: R. Freeman and L. Katz (eds.), *Differences and Changes in Wage Structures*, pp. 1-22. Chicago: University of Chicago Press.

Freeman, R. and R. Oostendorp (2000), *Wages around the World: Pay Across Occupations and Countries*, Working Paper 8058. Cambridge: National Bureau of Economic Research.

Freeman, R. and R. Schettkat (2000a), *Low Wage Services: Interpreting the US-German Difference*, Working Paper 7611. Cambridge: National Bureau of Economic Research.

Freeman, R. and R. Schettkat (2000b), *Skill Compression, Wage Differentials and Employment: Germany vs. the US*, Working Paper 7610. Cambridge: National Bureau of Economic Research.

Freeman, R. and R. Schettkat (2000c), *The Role of Wage and Skill Differences in US-German Employment Differences*, Working Paper 7474. Cambridge: National Bureau of Economic Research.

Fridberg, T and N. Ploug (2000), 'Public Attitudes to Unemployment in Different

European Welfare Regimes', in: D. Gallie and S. Paugam (eds.), *Welfare Regimes and the Experience of Unemployment in Europe*. Oxford: Oxford University Press.

Friez, A. and M. Julhès (1998), 'Séries Longues sur les Salaires', *Emploi-Revenus* no. 136. Paris: INSEE.

Fritzell, J. (1993), 'Income Inequality Trends in the 1980s: A Five-Country Comparison', *Acta Sociologica*, 36: 47-62.

Funken, K. and P. Cooper (1995), *Old and New Poverty: The Challenge for Reform*. London: Rivers Oram Press.

Galbraith, J. (1992), *The Culture of Contentment*. London: Penguin.

Galbraith, J. (1998), *Created Unequal*. New York: The Free Press.

Gallie, D. (1991), 'Patterns of Skill Change: Upskilling, Deskilling or the Polarisation of Skills?', *Work, Employment and Society*, 5, 319-351.

Gallie, D. (1999), 'Unemployment and Social Exclusion in the European Union', *European Societies*, 1-2, 139-167.

Gallie, D. (2000), 'The Labour Force', in: A. Halsey and J. Webb (eds.), *Twentieth Century British Social Trends*, London: Macmillan: 281-323.

Gallie, D., S. Jacobs and S. Paugam (2000), 'Poverty and financial hardship among the unemployed', in: D. Gallie and S. Paugam (eds.), *Welfare Regimes and the Experience of Unemployment in Europe*. Oxford: Oxford University Press.

Gallie, D., C. Marsh and C. Vogler (1994), *Social Change and the Experience of Unemployment*. Oxford: Oxford University Press.

Gallie, D., M. White, Y. Cheng and M. Tomlinson (1998), *Restructuring the Employment Relationship*. Oxford: Oxford University Press.

Gardiner, K. (1997), 'A Survey of Income Inequality over the Last Twenty Years – How does the UK compare?', in: P. Gottschalk, B. Gustafsson and E. Palmer (eds.), *Changing Patterns in the Distribution of Economic Welfare*, pp. 36-59. Cambridge: Cambridge University Press.

Garfinkel, I. and R. Haveman (1977), *Earnings Capacity, Poverty and Inequality*, New York: Academic Press.

Gaston, N. and D. Trefler (1994), 'Protection, trade and wages: Evidence from U.S. manufacturing', *Industrial and Labor Relations Review*, 47, 574-593.

Giddens, A. (1999), *The Third Way: the Renewal of Social Democracy*. Cambridge: Polity Press.

Giddens, A. (2000), *The Third Way and its Critics*. Cambridge: Polity Press.

Gittleman, M. and M. Joyce (1995), 'Earnings Mobility in the United States, 1967-91', *Monthly Labour Review*, September, 3-13.

Glyn, A. (1995), 'The Assessment: Unemployment and Inequality', *Oxford Review of Economic Policy*, 11 (1): 63-72.

Glyn, A. (2001), *Inequalities of employment and wages in OECD countries.* Discussion Paper, Institute of Economics and Statistics, Oxford University.

Glyn, A. and S. Machin (1997), 'Colliery Closures and the Decline of the UK Coal Industry', *British Journal of Industrial Relations,* 35 (2) 197-214.

Glyn, A. and R. Rowthorn (1988), 'European Unemployment, Corporatism and Structural Change', *American Economic Review,* 78, 194-199.

Glyn, A. and W. Salverda (2000a), 'Does Wage Flexibility Really Create Jobs?', *Challenge,* 43 (1) 32-43.

Glyn, A. and W. Salverda (2000b), 'Employment Inequalities', in: M. Gregory, W. Salverda and S. Bazen (eds.), *Labour Market Inequalities: Problems and Policies of Low-Wage Employment in International Perspective.* Oxford: Oxford University Press.

Goldin, C. and L. Katz (1998), *The Returns to Education across the 20th Century.* Working Paper 7126. Cambridge: National Bureau of Economic Research.

Goldthorpe, J.H. (2001), *Globalisation and Social Class.*

Goodin, R. (1988), *Reasons for Welfare: The Political Theory of the Welfare State.* Princeton: Princeton University Press.

Gordon, R.J. (2000), 'Does the "New Economy", Measure Up to the Great Inventions of the Past?', *Journal of Economic Perspectives,* 14: 49-74.

Gornick, J., M.K. Meyers and K.E. Ross (1997), 'Supporting the Employment of Mothers', *Journal of European Social Policy,* 7 (1) 45-70.

Gosling, A. (1996), 'Minimum Wages: Possible Effects on the Income Distribution', *Fiscal Studies,* 31-48.

Gosling A. and T. Lemieux (2001), *Labour Market Reforms and Changes in Wage Inequality in the United Kingdom and the United States.* Working Paper 8413. Cambridge: National Bureau of Economic Research.

Gosling, A. and S. Machin (1994), *Trade unions and the dispersion of earnings in British establishments,* Working Paper 4732. Cambridge: National Bureau of Economic Research.

Gosling, A., S. Machin and C. Meghir (1994), *The Changing Distribution of Male Wages in the UK, 1966-1992,* Institute of Fiscal Studies Working Paper W94/13.

Gottschalk, P. and M. Joyce (1998), 'Cross-National Differences in the Rise in Earnings Inequality: Market and Institutional Factors', *Review of Economics and Statistics,* 80, 489-502.

Gottschalk, P. and T. Smeeding (1997), 'Cross-National Comparisons of Earnings and Income Inequality', *Journal of Economic Literature,* 35, 633-687.

Gough, I., J. Bradshaw, J. Ditch, T. Eardley and P. Whiteford (1997), 'Social Assistance in OECD Countries', *Journal of European Social Policy* 7 (1) 17-44.

Granier, P. and J. Nyssen (1995), *Réduction des charges sociales sur les emplois non qualifiés, chômage et croissance*. GREQAN Document de Travail 95A05, Marseille: GREQAM.

Gravestein-Ligthelm, J.H., J. de Koning and C. Zandvliet (1988), *Evaluatie van de Wet Vermeend-Moor: Hoofdrapport 1997*. The Hague: Ministerie van Sociale Zaken.

Green, F. (1998), *The Value of Skills*, University of Kent, Department of Economics Discussion Paper no. 98/19.

Green, F., A. Felstead and D. Gallie (1998), *Changing Skill-Intensity: An Analysis Based on Job Characteristics*, Working paper.

Gregg, P. and S. Machin (1993), 'Is the Rise in UK Inequality Different?', in: R. Barrell (ed.), *Is the British Labour Market Different?*, Cambridge: Cambridge University Press.

Gregg, P. and A. Manning (1997), 'Skill-biased Change, Unemployment and Wage Inequality', *European Economic Review*, 41, 1173-1200.

Gregg, P. and J. Wadsworth (1996a), 'More Work in Fewer Households?', in: J. Hills (ed.), *New Inequalities: The Changing Distribution of Income and Wealth in the UK*. Cambridge: Cambridge University Press.

Gregg, P. and J. Wadsworth (1996b), *It Takes Two: Employment Polarisation in the OECD*, CEP Discussion Paper.

Gregg, P. and J. Wadsworth (2001), 'Everything You Wanted to Know about Workless Households but were afraid to Ask: Worklessness and Polarisation at the Household Level', *Oxford Bulletin of Economics and Statistics*, 63, special issue.

Gregory, M. and P. Elias (1994), 'Earnings Transitions of the Low-paid in Britain, 1976-91: A Longitudinal Study', *International Journal of Manpower*, 15 (2/3) 170-188.

Grubb, D. (1994), 'Direct and Indirect Effects of Active Labour Market Policies in OECD countries', in: Barrell, R. (ed.), *The UK Labour Market, Comparative Aspects and Institutional Developments*. Cambridge: Cambridge University Press.

Gustafsson, B., R. Aaberge, A. Cappelen, P.J. Pedersen, N. Smith and H. Uusitalo (1999), 'The distribution of Income in the Nordic Countries: Changes and Causes', in: M. Kautto, M. Heikkilä, B. Hvinden, S. Marklund and N. Ploug (eds.), *Nordic Social Policy*. London: Routledge.

Gustafsson, B. and M. Hohansson (1999), 'In Search of Smoking Guns: What Makes Income Inequality Vary Over Time in Different Countries?', *American Sociological Review*, 64, 585-605.

Gustafsson, B. and H. Uusitalo (1990), 'Income Distribution and Redistribution during Two Decades: Experiences from Finland and Sweden', in: I. Persson (ed.), *Growing Equality in the Welfare State*. Oxford: Oxford University Press.

Hagenaars, A., K. de Vos and M.A. Zaidi (1994), *Poverty Statistics in the Late 1980s: Research Based on Micro-data*. Luxembourg: Office for Official Publications of the European Communities.

Hahn, F.H. (1998), 'Reconsidering Free Trade', in: G. Cook (ed.), *The Economics and Politics of International Trade, Freedom and Trade*, vol. II. London: Routledge.

Hall, P. (2002), 'The Comparative Political Economy of the "Third Way"', in: O. Schmidtke (ed.), *The Third Way Transformation of Social Democracy:* Aldershot: Ashgate.

Hamermesh, D.S. (1993), *Labor Demand*. Princeton: Princeton University Press.

Hamermesh, D.S. and G.A. Pfann (1996), 'Adjustment Costs in Factor Demand', *Journal of Economic Literature*, 1264-1292.

Hanson, G. and A. Harrison (1995), *Trade, Technology and Wage Inequality*, Working Paper 5110. Cambridge: National Bureau of Economic Research.

Haskel, J. (1996), 'The Decline in Unskilled Employment in UK Manufacturing', Centre for Economic Policy Research, Discussion Paper No.1356.

Haskel, J. (1999), 'Small Firms, Contracting-out, Computers and Wage Inequality: Evidence from UK Manufacturing', *Economica*, 66, 1-21.

Haskel, J. and Y. Heden (1998), *Computers and the Demand for Skilled Labour: Industry and Establishment-Level Panel Evidence for the UK*, Discussion Paper no. 384, Economics Department, Queen Mary and Westfield College.

Haskel, J. and M. Slaughter (1998), *Does the Sector Bias of Skill-biased Technical Change Explain Changing Wage Inequality?*, Discussion Paper 386, Economics Department, Queen Mary and Westfield College.

Hauser, R. and I. Becker (2001), *Einkommensverteilung im Querschnitt und im Zeitverlauf 1973-1998*. Bonn: Bundesministerium für Arbeit und Sozialordnung.

Haveman, R. (1996), 'Reducing Poverty while Increasing Employment: A Primer on Alternative Strategies and a Blueprint', *The OECD Jobs Study Working Paper 7*. Paris: OECD.

Haveman, R. and A. Bershadker (1998), 'Reliance as Poverty Criterion: Trends in Earnings Capacity Poverty, 1975-1992', *American Economic Review*, May 1998.

Haveman, R and R. Hollister (1991), 'Direct Job Creation: Economic Evaluation and Lessons for the United States and Western Europe', in: A. Björklund et al. (eds.), *Labour market and unemployment insurance*. Oxford: Clarendon Press.

Heckman, J., R. Lalonde and J. Smith (1999), 'The Economics and Econometrics of Active Labour Market Programs', in: O. Ashenfelter and D. Card (eds.), *Handbook of Labour Economics*, vol. 3. Amsterdam: North-Holland.

Heckman, J., L. Lochner and R. Cossa (2002), *Learning-by-doing vs. On-the-job-training: Using variation induced by the EITC to distinguish between models of skill formation*, Working Paper 9083. Cambridge: National Bureau of Economic Research.

Heidenheimer, A., Heclo, H. and T. Adams (1990), *Comparative Public Policy: The Politics of Public Choice in America, Europe and Japan*, New York: St. Martins Press.

Hemerijck, A. (1999), 'Prospects for Inclusive Social Citizenship in an Age of Structural Inactivity', MPifG Working Paper 99/1.

Hemerijck, A. (2002), 'The Self-Transformation of the European Social Model(s)', in: G. Esping-Andersen, D. Gallie, A. Hemerijck and J. Myles (eds.), *Why we Need a New Welfare State*. Oxford: Oxford University Press.

Hemerijck, A. and M. Schludi (2000), 'Sequences of Policy Failures and Effective Policy Responses', in: F.W. Scharpf and V. Schmidt (eds.), *Welfare and Work in the Open Economy – From Vulnerability to Competitiveness*. Oxford: Oxford University Press.

Hemerijck, A., Unger, B. and Visser, J. (2000), How Small Countries Negotiate Change: Twenty-Five Years of Policy Adjustment in Austria, the Netherlands, and Belgium, in: F.W. Scharpf and V. Schmidt (eds.), *Welfare and Work in the Open Economy – Diverse Responses to Common Challenges*, Oxford: Oxford University Press.

Hemerijck, A. and J. Visser (1999), 'The Dutch Model: an Obvious Candidate for the "Third Way"', *Arch. Europ. Sociol*, 42 (1).

Hendrickx, K., B. Hertveldt and L. Masure (1997), *Doorlichting van verscheidene alternatieven ter herformulering van de Maribel-bijdrageverminderingen*. Brussels: Federaal Planbureau.

Herrnstein, R.J. and C. Murray (1996), *The Bell Curve: Intelligence and Class Structure in American Life*. New York: Simon and Schuster.

Hey, J. (1989), *Current Issues in Microeconomics*. Houndmills: MacMillan.

Hoff, S. (2003), 'Van uitkering naar arbeid: de rol van het inkomen', *Sociaal en Cultureel Planbureau*, Armoedemonitor 2003. The Hague: CBS.

Hoge Raad voor de Werkgelegenheid (1999), *Verslag*. Brussels: Ministerie van Tewerkstelling en Arbeid.

Holderbeke, F. (1994), 'Conjunctuur en arbeidsmarktindicatoren', *Nieuwsbrief Steunpunt WAV*, 4 (1) 37-46.

Horrigan, M. and R. Mincey (1993), 'The Minimum Wage and Earnings and Income Inequality', in: S. Danziger and P. Gottschalk (eds.), *Uneven Tides: Rising Inequality in America*, pp. 251-275. New York: Russell Sage Foundation.

Huber, E. and J.D. Stephens (2000), 'Welfare State and Production Regimes in the Era of Retrenchment', in: P. Pierson (ed.), *The New Politics of the Welfare State*. Oxford: Oxford University Press.

Hughes, G. and B. Nolan (1998), *Competitive and Segmented Labour Markets and Exclusion from Retirement Income*. Paper for LoWER Conference, Groningen.

Hui, W. and P. Trivedi (1986), Duration Dependence, Targeted Employment Subsidies and Unemployment Benefits, *Journal of Public Economics* 31: 105-129.

Inglehart, R. (1990), *Culture Shift in Advanced Society*. Princeton: Princeton University Press.

Institute of Social Studies Advisory Service (1990), *Poverty in Figures: Europe in the Early 1980s*. Luxembourg: Eurostat.

Ires (1996), 'Emploi et chômage: les politiques belges a l'épreuve des faits', *Journée d'étude de l'IRES*, 23 Octobre 1996, Louvain-la-Neuve.

Iversen, T. and T.R. Cusack (2000), 'The Causes of Welfare State Expansion. Deindustrialisation or Globalisation?', *World Politics*, 52, 313-349.

Iversen, T. and D. Soskice (2001), *Two Worlds of Capitalism: Ricardo versus Heckscher-Ohlin*.

Iversen, T. and A. Wren (1998), 'Equality, Employment and Budgetary Restraint, The Trilemma of the Service Economy', *World Politics*, 50, 507-546.

Jäntti, M. and S. Danziger (2000), 'Income Poverty in Advanced Countries', in: A. Atkinson and F. Bourguignon (eds.), *Handbook of Income Distribution*. Amsterdam: Elsevier.

Jenkins, S. (1991), 'Poverty Measurement and the Within-Household Distribution: Agenda for Action', *The Journal of Social Policy*, 20 (4) 457-483.

Jensen, P. and M. Verner (1997), *Do Low-Wage Individuals Experience More Unemployment?*, Paper for LoWER Conference, London.

Johnson, G. (1997), 'Changes in Earnings Inequality: The Role of Demand Shifts', *Journal of Economic Perspectives*, 11, 41-54.

Johnson, G. and F. Stafford (1999), 'The labour market implications of international trade', in: O. Ashenfelter and D. Card (eds.), *Handbook of Labour Economics*, vol. 3, Amsterdam: North-Holland.

Jongen, E.L.W. (1998), *Vouchers for the Long-term Unemployed: a Simulation with MIMIC*, Research Memorandum no. 139. The Hague: Centraal Planbureau.

Jongen, E.L.W. (1999), 'What Can we Expect from Subsidies for the Long-term Unemployed?', *De Economist*, 147 (2) 205-228.

Juhn, C. (1999), 'Wage Inequality and Demand for Skill: Evidence from Five Decades', *Industrial and Labour Relations Review*, 52, 424-443.

Juhn, C., K.M. Murphy and B. Pierce (1993), 'Wage Inequality and the Rise in Returns to Skill', *Journal of Political Economy*, 101, 410-442.

Kahn, L. (2000), 'Wage Inequality, Collective Bargaining and Relative Employment 1985-94: Evidence from 15 OECD Countries', *The Review of Economics and Statistics*, 82 (4): 564-579.

Kaldor, N. (1936), 'Wage Subsidies as a Remedy for Unemployment', *Journal of Political Economy*, 44 (6): 721-742.

Kanbur, R. (2000), 'Income Distribution and Development', in: A. Atkinson and F. Bourguignon (eds.) *Handbook of Income Distribution*. Amsterdam: Elsevier.

Karoly, L.A. (1994), 'The Trend in Inequality Among Families, Individuals, and Workers in the United States: A Twenty-Five Year Perspective', in: S. Danziger and P. Gottschalk (eds.), *Uneven Tides*. New York: Russell Sage Foundation.

Katz, L. (1998), 'Wage Subsidies for the Disadvantaged', in: Freeman, R. and P. Gottschalk, *Generating Jobs: How to Increase Demand for Less-Skilled Workers*. New York: Russell Sage Foundation.

Katz, L. (1999), *Technological Change, Computerization and the Wage Structure*, mimeo, Department of Economics, Harvard University.

Katz, L. and D. Autor (2000), 'Changes in the Wage Structure and Earnings Inequality', in: O. Ashenfelter and D. Card. (eds.), *The Handbook of Labour Economics*, vol. 3. Amsterdam: North-Holland.

Katz, L., G. Loveman and D. Blanchflower (1993), *A Comparison of Changes in the Structure of Wages in Four OECD countries*. Working paper 4297. Cambridge: National Bureau of Economic Research.

Katz, L.F. and K.M. Murphy (1992), 'Changes in Relative Wages, 1963-1987: Supply and Demand Factors', *Quarterly Journal of Economics*, 107, 35-78.

Katz, L. and A. Revenga (1989), 'Changes in the structure of wages: The United States vs Japan', *Journal of the Japanese and International Economies*, 3, 522-533.

Kaus, M. (1992), *The End of Equality*, New York: Basic Books.

Keese, M., M. Gittelman and E. Stancanelli (1997), *Do Minimum Wages Work?* Paper for LoWER Conference, Milan.

Keese, M. and P. Swaim (1997), *The Incidence and Dynamics of Low-Wage Employment in OECD Countries*. Paper presented at the European Low-Wage Employment Research Network Conference on the Problems of Low-Wage Employment, 31 January-1 February, Bordeaux.

Kenworthy, L. (2004), *Egalitarian Capitalism? Jobs, Incomes and Inequality in Affluent Countries*. New York: Russell Sage Foundation.

Keynes, J.M. (1935), *The General Theory of Employment, Interest and Money*. Cambridge: Cambridge University Press.

Kiley, M.T. (1999), 'The Supply of Skilled Labour and Skill-Biased Technological Progress', *Economic Journal*, 109, 708-724.

Kleinknecht. A. and Naastepad (n.d.), *How the Netherlands achieved full employment*. Working Paper Delft University of Technology.

Knegt, R. (2000), *Evaluatie Ontslagvergunningsprocedure RDA*. The Hague: Ministerie SZW/ Elsevier.

Koevoets, W. (2000), 'De effectiviteit van vermindering van patronale bijdragen: micro-economische analyse van tewerkstellingseffecten van het jongerenbanenplan', *Belgisch Tijdschrift voor Sociale Zekerheid*.

Kohli, M., M. Rein and A. Guillemard (1993), *Time for Retirement*. Cambridge: Cambridge University Press.

Konings, J. and F. Roodhooft (1997), 'How Elastic is the Demand for Labour in Belgian Enterprises? Results from Firm Level Accounts Data, 1987-1994', *De Economist*, 145: 229-241.

Korpi, W. (2000), 'Faces of Inequality: Gender, Class and Patterns of Inequality in Different Types of Welfare States', *Social Politics*, pp. 127-191.

Kramarz, F. and T. Philippon (1999), *The Impact of Differential Payroll Tax Subsidies on Minimum Wage Employment*. Paris: CREST.

Kraus, F. (1981), 'The Historical Development of Income Inequality in Western Europe and the United States', in: P. Flora and A.J. Heidenheimer (eds.), *The Development of Welfare States in Europe and America*. New Brunswick: Transaction Books.

Krueger, A. (1993), 'How Computers Have Changed the Wage Structure: Evidence from Microdata, 1984-1989', *Quarterly Journal of Economics*, 108, 33-60.

Krueger, A. (2002), 'Inequality, Too Much of a Good Thing?', in: J.J. Heckman and A.B. Krueger (eds.), *Inequality in America: What Role for Human Capital Policies*. Cambridge: MIT Press.

Krueger, A. and J.-S. Pischke (1997), *Observations and Conjectures on the US Employment Miracle*, Working Paper 6146. Cambridge: National Bureau of Economic Research.

Krugman, P. (1995a), 'Growing World Trade: Causes and Consequences', *Brookings Papers*, 1: 327-62.

Krugman, P. (1995b), *Technology, Trade and Factor Prices*. Working Paper 5355. Cambridge: National Bureau of Economic Research.

Kuipers, S. (2006), *The Crisis Imperative: Crisis Rhetoric and Welfare State Reform in Belgium and the Netherlands in the Early 1990s*, Amsterdam: Amsterdam University Press.

Laffargue, J.P. (1999), *Financement d'une baisse de cotisations sociaux employeurs sur le travail peu qualifié*, Cepremap Document de Travail 9913. Paris: CEPREMAP.

Lamberts, M. (1993), *Zij vragen zoveel aandacht, mijnheer. Tewerkstellings- en aanwervingsbeleid ten aanzien van laaggeschoolden en kansarmen*. Leuven: HIVA.

Lang, K. (1998), 'The Effect of Trade Liberalisation on Wages and Employment: The Case of New Zealand', *Journal of Labor Economics*, 16, 792-814.

Laroque, G. and B. Salanié (1999), *Breaking Down Married Female Non-Employment in France*, CEPR Discussion Paper 2239.

Lattimore, R. and P. Wooding (1996), 'International trade', in: B. Silverstone, A. Boılard and R. Lattimore (eds.), *A Study of Economic Reform: The Case of New Zealand*, pp. 315-353. Amsterdam: North-Holland.

Lauwereys, L., N. Matheus and I. Nicaise (2000), *De sociale tewerkstelling in Vlaanderen: doelgroepenbereik, kwaliteit en doelmatigheid*. Leuven/Brussels: HIVA-DWTC.

Lawrence, R. and M. Slaughter (1993), 'International Trade and American Wages in the 1980s: Giant Sucking Sound or Small Hiccup?', *Brookings Papers on Economic Activity*, 2, 161-226.

Lawson, R. and W.J. Wilson (1995), 'Poverty, Social Rights and the Quality of Citizenship', in: K. McFate, R. Lawson and W. Wilson (eds.), *Poverty, Inequality, and the future of social policy: Western States in the New World Order*. New York: Russell Sage.

Layard, R., D. Piachaud, M. Stewart et al. (1978), *The Causes of Poverty*. London: HMSO.

Leamer, E. (1996), *In search of Stolper-Samuelson effects on U.S. wages*, Working Paper 5427. Cambridge: National Bureau of Economic Research.

Lee, D.S. (1999), 'Wage inequality in the United States During the 1980s: Rising Dispersion or Falling Minimum Wage?', *Quarterly Journal of Economics*, 114: 977-1023.

Levy, F. (1996), 'With What Skills are Computers a Complement?', *American Economic Review: Papers and Proceedings*, 86, 258-262.

Lin, W., P.K. Robins, D. Card, K. Harknett and S. Lui-Gurr (1998), *When Financial Incentives Encourage Work: Complete 18-Month Findings from the Self-Sufficiency Project*. Ottawa: Social Research and Demonstration Corporation.

Lindbeck, A. and D. Snower (1996), 'Reorganization of Firms and Labor Market Inequality', *American Economic Review: Papers and Proceedings*, 86, 315-321.

Lindert, P.H. (2000), 'Three Centuries of Inequality in Britain and America', in: A. Atkinson and F. Bourguignon (eds.), *Handbook of Income Distribution*. Amsterdam: Elsevier.

Lindert P.H. and J.G. Williamson (2001), *Does Globalisation Make the World More Unequal?*, Working Paper 8228. Cambridge: National Bureau of Economic Research.

Lloyd-Ellis, H. (1999), 'Endogenous Technological Change and Wage Inequality', *American Economic Review*, 89, 47-77.

Loprest, P. (1999), *How Families that Left Welfare are Doing: A National Picture*. Washington, D.C.: Urban Institute.

Lucifora, C. (2000), 'Wage Inequalities and Low Pay: The Role of Labour Market Institutions', in: M. Gregory, W. Salverda and S. Bazen (eds.), *Labour Market Inequalities: Problems and Policies of Low-Wage Employment in International Perspective*. Oxford: Oxford University Press.

Machin, S. (1996a), 'Changes in the Relative Demand for Skills in the UK Labour Market', in: A. Booth and D.J. Snower (eds.), *Acquiring Skills: Market Failures, Their Symptoms and Policy Responses*. Cambridge: Cambridge University Press.

Machin, S. (1996b), 'Wage Inequality in the UK', *Oxford Review of Economic Policy*, 12, 47-64.

Machin, S. and A. Manning (1994), 'Minimum Wages, Wage Dispersion and Employment: Evidence from the UK Wages Councils', *Industrial and Labor Relations Review*, 47, 319-329.

Machin, S. and A. Manning (1996), 'Employment and the Introduction of a Minimum Wage in Britain', *Economic Journal*, 667-676.

Machin, S. and A. Manning (1999), 'Long Term Unemployment in Europe', in: O. Ashenfelter and D. Card (eds.), *Handbook of Labour Economics*, vol. 3. Amsterdam: North-Holland.

Machin, S. and J. Van Reenen (1998), 'Technology and Changes in Skill Structure: Evidence for 7 OECD countries', *Quarterly Journal of Economics*, 113 (4) 1215-1244.

Mahy, B., L. Ockerman, D. Wala, Y.-B. Minette, V. Vandeville (1996), *Evaluation des politiques de résorption du chômage de longue durée: offre et demande de travail*. Brussels: DWTC.

Malinvaud, E. (1998), *Les cotisations sociales à la charge des employeurs: analyse économique*. Rapport au Premier Ministre, Conseil d'Analyse Economique, Paris.

Manacordan, M. (1999), *Changes in the Returns to Education and the Scala Mobile, Italy: 1978-1992*. Paper presented at the IEA World Congress Session on Inequality, Argentina, Aug. 27.

Manacordan, M. and A. Manning (1999), *Just Can't Get Enough: More on Skill-Biased Change and Labour Market Performance*, CEP Discussion Paper 412, Centre for Economic Performance, LSE.

Manning, A. (2003), *Monopsony in Motion: Imperfect Competition in Labor Markets*. Princeton: Princeton University Press.

Marsh, A. and S. McKay (1993), *Families, Work and Benefits*. London: Policy Studies Institute.

Martin, B. (1995), *Away from Equality: Change in Personal Incomes, 1951 to 1991*, Discussion Paper 20, Population Studies Centre, University of Waikato.

Martin, J.P. (1996), 'Measures of Replacement Rates for the Purpose of International Comparisons: A Note', *OECD Economic Studies*, 26, 99-115.

Martin, J.P. (1998), *What Works among Active Labour Market Policies: Evidence from OECD Countries Experiences*, Labour Market and Social Policy Occasional Papers 35. Paris: OECD.

Marx, I. (2001), 'Job subsidies and cuts in employers' social security contributions: The verdict of empirical evaluation studies', *International Labour Review*, 140 (1) 69-85.

Marx, I. and W. Salverda (2005), *Low-Wage Employment in Europe: Perspectives for Improvement*. Leuven: Acco.

Marx, I. and G. Verbist (1998), 'Low-Paid Work and Poverty: A Cross-Country Perspective', in: S. Bazen, M. Gregory and W. Salverda (eds.), *Low-Wage Employment in Europe*, pp. 63-86. London: Edward Elgar.

Mau, S. (2001), *Patterns of Popular Support for the Welfare State: A Comparison of the United Kingdom and Germany*, WZB Working Paper FS III 01-405. Berlin: WZB.

McIntosh, S. and H. Steedman (2002), *Low Skills: A Problem for Europe*. Final Report to DGXII of the European Commission on the NEWSKILLS Programme of Research Education and Training: New Job Skill Needs and the Low-skilled.

Mead, L. (1986), *Beyond Entitlement: the Social Obligation of Citizenship*. New York: Free Press.

Meyer, B. and D. Rosenbaum (1999), *Welfare, the EITC, and the Labour Supply of Single Mothers*, Working Paper 7363. Cambridge: National Bureau of Economic Research.

Ministerie van Sociale Zaken (2002), *Sociale Nota*, The Hague.

Ministerie van Tewerkstelling en Arbeid (1997), *Het Federaal Werkgelegenheidsbeleid: Evaluatierapport 1997*. Brussels.

Ministerie van Tewerkstelling en Arbeid (1999), *Het Federaal Werkgelegenheidsbeleid: Evaluatierapport 1998*. Brussels.

Ministerie van Tewerkstelling en Arbeid (2000), *Het Federaal Werkgelegenheidsbeleid*. Brussels.

Mishel, L. and J. Bernstein (2003), *The State of Working America 2002-2003*. Armonk, NY: M.E. Sharpe.

Mok, A. (1999), *Arbeid, bedrijf en maatschappij*, Houten: Educative Partners Nederland

Mot, E., A. Paape, F. van Puffelen and B. Schumacher (1992), *Werking van de Wet Loonkostenreductie op Minimumloonniveau: een evaluatieonderzoek*. The Hague: Ministerie van Sociale Zaken.

Mühlau, P. and W. Salverda (2000), *Employment Effects of Low-Wage Subsidies: The case of 'SPAK', in the Netherlands*.

Murnane, R., J. Willett and F. Levy (1995), 'The Growing Importance of Cognitive Skills in Wage Determination', *Review of Economics and Statistics*, 77 (2) 251-266.

Murphy, K., W. Riddell and P. Romer (1998), 'Wages, Skills and Technology in the United States and Canada', in: E. Helpman (ed.), *General Purpose Technologies*. Cambridge: MIT Press.

Murphy, K. and R. Topel (1997), Unemployment and Non-Employment, *American Economic Association Papers and Proceedings*: 295-300.

Murray, C. (1984), *Losing Ground: American Social Policy, 1950-1980*. New York: Basic Books.

Neumark, D. and D. Reed (2002), *Employment Relationships in the New Economy*, Working Paper 8910. Cambridge: National Bureau of Economic Research.

Neumark, D. and W. Wascher (1995), *The Effect of New Jersey's Minimum Wage Increase on Fast-Food Employment: A Revaluation Using Payroll Records*, Working Paper 5524. Cambridge: National Bureau of Economic Research.

Neumark, D. and W. Wascher (1996), *Is the Time-series Evidence on Minimum Wage Effect Contaminated by Publication Bias?*, Working Paper 5631. Cambridge: National Bureau of Economic Research.

Neumark, D. and W. Wascher (1997), *Do Minimum Wages Fight Poverty?* Working Paper 6127. Cambridge: National Bureau of Economic Research.

Nicaise, I. (1996a), 'Een win-win operatie: arbeidsmarktstrategieën voor laaggeschoolden', *Nieuwsbrief WAV*, 6 (3) 29-38.

Nicaise, I. (1996b), 'Vis geven of leren vissen? Sociale kosten-baten analyse van de TOK-projecten van de OCMW's', *Belgisch Tijdschrift voor Sociale Zekerheid*, 38 (4) 923-937.

Nicaise, I., J. Bollens, L. Dawes, S. Laghaei, L. Thaulow, M. Verdié and A. Wagner (1995), *Labour Market Policies for the Poor in Europe: Pitfalls and Dilemmas – and How to Avoid Them*. Avebury: Aldershot.

Nickell, S. (1997), 'Unemployment and Labour Market Rigidities: Europe versus North America', *Journal of Economic Perspectives*, 11 (3) 55-74.

Nickell, S. (1998), 'The Collapse in the Demand for the Unskilled: What Can Be Done', in: R. Freeman and P. Gottschalk (eds.), *Generating Jobs: How to Increase Demand for Less-Skilled Workers*. New York: Russell Sage Foundation.

Nickell, S. (1998), 'Unemployment: Questions and Some Answers', *The Economic Journal*, 108, 802-16.

Nickell, S. and B. Bell (1995), 'The Collapse in the Demand for the Unskilled and Unemployment Across the OECD', *Oxford Review of Economic Policy*, 11 (1) 40-62.

Nickell, S. and B. Bell (1996), 'Changes in the Distribution of Wages and Unemployment in OECD Countries', *American Economic Review*, 86 (2) 302-308.

Nickell, S. and B. Bell (1997), 'Would Cutting Payroll Taxes on the Unskilled have a Significant Impact on Unemployment?', in: D.J. Snower and G. de la Dehesa (eds.), *Unemployment Policy: Government Options for the Labour Market.* Cambridge: Cambridge University Press.

Nickell, S and R. Layard (1999), 'Labour Market Institutions and Economic Performance', in: O. Ashenfelter and D. Card (eds.), *Handbook of Labour Economics,* vol. 3. Amsterdam: North-Holland.

Nolan, B. (1998a), *Low Pay in Ireland.* Dublin: Stationery Office.

Nolan, B. (1998b), 'Low Pay, the Earnings Distribution and Poverty in Ireland 1987-94', in: S. Bazen, M. Gregory and W. Salverda (eds.), *Low Wage Employment in Europe.* London: Edward Elgar.

Nolan, B. and I. Marx (2000), 'Low Pay and Household Poverty', in: M. Gregory et al. (ed.), *Labour Market Inequalities: Problems and Policies of Low-wage Employment in International Perspective,* pp. 100-119. Oxford: Oxford University Press.

Nolan, B. and D. Watson (1998), *Women and Poverty in Ireland.* Dublin: Oak Tree Press.

Nolan, B. and C.T. Whelan (1996), *Resources, Deprivation and Poverty.* Oxford: Clarendon Press.

OECD (1993), *Employment Outlook.* Paris: OECD.

OECD (1994), *The Jobs Study: Evidence and Explanations Part I Labour Market Trends and Underlying Forces of Change.* Paris: OECD.

OECD (1995a), *Income Distribution in OECD Countries.* Paris: OECD.

OECD (1995b), *The OECD Jobs Study: Taxation. Employment and Unemployment.* Paris: OECD.

OECD (1995), *Education at a Glance.* Paris: OECD.

OECD (1995), *Employment Outlook.* Paris: OECD.

OECD (1996a), *Employment Outlook.* Paris: OECD.

OECD (1996b), *OECD Economic Survey: United Kingdom 1995/1996.* Paris: OECD.

OECD (1997a), *Employment Outlook.* Paris: OECD.

OECD (1997b), *OECD Economic Survey: Belgium.* Paris: OECD.

OECD (1997c), *Policies for Low-paid Workers and Unskilled Job Seekers.* Paris: OECD.

OECD (1998a), *Benefit systems and Work Incentives.* Paris: OECD.

OECD (1998b), *Employment Outlook.* Paris: OECD.

OECD (1999a), *Benefit Systems and Work Incentives.* Paris: OECD.

OECD (1999b), *Employment Outlook.* Paris: OECD.

OECD (2000), 'Rewarding work', *Employment Outlook.* Paris: OECD.

OECD (2001), 'When Money is Tight: Poverty Dynamics in OECD Countries', *Employment Outlook*. Paris: OECD.
OECD (2002a), *Economic Survey of the Netherlands*. Paris: OECD.
OECD (2002b), *Employment Outlook*, Paris: OECD.
OECD (2002c), *Vieillir au Travail: Comment Promouvoir l'Emploi des plus de 50 ans en Belgique?* Paris: OECD.
OECD (2003), *Employment Outlook*. Paris: OECD.
O'Higgins, M. and S. Jenkins (1990), 'Poverty in the EC: Estimates for 1975, 1980 and 1985', in: R. Teekens and B. Van Praag (eds.), *Analysing Poverty in the European Community*. Luxembourg: Eurostat.

Pedersen, P. and N. Westergard-Nielsen (1993), 'Unemployment: A Review of the Evidence from Panel Data', *OECD Economic Studies*, 20, 65-95.
Pereira P.T. and P.S. Martins (2000), *Does Education Reduce Wage Inequality? Quantile Regressions Evidence from Fifteen European Countries*, Discussion Paper 120, IZA Bonn Germany.
Pettersen, P. (1995), 'The Welfare State: The Security Dimension', in: O. Borre and E. Scarbrough (eds.), *The Scope of Government*. Oxford: Oxford University Press.
Phelps, E. (1994), *Structural Slumps: The Modern Equilibrium Theory of Unemployment, Interest and Assets*. Cambridge: Harvard University Press.
Phelps, E. (1997a), *Rewarding Work*. Cambridge: Harvard University Press.
Phelps, E. (1997b), 'Wage Subsidy Programmes: Alternative Designs', in: D.J. Snower and G. de la Dehesa (eds.), *Unemployment Policy: Government Options for the Labour Market*. Cambridge: Cambridge University Press.
Pierson, P. (1996), 'The New Politics of the Welfare State', *World Politics*, 48, 143-179.
Pierson, P. (2001), 'Coping with Permanent Austerity: Welfare State Restructuring in Affluent Democracies', in: Paul Pierson (ed.) *The New Politics of the Welfare State*. Oxford: Oxford University Press.
Piketty, T. (1999), 'Can Fiscal Redistribution undo Skill-Biased Technical Change? Evidence from the French Experience', *European Economic Review*, 43, 839-851.
Pontuson, J. (2005), *Inequality and Prosperity: Social Europe vs. Liberal America*. Ithaca: Cornell University Press.
Prasad, E. (2002), *Wage Inequality in the United Kingdom, 1975-1999*, IZA Discussion Paper 510.
Pryor, F. and D. Schaffer (1999), *Who's Not Working and Why*. Cambridge: Cambridge University Press.

Reich, R. (1991), *The Work of Nations: Preparing Ourselves for 21st Century Capitalism*. New York: Simon and Schuster.

Richardson, J. (1995), 'Income Inequality and Trade: How to Think, What to Conclude', *Journal of Economic Perspectives*, 9 (3) 33-54.

Richardson, J. (1998), *Do Wage Subsidies Enhance Employability? Evidence from Australian Youth*. Discussion Paper 387. London School of Economics, Centre for Economic Performance.

Rifkin, J. (1995), *The End of Work. The Decline of the Global Labor Force and the Dawn of the Post-Market Era*. New York: Putnam.

Ritakkalio, V.-M. (2001), *Trends of Poverty and Income Inequality in Cross-National Comparison*. Luxembourg Income Study Working Paper 272.

Rivera-Batiz, F.L. (1992), 'Quantitative Literacy and the Likelihood of Employment Among Young Adults', *Journal of Human Resources*, 27, 313-328.

Roemer, J., R. Aaberge, U. Colombino, J. Fritzell, S.J. Jenkins, I. Marx, M. Page, E. Pommer, J. Ruiz-Castillo, M.J. San Segundo, T. Tranaes, G. Wagner and I. Zubiro (2003), 'To what extent do fiscal regimes equalise opportunities for income acquisition among citizens?', *Journal of Public Economics*, 87, 539-565.

Roller, E. (1999), 'Shrinking the Welfare State: Citizens', Attitudes towards Cuts in Social Spending in the 1990s', *German Politics*, 8 (1) 21-39.

Roorda, W. and E. Vogels (1998), 'Werknemerstoeslagen versus loonkostensubsidies', *Economisch-Statistische Berichten*, 13, 126-129.

Rosanvallon, P. (1995), *La Nouvelle Question Sociale: Repenser l'Etat Providence*. Paris: Seuil.

Rosen, S. (1996), 'Public Employment and the Welfare State in Sweden', *Journal of Economic Literature*, 34, 729-740.

Rowthorn, R. and R. Ramaswamy (1999), 'Growth, Trade and Deindustrialisation', *IMF Staff Papers*, 46 (1) 18-41.

Rijksdienst voor Arbeidsvoorziening (2000), *Jaarboekverslag*, Brussels: RVA.

Sachs, J. and H. Shatz (1996), 'U.S. Trade with Developing Countries and Wage Inequality', *American Economic Review: Papers and Proceedings*, 86, 234-239.

Saint-Paul, G. (1996), 'Are the Unemployed Unemployable', *European Economic Review*, 40, 1501-1519.

Sandmo, A. (2002), *Globalisation and the Welfare State: More Inequality – Less Redistribution?*, Discussion Paper 04/02. Norway: Norwegian School of Economics and Business Administration.

Scarpetta, S. (1996), 'Assessing the Role of Labour Market Policies and Institutional Settings on Unemployment: A Cross-Country Study', *OECD Economic Studies*, 26, 43-98.

Scharpf, F.W. and V. Schmidt (2000), *Welfare and Work in the Open Economy – From Vulnerability to Competitiveness*. Oxford: Oxford University Press.

Schmitt, J. (1995), 'The Changing Structure of Male Earnings in Britain, 1974-1988', in: R. Freeman and L. Katz (eds.), *Changes and Differences in Wage Structures*. Chicago: University of Chicago Press.

Schokkaert, E. and F. Spinnewyn (1995), 'Fundamenten van Sociale Zekerheid: Solidariteit en Verzekering, Overheid en Markten', in: M. Despontin and M. Jegers (eds.), *De Sociale Zekerheid Verzekerd?*, Brussels: VUBPRESS.

Schokkaert, E. and J. Sweeney (1999), 'Social Exclusion and Ethical Responsibility: Solidarity with the Least Skilled', *Journal of Business Ethics*, 21 (2) 251-268.

Schokkaert, E., M. Verhue and G. Pepermans (2000), 'Vlamingen over het pensioensysteem', in: P. Pestieau, L. Gevers, V. Ginsburgh, E. Schokkaert and B. Cantillon (eds.), *De toekomst van onze pensioenen*. pp. 55-75. Leuven: Garant.

Scholz, J.K. (1996), 'In-Work Benefits in the United States: The Earned Income Tax Credit', *The Economic Journal*, 1, 130-141, 159-169.

Sianesi, B. (2002), *Differential Effects of Swedish Active Labour Market Programmes for Unemployed Adults during the 1990's*. IFAU Working Paper 5.

Siebert, H. (1997), 'Labour Market Rigidities: At the Root of Unemployment in Europe', *Journal of Economic Perspectives*, 11 (3) 37-54.

Slaughter, M. (1998), 'What are the Results of Product Price Studies and what can we Learn from their Differences?', Working Paper 6591. Cambridge: National Bureau of Economic Research.

Slaughter, M. and P. Swagel (1997), *The Effect of Globalization on Wages in the Advanced Economies*. Staff Studies for the World Economic Outlook. Washington: International Monetary Fund.

Sloane, P. and I. Theodossiou (1996), 'Earnings Mobility, Family Income and Low Pay', *The Economic Journal*, 657-66.

Smeeding, T., K. Ross, M. O'Connor and M. Simon (1998), *The Economic Impact of the Earned Income Tax Credit*, Center for Policy Research, Maxwell School of Public Policy, Syracuse University.

Sneessens, H. (1999), 'Technological Bias and Unemployment: A Macroeconomic Perspective'.

Sneessens, H. en F. Shadman (2000), 'Analyse macro-économique des effets de réductions ciblées des charges sociales', *Revue Belge de Securité Sociale*, 3: 613-630.

Snower, D.J. (1994), 'Converting Unemployment Benefits into Employment Subsidies', *AEA Papers and Proceedings*, 84: 65-70.

Snower, D.J. (1996), 'The Low-Skill, Bad-Job Trap', in: A. Booth and D.J. Snower (eds.), *Acquiring Skills: Market Failures, Their Symptoms and Policy Responses*. Cambridge: Cambridge University Press.

Snower, D.J. (1997), 'The Simple Economics of Benefit Transfers', in: D.J. Snower and G. de la Dehesa (eds.), *Unemployment Policy: Government Options for the Labour Market*. Cambridge: Cambridge University Press.

Snower, D.J. (1998), 'Causes of Changing Earnings Inequality', *Income Inequality: Issues and Policy Options*, pp. 69-134. Kansas City: Federal Reserve Bank of Kansas City.

Soskice, D. (1990), 'Wage Determination: The Changing Role of Institutions in the Advanced Industrialised Countries', *Oxford Review of Economic Policy*, 6 (4).

Standing, G. (1999), *Global Labour Flexibility: Seeking Distributive Justice*. London: MacMillan.

Statistics Finland (1999), *Income Distribution Statistics*, 1997, Statistics Finland: Helsinki.

Statistics New Zealand (1999), *Incomes*. Wellington: Statistics New Zealand.

Steedman, H., A. Green, O. Bertrand, A. Richter, M. Rubin and K. Weber (1997), *Assessment, Qualifications and Standards: the UK compared to France, Germany, Singapore and the US: A Technical Report*. Centre for Economic Performance.

Stewart, M. and J. Swaffield (1998), 'The Earnings Mobility of Low-paid Workers in Britain', in: R. Asplund, P.J. Sloane and I. Theodossiou (eds.), *Low Pay and Earnings Mobility in Europe*. Cheltenham: Edward Elgar.

Sutherland, H. (1997). *A National Minimum Wage and In-Work Benefits*. Employment Policy Institute.

Taylor-Gooby, P. (1998), 'Commitment to the Welfare State', in: Jowell et al. (eds.), *Social Attitudes 15th Report. How Britain Differs*. Aldershot: Ashgate.

Topel, R. (1997), 'Factor Proportions and Relative Wages: The supply-side Determinants of Wage Inequality', *Journal of Economic Perspectives*, 11: 55-74.

United Kingdom, Department of Social Security (1994), *Social Security Statistics*. London: HMSO.

Uusitalo, H. (1998), *Changes in Income Distribution during a Deep Recession and After*. Helsinki: STAKES.

Van den Bosch, K. (1993), 'Poverty measures in Comparative Research', in: J. Berghman and B. Cantillon (eds.), *The European Face of Social Security. Essays in Honour of Herman Deleeck*. pp. 3-23. Aldershot: Avebury.

Van den Bosch, K. (2001), *Identifying the Poor: Using Subjective and Consensual Measures*, Aldershot: Ashgate.

Van den Bosch, K., T. Callan, J. Estivill, P. Hausman, B. Jeandidier, R. Muffels and J. Yfantopoulos (1993), 'A Comparison of Poverty in Seven European Countries and Regions using Subjective and Relative Measures', *Journal of Population Economics*, 6: 235-259.

Van der Linden, B. (1997), 'Effets des Formations Professionnelles et des Aides à L'embauche: Exploitation d'une Enquête Auprès d'Employeurs Belges', *Economie et Prévision.* 131: 113-130.

Van Hoorebeeck, B. et al. (2002), *Validiteitsproblemen van de Belgische ECHP-data.* Antwerp: Centrum voor Sociaal Beleid.

Van Nes, P.J., E.A.M. Stotijn and J.J. van Velden (1998), *Evaluatie van het gebruik van de afdrachtskorting lage lonen.* The Hague: Ministerie van Sociale Zaken en Werkgelegenheid.

Van Oers, F.M., R.A. de Mooij, J.J. Graafland and J. Boone (1999), *An Earned Income Tax Credit in the Netherlands: Simulations with the MIMIC Model.* The Hague: Centraal Planbureau.

Van Oorschot, W. (1999), *The Legitimacy of Welfare: a Sociological Analysis of the Motives for Contributing to Welfare Schemes,* WORC-paper series 99.11.22, WORC/TISSER, Tilburg.

Van Oorschot, W. (2002), *Flexibility and Security for the Workers and Careers in the Netherlands: Trends, Policies and Outcomes,* Report Social and Behavioural Sciences, Department of Sociology, Tilburg University,

Van Ours, J. (2002), *The Locking-in Effect of Subsidised Jobs.* IZA Discussion Paper 527.

Van Polanen Petel, V.C.A., T.W. Hu, J. de Koning and C. van der Veen (1999), *Werkgelegenheidseffecten van de SPAK en VLW.* Rotterdam: NEI.

Van Trier, W. (1999), 'Evaluatie van het arbeidsmarktbeleid: bouwstenen voor een beleidsrelevant analysekader', *Nieuwsbrief Steunpunt WAV,* 9 (1-2) 121-124.

Vandenbroucke, F. (2001), 'The Active Welfare State: A European Ambition', *Documentatieblad van het Ministerie van Financiën,* 3, 3-16.

Verbist, G. (2002*), The Redistributive Effect of Personal Income Taxes in Belgium.* Ph.D. Thesis, Universiteit Antwerp.

Verhue, M., E. Schokkaert and E. Omey (1997), *De kloof tussen laag- en hooggeschoolden en de politieke houdbaarheid van de Belgische werkloosheidsverzekering: een empirische analyse,* Universiteit Gent (Fac. Economische en Toegepaste Economische Wetenschappen) Working Paper 36.

Visser, J. (2002), 'The First Part-time Economy in the World: a Model to be Followed?', *Journal of European Social Policy,* 12 (1) 23-43.

Visser J. and A. Hemerijck (1997*), A Dutch Miracle.* Amsterdam: Amsterdam University Press.

Vlaamse Dienst voor Arbeidsbemiddeling (VDAB), *Trends en Cijfers.* Brussels.

Vleugels, I., T. Ergo, J. Bollens, F. Heylen and I. Nicaise (1998), *Leven na de dop. Een onderzoek naar de haalbaarheid en effectiviteit van Opleidings- en Werkervaringsgaranties voor Langdurig Werklozen.* Leuven: HIVA.

Vrieze, G., A. Mok and F. Smit (2003), *Beroepscultuur en beroepsethiek in ROC's: Een onderzoek bij Gilde Opleidingen en ROC Westerschelde*, Nijmegen: ITS.

Wallerstein, M. (1999), 'Wage Setting Institutions and Wage Inequality in Advanced Industrial Societies', *American Journal of Political Science*, 43 (3) 649-680.

White, S. (2001), *New Labour and the Future of Progressive Politics*. London: Macmillan.

Whitehouse, E. (1996), 'Designing and Implementing In-Work Benefits', *The Economic Journal*, 1, 130-141.

Willensky, H. (1975), *The Welfare State and Equality: Structural and Ideological Roots of Public Expenditure*. Berkeley: University of California Press.

Wood, A. (1994), *North-South Trade, Employment and Inequality: Changing Fortunes in a Skill-Driven World*. Oxford: Clarendon Press.

Wood, A. (1995), 'How Trade Hurt Unskilled Workers', *Journal of Economic Perspectives*, 9, 57-80.

Wood, A. (1998), 'Globalisation and the Rise in Labour Market Inequalities', *The Economic Journal*, 108, 1463-1482.

Woodbury, S. and R. Spiegelman (1987), 'Bonuses to Workers and Employers to Reduce Unemployment: Randomized Trials in Illinois', *American Economic Review*, 77 (4) 513-530.

Wouters, M., R. Van Meensel and I. Nicaise (1994), *De TOK-projecten en hun cursisten, drie jaar later*. Leuven: HIVA.

Young, M. (1958), *The Rise of Meritocracy 1870-2033*. London: Penguin.

Zeitlin, J. and D.M. Trubeck (2003), *Governing Work and Welfare in the New Economy. European and American Experiments*. Oxford: Oxford University Press.

Zilliak, J. (2002), 'Social Policy and the Macroeconomy: What Drives Welfare Caseloads?', *Focus*, 22, 1, 29-34.

Zijderveld, A. (1979), 'Het ethos van de verzorgingsstaat', *Sociale Wetenschappen*, 22 (3) 179-203.

Index

Acemoglu, D. 69-70, 84, 87, 92
activation 168
active labour market policies 18, 20, 123, 170, 201
active welfare state 18-20, 168-169, 186, 188
anti-poverty policies 115, 117-118, 120, 123-125, 132, 169, 182, 190, 221, 234, 241
Ashenfelter, O. 24
Atkinson, A. 31-32, 51, 69, 83, 92-93, 113-114, 137, 206, 208
Australia 66, 73, 91, 99-101, 106-108, 137, 171-176, 180, 205-206, 213-215
Autor, D. 84, 87

Baldwin, P. 26, 156
Barr, N. 29, 156
Belgium 11, 19, 24, 30, 38-42, 44-46, 48-49, 52-55, 58, 70, 72, 98-108, 111, 117, 123-124, 126-128, 130-132, 134-143, 146-156, 159-160, 162-163, 169-172, 174-176, 180, 182, 185, 187, 190-191, 201-203, 205-209, 214-215, 233, 239
benefit dependency 9-10, 17-18, 30-33, 53-55, 58, 61, 77, 119, 135, 148, 168-170, 181, 184, 188-189, 194, 201, 218-219, 223-224, 228, 236, 240

benefit termination 131-132, 136, 149
Bershadker, A. 56-58
Beveridge; W. 25
Bismarckian systems 124, 129, 163, 236, 239
Blank, R. 76, 118, 168-169, 221-222, 224-225, 227
Blau, F. 77, 90-91
Blundell, R. 51, 149
Boeri, T. 27
Bogaerts, K. 52, 131, 147-149
Bonoli, G. 169
breadwinner model 9, 12, 14-16, 25-26, 38-39, 45, 49-51, 53, 63, 74, 124-125, 127-129, 140, 143, 145-146, 149, 162, 183-184, 194, 229-230
Burniaux, J-M. 32, 173, 175-176, 192
Burtless, G. 82, 212-213

Canada 33-37, 66, 71, 73, 76, 87, 89, 92, 99-101, 106-108, 137, 171-176, 180, 219, 228
Cantillon, B. 20, 31, 41, 55, 133, 135, 143-145, 183, 190-191, 233
Card, D. 76, 85, 91-92, 118, 153, 225, 228
child care 52, 57-58, 80, 118, 146, 148, 169-170, 181, 194, 222, 224, 226

De Beer, P. 188, 190-191, 193, 202, 206
De Lathouwer, L. 52, 130-131, 133, 146-149, 181, 191
De Swaan, A. 27-28
deindustrialisation 10, 38, 55, 153, 237
Deleeck, H. 20, 130
Denmark 30, 67, 70-71, 73, 84, 100, 102-105, 114, 128, 135, 137-138, 174-176
deregulation 169, 185
deserving poor 27
dual-earnership 12, 106-108, 184-186, 230

early retirement 30, 39, 52-55, 125-129, 135, 140, 181, 187
earnings inequality 11, 13-14, 29, 45, 68-74, 76-77, 81, 84-85, 87-93, 97-98, 113, 118, 170, 185-186, 236, 238
education system 77, 88
educational attainment 27, 39-40, 44, 47-49, 51, 57-58, 64-65, 70-72, 78, 86, 91, 179, 193
efficiency 123-125, 129, 136, 156, 205
EITC 117-118, 169, 218-232
employers' contributions 32, 102, 109, 118, 123, 201-207, 209, 211-212, 214-215, 217-218, 226, 230, 240
employment growth 18, 31, 62-63, 65-66, 76, 172-173, 167-168, 174, 179-180, 182, 186-190, 192-193, 195, 210-212, 219, 224, 236, 239
equity NA
Esping-Andersen, G. 2, 11, 23, 38-39, 75, 126, 178, 184, 235
European Commission 32
European Union 11, 62-63, 66-67, 89, 101, 104-105, 109, 116, 126-127, 167, 178, 182-183, 187, 194

evaluation studies 201, 203, 206-207, 210, 212, 214, 216-217, 228, 230, 232-233, 240

Ferrera, M. 23
financial incentives 17, 77, 108, 117-118, 120, 126, 145, 147-149, 151, 179, 181, 194, 205-206, 207n, 208-209, 217-219, 223, 228, 232-234, 241
Finland 69-70, 73, 99-101, 106-108, 137, 171, 174-176
Förster, M. 32, 99, 137, 171-172, 183, 192
France 10, 30, 34-37, 69, 71, 73, 76, 84, 87, 99-100, 102-105, 128, 137, 139, 152, 154-155, 170-172, 174-176, 180, 185, 202, 211-212, 214-215, 233, 235
Freeman, R. 28, 76-77, 83, 89-92, 118
full-employment 13, 18, 25-27, 62, 123-124, 236-237

Gallie, D. 11, 65, 138-139
Germany 30, 34-37, 66, 69-70, 73, 76, 84, 87-89, 91, 99-108, 112, 128, 137, 138, 170-172, 174-177, 180, 185, 187, 215
globalisation 2, 10, 23, 38, 61, 68, 78, 81, 83-84, 153
Glyn, A. 62-63, 71-75, 78, 89
gradual change 15, 19, 117, 124, 134, 148, 156, 162-163, 221, 224, 232, 237, 239
Gregg, P. 87, 179, 181, 186

Haveman, R. 56-58
Hemerijck, A. 2, 11, 13, 20, 27, 75, 126, 169, 186-187, 189

household income 32, 48, 51, 101-102, 104-106, 111, 115, 125, 131, 136, 138-140, 159, 162, 184-185, 194, 228-229

in-work poverty 18, 97-98, 100, 117, 183, 236, 239
income distribution 18, 32, 104-105, 113, 158, 162, 169, 172, 191, 193, 227
incremental change 14-17, 123-124, 147, 156, 163, 167
international trade 11, 15, 19, 51, 54-55, 63, 65, 68, 73, 78-83, 93, 127, 157, 189, 203-204
Ireland 69, 73, 75, 102-105, 109-111, 116, 128, 172, 180, 201, 205-206, 208-209
Italy 67, 73, 91, 99-100, 102-105, 128, 137-139, 171-172, 174-177, 179-180, 184-185
Iversen, T. 13, 23, 75, 153, 237

Japan 73, 79, 84, 172, 180
job destruction 31, 53, 67, 119, 126-127, 210-211, 217
jobless growth 62

Kahn, L. 77, 82, 90-91
Katz, L. 84, 86-87, 91, 203, 211-213, 216
Kenworthy, L. 186
knowledge economy 62, 79, 94, 238

labour demand 9, 11-13, 15, 18-21, 24-25, 53-54, 56, 61-62, 64-65, 75-76, 78, 80-84, 86-89, 92-93, 97, 123, 146, 148, 154, 193, 201-203, 211, 233, 236-238, 240
labour market flexibility 76-77, 184-185, 227

labour supply 39, 117, 147, 149, 153, 201, 218-219, 224-225, 229-231
legitimacy 2, 13, 24, 27, 72, 123, 145, 149, 156-157, 160-161, 170, 203, 231, 236, 240
less-skilled workers 11-16, 18-21, 23-24, 26, 38-39, 41-49, 51-54, 56-58, 61-62, 65, 67-68, 70-72, 74-83, 86-87, 89-94, 97, 123, 146, 148-149, 159, 170, 184-185, 189-190, 193, 202-204, 206, 209, 223, 227, 235-239
living standard 12, 15, 32, 39, 41-42, 44-46, 49-51, 57, 114-115, 119, 129, 142-146, 182, 184, 190, 192-193, 195, 218, 221, 240
lone parent households 12, 33, 177, 194, 220, 227, 229, 232
low-paid employment 11, 15, 18, 20, 23, 27-28, 32, 52, 57, 62-63, 65-67, 71, 73, 75-79, 86, 90, 93, 97-120, 128, 146, 148, 169-170, 183-186, 189, 201, 204-205, 207-208, 211-212, 217-223, 225, 227, 229-233, 235, 237, 239-241

Machin, S. 186
make work pay 19, 168-169, 182, 201, 220-221
means-tested programmes 16, 114, 119, 130, 179
minimum wage 12, 15-16, 28, 38-39, 52, 75, 81, 93, 98, 116-120, 143, 145-155, 169, 182, 184-186, 189-195, 204, 207, 211-212, 221-222, 224-226, 232, 241

Netherlands 18-19, 30, 67, 70, 73, 75, 87, 89, 99-108, 110, 112, 128, 135, 137-138, 150, 152, 154-155, 161, 167-

168, 171-172, 174-177, 180-181, 185-195, 202, 204, 206-210, 212, 239
New Zealand 69, 71, 73
Nickell, S. 70-72, 76, 88-89, 202
Nolan, B. 32, 69, 97n, 110, 116
non-deserving poor 27, 160
non-employment 29, 55-56, 58, 70-71, 75, 77-78, 114, 117, 119, 137, 139, 149, 154, 173, 177-181, 184-185, 191, 193-195, 220, 223, 225-226, 237
Norway 70-71, 73, 91, 100, 137, 151, 172, 174-176, 180

OECD 9, 18, 24, 30-32, 53, 58, 62-67, 69-72, 74-78, 83-84, 87, 91, 98-99, 101-103, 105, 109-110, 112, 118, 126, 128, 135, 137-138, 146, 151-152, 154-155, 167, 169, 171-173, 175-181, 183, 185-187, 189, 191-192, 195, 201-203, 206, 208, 215, 220, 233, 237
Open Method of Coordination 18, 167

pensions 29, 109, 114-115, 125, 158
Phelps, E. 202
Pierson, P. 14, 162
Piketty, T. 23
Pontuson, J. 94
post-industrial economy 10-11, 38-39, 62, 79, 85, 127, 140, 146, 161, 236, 238
poverty 9-10, 12-15, 17-18, 20, 24, 28, 31-37, 39, 41-43, 48-49, 51-52, 54-59, 61, 74, 95, 97-120, 123-127, 129, 131-132, 136-146, 148, 156, 163, 167, 169-176, 180, 182-187, 190-195, 219, 221, 222, 226-228, 234, 236-237, 239-241
poverty threshold 12, 17, 119, 131, 141-146, 148, 172, 182, 184, 190-191, 193, 195

public support 124, 157, 160-162, 179

redistribution 13, 25-26, 28-29, 55-56, 61, 65, 92, 116, 125, 162, 219, 236-237, 239
regular labour market 213, 215-216, 218
Reich, R. 23, 78-80
Rifkin, J. 23, 62
Rosanvallon, P. 10, 23, 235

Salverda, W. 71-74, 78, 89, 97n, 212
Schokkaert, E. 54, 127, 157, 160
self-reliance 17, 20-21, 23, 25, 30-31, 48, 51-52, 55-58, 78, 93, 123, 168-169, 220, 236-237
service economy 13, 19, 23, 28, 39, 54, 62-64, 66-67, 76, 79-81, 119, 184, 190, 204, 236-237
single mothers 11, 56, 117, 220, 224-227, 229
skills 11, 39-40, 53-54, 63, 65, 79, 82, 84-87, 89-92, 94, 127, 169, 193, 202, 235, 238, 240
Smeeding, T. 31-32, 137, 227
Snower, D.J. 23, 84-85, 202, 217
social assistance 15-17, 30, 114, 116, 123, 132, 136-137, 163, 167, 187-188, 191-192, 194, 213, 220
social inclusion 168, 194-195
social insurance 14-17, 26, 29, 67, 81, 114, 123-125, 129-130, 134, 136, 148, 156-158, 160, 162-163, 167, 222, 236, 239
social norms 86, 90, 92
social security 14-17, 25-26, 29, 32, 38-39, 45-46, 48-52, 69, 102, 117, 123, 125-127, 143, 145-146, 149, 156, 158-159, 162, 184, 188, 203-204, 207, 216-218, 221, 229, 239

social security contributions 32, 45-
    46, 102, 109, 118, 123, 147-148, 158,
    201-203, 205-207, 209, 211-212,
    214-215, 217-218, 226, 230, 240
social transfers 51, 108
socio-demographic 10-12, 33, 56,
    124-125, 170, 194, 232, 237
solidarity 2, 26-28, 51, 124, 129,
    148, 153, 156-157, 159-160
Spain 2, 30, 67, 71, 73, 100, 102-105,
    128, 137-138, 155, 174, 177, 179,
    184, 202
Spinnewyn, F. 157, 160
stigmatization 216-218, 222
Sweden 30, 33-37, 66-67, 69-71, 73,
    84, 89, 91-92, 98-101, 106-108,
    137, 171-172, 174-176, 183
Switzerland 73, 91

targeting 115, 117, 158
tax credits 18, 97, 117, 119, 123, 169-170,
    201, 211-213, 218, 220-222, 229, 233
taxes 14, 26, 29, 32, 34, 36, 51, 108-
    109, 147-149, 218, 226
technological change 10, 19, 23, 27,
    38, 55, 61, 68, 78-79, 81, 83-88, 92-
    93, 153, 235, 237
Third Way 18, 168-169, 186, 237
trade-off 55, 71, 75, 78, 86, 171, 238

UK 25, 27, 30, 65-73, 75, 84-89, 91-93,
    99-108, 110, 112-113, 116, 118, 128,
    137-139, 153, 155, 169, 171-176, 177,
    179-181, 185-186, 201-202, 205-206,
    208-210, 219, 229-231, 233
unemployment 9-11, 13, 15-18, 20,
    25-31, 39, 43, 45, 52-55, 65-66,
    70-71, 75-78, 81, 86, 88-89, 97,
    109, 111, 113-118, 123-132, 134-137,
    140-141, 147-149, 151, 153, 156-160,
    162, 168, 170, 177, 179, 184, 187,
    194, 202, 205, 209, 216, 219, 223-
    224, 227, 235-236, 238
unemployment insurance 16-17, 25,
    123-126, 129-136, 139-150, 157-
    160, 162-163
upskilling 23, 42, 93-94, 238
US 18, 33-37, 56-58, 63, 65-73, 75-
    77, 79, 81-92, 98-110, 112, 116-118,
    137, 153-155, 161, 168-176, 180,
    183-185, 187, 201-202, 211n, 212,
    216, 218-227, 229-232, 238

Van den Bosch, K. 31-32, 183
Van Oorschot, W. 27, 161
Vandenbroucke, F. 169
Verbist, G. 97n, 233
Visser, J. 2, 186-189

Wadsworth, J. 179, 181, 186
wage flexibility 77, 97, 119, 185
wage floors 81, 241
wage subsidies 18, 20, 55, 94, 120,
    123, 160, 169-170, 201-203, 205-
    206, 208-210, 212-219, 225, 230-
    234, 237, 240
welfare state 2, 9-14, 16, 18-20,
    23-29, 38-39, 45-46, 58, 62-63, 75,
    119, 142, 145, 156, 160-163, 168-
    169, 184, 186-189, 235-237
welfare state regime 13, 24-25, 130,
    151, 236
welfare-to-work 231
Wood, A. 81-82
"work, work, work" 18, 167
workless households 173-174, 177-
    182, 190, 195, 239
Wren, A. 13, 23, 75, 237

Zeitlin, J. 168

CHANGING WELFARE STATES

PREVIOUSLY PUBLISHED

Jelle Visser and Anton Hemerijck, *A Dutch Miracle. Job Growth, Welfare Reform and Corporatism in the Netherlands*, 1997 (ISBN 978 90 5356 271 0)

Christoffer Green-Pedersen, *The Politics of Justification. Party Competition and Welfare-State Retrenchment in Denmark and the Netherlands from 1982 to 1998*, 2002 (ISBN 978 90 5356 590 2)

Jan Høgelund, *In Search of Effective Disability Policy. Comparing the Developments and Outcomes of the Dutch and Danish Disability Policies*, 2003 (ISBN 978 90 5356 644 2)

Maurizio Ferrera and Elisabetta Gualmini, *Rescued by Europe? Social and Labour Market Reforms from Maastricht to Berlusconi*, 2004 (ISBN 978 90 5356 651 0)

Martin Schludi, *The Reform of Bismarckian Pension Systems. A Comparison of Pension Politics in Austria, France, Germany, Italy and Sweden*, 2005 (ISBN 978 90 5356 740 1)

Uwe Becker and Herman Schwartz (eds.), *Employment 'Miracles'. A Critical Comparison of the Dutch, Scandinavian, Swiss, Australian and Irish Cases Versus Germany and the US*, 2005 (ISBN 978 90 5356 755 5)

Sanneke Kuipers, *The Crisis Imperative. Crisis Rhetoric and Welfare State Reform in Belgium and the Netherlands in the Early 1990s*, 2006 (ISBN 978 90 5356 808 8)

Anke Hassel, *Wage Setting, Social Pacts and the Euro. A New Role for the State*, 2006 (ISBN 978 90 5356 919 1)